Reclaiming the Rural

Reclaiming the Rural

Essays on Literacy, Rhetoric, and Pedagogy

Edited by
Kim Donehower,
Charlotte Hogg, and
Eileen E. Schell

Southern Illinois University Press
Carbondale and Edwardsville

15   14   13   12   4   3   2   1

Library of Congress Cataloging-in-Publication Data
Reclaiming the rural : essays on literacy, rhetoric,
and pedagogy / edited by Kim Donehower, Charlotte Hogg, and Eileen E. Schell.
        p. cm.
Includes bibliographical references and index.
ISBN-13: 978-0-8093-3065-2 (pbk. : alk. paper)
ISBN-10: 0-8093-3065-2 (pbk. : alk. paper)
ISBN-13: 978-0-8093-3066-9 (ebook)
ISBN-10: 0-8093-3066-0 (ebook)
1. English language—Rhetoric—Study and teaching (Higher)—United States. 2. Academic writing—Study and teaching (Higher)—United States.
3. Rural population—Education—United States.
4. Country life—United States. I. Donehower, Kim.
II. Hogg, Charlotte, [date]. III. Schell, Eileen E.
PE1405.U6R45 2007
808'.0420711—dc22   2011014518

*To those struggling to sustain rural communities,
businesses, farms, and schools*

Contents

Section III: Pedagogies

Contents

Preface

Kim Donehower, Charlotte Hogg, and Eileen E. Schell

In 2007 we coauthored *Rural Literacies* to urge the fields of composition, rhetoric, and literacy studies to consider the complexities of rural literacies in classrooms and communities. We wanted to move the field beyond three metaphors, first delineated by Henry Shapiro:

- preservation: the inclination to isolate and celebrate what has been deemed essentially rural as a way to resist and separate from that which is urban;
- abandonment: the drive to allow that which is considered rural to return to a state of nature;
- modernization: the impulse to convert that which is considered rural to align with urban and suburban culture, technology, economy, and so on.

These metaphoric lenses often create dualistic narratives, depicting rural places and people as lacking educational, economic, and cultural resources, or celebrating and mythologizing our rural past and character. We argued for sustainability as a better metaphor for the kind of mutual identification that rural, urban, and suburban communities need to exercise.

Our own rural and agrarian backgrounds fueled this agenda. Kim's family hails from a small town in southern Appalachia; Charlotte spent most of her formative years in Paxton, Nebraska; Eileen grew up on a third-generation family farm near the small town of Cashmere in eastern Washington state. Our self-identification as people connected to rural areas and as teachers of rural students led us to critically examine how the field of rhetoric and composition studies acknowledges the concept of the rural—or not. We were particularly concerned that rhetoric and composition scholarship tended to ignore or dismiss rural students and communities, either because such scholarship was focusing on other groups or had historically neglected such populations in favor of inner-city populations, or, worse yet, was buying into some long-perpetuated stereotypes about the rural.

As a focus on urban literacies and rhetorics came to prevail in composition and rhetoric, scholars began to deploy the metaphor of the city as a focal point for scholarship in the field (see Reynolds; Friend; and McComiskey and Ryan). However, our field's preoccupation with the literacies and rhetorics of the city may come at the expense of the 56 million Americans who live in rural areas. This need not be the case if scholars of urban and rural literacies interrogate the social, economic, and political interconnections that bind our different communities together.

For example, when David Fleming examines Chicago's Cabrini Green urban revitalization project in *City of Rhetoric*, his concerns about democratic living in cities apply to rural issues as well. Fleming argues that "no 'indirect' effect of places is more important for the development and exercise of civic capacities than the quality and character of neighborhood schools" (189); the same could be said of rural towns that lose schools to consolidation. Similarly, Douglas Reichert Powell's *Critical Regionalism*, in which place or region is not fixed but is "always at some level an attempt to persuade as much as . . . to describe," provides a framework with which to reconsider how scholarship on rural, urban, and suburban spaces can be brought together in an ongoing conversation rather than being isolated in separate camps (21). Key chapters in *Reclaiming the Rural* indicate how different constituencies negotiate rhetorically in the ways Fleming and Powell describe. The phrase *reclaiming the rural* means considering how rural spaces and people relate—through representation or interaction—to urban and suburban areas and ultimately to the global community.

We saw *Rural Literacies* as the start of a conversation, joining in with fellow scholars such as Katherine Kelleher Sohn (*Whistlin' and Crowin' Women of Appalachia: Literacy Practices since College*, 2006), Jacqueline Edmondson (*Prairie Town: Redefining Rural Life in the Age of Globalization*, 2003), and Robert Brooke (*Rural Voices: Place Conscious Education and the Teaching of Writing*, 2003). These texts, in part, rely upon qualitative research in rural communities; we believe, as many literacy scholars do, that "little narratives" (see Daniell) allow us to see, in the most textured ways, how, as Deborah Brandt argues, "literacy is always in flux" ("Accumulating Literacy" 666).

After the publication of *Rural Literacies*, we heard from rural, urban, and suburban educators who told us that the book began to fill a gap for them in rhetoric and composition scholarship; graduate students wrote to us about their projects on rural literacies and rhetorics and sought our advice. From our desire to expand our initial research to include a broader set of sites, populations, perspectives, and methodologies, the idea for *Reclaiming the Rural* was born.

Our working assumption in *Rural Literacies*, as now, is that *literacy* can be defined broadly as "skills and practices needed to gain knowledge, evaluate and interpret that knowledge, and apply [that] knowledge to accomplish particular goals." Here *reading* refers to "the ability to gather and process knowledge from a variety of 'texts'"; *writing* we take to mean "the ability to transform knowledge . . . just as writers transform ideas and information to accomplish rhetorical goals." *Rural literacies*, more specifically, are "the particular kinds of literate skills needed to achieve the goals of sustaining life in rural areas" (4). In *Reclaiming the Rural*, contributors build upon these definitions to explore other ideas, ranging from Deborah Brandt's definition of *literacy sponsors* as those who "set the terms for access to literacy" ("Sponsors of Literacy" 166–67); to Sylvia Scribner's metaphors of literacy as adaptation, power, and a state of grace; to Morris Young's reconsideration of the literacy narrative as an "act to confirm, transform, or even reject a person's participation in culture, raise questions about community identity and membership, or encourage participation of not only the writer but also the reader in making meaning" (35).

Reclaiming the Rural also achieves more breadth than *Rural Literacies* in terms of locale, with research based in multiple regions of the United States, Mexico, and Canada, but as any collection must be, it is limited in its scope. We include here a segment on land-based rhetorics and economies that addresses agriculture, but there could also have been a section investigating other natural-resource industries in rural areas: forestry, mining, oil and natural gas exploration, and fishing, among others. All the locales considered in this volume are situated in North America; we hope future work will widen that geographic scope and join with researchers who are beginning to examine both global and transnational understandings of rhetorics and literacies (Canagarajah; Hesford and Schell).

Our contributors employ a range of methodologies, including rhetorical analyses of economies and environments, media, and public spaces; classroom-based research; historical analysis and archival work; and qualitative research that illuminates and complicates historical contributions by rural people and organizations. Through these various methodologies, researchers in this collection help us consider how we might more productively navigate the clashes (or tacit acceptance) found in the intersections between neoliberal rhetorics and the realities of rural life and work. They engage and challenge the unfortunate binary between manual labor and intellectual work that has been propagated by political "red state/blue state" rhetorics, which distinguishes between the everyday practices of making a living in rural communities and the practices of reflection and meaning-making.

When we sent out the initial query for proposals, we asked for research into the realities of rural literacies and rhetorics against pervasive stereotypes that overlook race, class, gender, sexual orientation, place, or religion. According to Kenneth M. Johnson, in 2000, minority populations "made up 40 percent of the population residing in metropolitan counties; 22 percent in suburban counties, and in rural areas, 17 percent." However, "between 1990 and 2000 . . . in nonmetropolitan counties that were not adjacent to metropolitan areas, minorities accounted for 48 percent of the [population] increase" (25). Amid these shifts in rural population, the debates over immigration and English-only laws, and post-Katrina realities of rural and urban poverty, it is apparent that we need further research into diverse rural populations. Included in this book are chapters on indigenous peoples in the rural United States and Canada (see essays by Cori Brewster; Marcia Kmetz; and Valerie Mulholland), Mexican and Indohispano communities (essays by Damián Baca; and Susan V. Meyers), rural women (essays by Jane Greer; and Carolyn Ostrander), and poverty and race (essay by Christian Z. Goering, David A. Jolliffe, Laine Gates, Kelly Riley, and Hillary Swanton). Even as these essays contribute much-needed research, we acknowledge that a great deal more work needs to be done.

The lack of research on diverse rural populations in our field mirrors the dearth in rural sociology, as lamented in Brown and Swanson's collection, *Challenges for Rural America in the Twenty-First Century*. Rogelio Saenz and Cruz C. Torres contend that "our existing knowledge about rural Latinos is woefully inadequate," despite the fact that "Latinos have a long and well-established presence in rural areas . . . extending back to the nineteenth century," and the assumption that these populations reside only in urban areas or are migrating to urban areas from rural areas is false (70, 69). More research is needed that explores the interactions—both clashing and harmonious—among diverse populations in rural areas as demographics continue to shift. Further, research is greatly needed on the rural South, where 91 percent of rural African Americans reside and the poverty rate for black children is 41 percent, compared to "a rate of 34.6 percent for African American children in Southern cities and 21 percent for rural Southern white children" (Carolyn Rogers cited in Harris and Worthen 39). Goering et al. in this collection point to the challenges that can emerge in the classroom when trying to highlight issues of race and poverty in the South. Our hope is that this piece and others can further the conversation on rurality, race, and class and can serve to remind scholars and teachers of further research that needs to be undertaken.

Without a doubt, this is an important time to be working on rural literacies, rhetorics, and pedagogies as we confront environmental and economic challenges of unprecedented scope and impact: global climate change, the end of peak oil, rising food prices, and a worldwide economic recession, to name a few. How rural communities will participate with urban and suburban communities in fostering the kinds of literacies needed for global citizenship and sustainable economic development is a challenge that scholars in rhetoric and composition are taking up already. As the essays in this collection demonstrate, rural people and organizations have long worked to reclaim the rural, despite media representations that sometimes still erase the ways that rural people, spaces, and collectivities across regions and locales must work together in a global culture. Online spaces, such as Reimagine Rural, Blog for Rural America, The Daily Yonder, and the Rural Womyn Zone have become resource hubs of literate and rhetorical activity by and for rural people. For scholars and teachers, it is critical to engage literacies and rhetorics that economically, historically, and pedagogically reclaim the rural in productive ways. We hope this volume offers readers insight into the ways you might reclaim the rural in your own work.

Works Cited

"About the Center for Rural Affairs." Center for Rural Affairs. Web. 16 June 2009.

Brandt, Deborah. "Accumulating Literacy: Writing and Learning to Write in the Twentieth Century." *College English* 57 (Oct. 1995): 649–68. Print.

——."Sponsors of Literacy." *College Composition and Communication* 49.2 (1998): 165–85. Print.

Canagarajah, Suresh. *A Geopolitics of Academic Writing*. Pittsburgh: U of Pittsburgh P, 2002. Print.

Daniell, Beth. *A Communion of Friendship: Literacy, Spiritual Practice, and Women in Recovery*. Carbondale: Southern Illinois UP, 2003. Print.

Donehower, Kim, Charlotte Hogg, and Eileen E. Schell. *Rural Literacies*. Carbondale: Southern Illinois UP, 2007. Print.

Fleming, David. *City of Rhetoric: Revitalizing the Public Sphere in Metropolitan America*. Albany: State U of New York P, 2009. Print.

Friend, Christy. "From the Contact Zone to the City: Iris Marion Young and Composition Theory." *JAC: Journal of Advanced Composition* 19.4 (Winter 1999): 657–76. Print.

Harris, Rosalind P., and Dreamal Worthen. "African Americans in Rural America." *Challenges for Rural America in the Twenty-first Century*. Ed. David L. Brown and Louis E. Swanson. University Park: Pennsylvania State UP, 2003. 32–42. Print.

Hesford, Wendy, and Eileen E. Schell. "Introduction: Configurations of Transnationality—Locating Feminist Rhetorics." *College English* 70.5 (2008): 461–71. Print.

Johnson, Kenneth M. "Unpredictable Directions of Rural Population Growth and Migration." *Challenges for Rural America in the Twenty-first Century*. Ed. David L. Brown and Louis E. Swanson. University Park: Pennsylvania State UP, 2003. Print.

McComiskey, Bruce, and Cynthia Ryan, eds. *City Comp: Identities, Spaces, Practices*. Albany: State U of New York P, 2003. Print.

Powell, Douglas Reichert. *Critical Regionalism: Connecting Politics and Culture in the American Landscape*. Chapel Hill: U of North Carolina P, 2007. Print.

Reynolds, Nedra. "Composition's Imagined Geographies: The Politics of Space in the Frontier, City, and Cyberspace." *College Composition and Communication* 50.1 (1998): 12–35. Print.

Saenz, Rogelio, and Cruz C. Torres. "Latinos in Rural America." *Challenges for Rural America in the Twenty-first Century*. Ed. David L. Brown and Louis E. Swanson. University Park: Pennsylvania State UP, 2003. 57–70. Print.

Shapiro, Henry. *Appalachia on Our Mind: The Southern Mountains and Mountaineers in the American Consciousness, 1870–1920*. Chapel Hill: U of North Carolina P, 1978. Print

Young, Morris. *Minor Re/Visions: Asian American Literacy Narratives as a Rhetoric of Citizenship*. Carbondale: Southern Illinois UP, 2004. Print.

Reclaiming the Rural

Introduction: Reclaiming the Rural

Kim Donehower, Charlotte Hogg, and Eileen E. Schell

> Other people don't like to say bad things
> about rural areas. So I will.
> —Michael Katz, qtd. in Berkes

In 2009, as part of the U.S. federal economic stimulus package, President Barack Obama announced a 7.2 billion dollar expansion of rural broadband Internet access to reach the "underserved" (Berkes). Many rural areas lack broadband access and have only slow dial-up access or no Internet access at all. In an age when information technology is vital to the growth and development of small businesses and local economies, as well as our nation and our world, those who have little or no access to the Internet are being left behind on the wrong side of the "digital divide."

The federal investment in rural broadband access has its fair share of opponents. Michael Katz, former Federal Communication Commission economic spokesperson and now a professor of business at New York University, argued at an American Enterprise Institute panel on 10 February 2009, summarized in a conference report, that "Congress may even be harming the environment by promoting and subsidizing rural broadband access." Rural people, Katz argued, are living an "environmentally hostile lifestyle" (qtd in Eboch) because energy is used inefficiently in sparsely populated areas. Katz noted that "studies have shown that living in a city is a good thing." (qtd in Eboch) since it "takes less energy to heat a multi-unit dwelling, and localized public transportation is far more environmentally friendly than a long car commute from a rural location." Eboch, summarizing Katz's comments, noted that it "would be a mistake to encourage a multibillion dollar subsidy that is simply 'lining the pockets of rural telecos and rural landowners' while distorting environmental incentives." While it is appropriate for commentators like Katz to question the government's federal stimulus plan, his comments about rural areas are fueled by two major assumptions: that rural communities and rural people are a drain on federal resources and that they are energy inefficient—a set of assumptions not supported by actual research on rural life and economies.

Katz was not alone in his concerns. The *New York Times* referred to rural broadband as a potential "cyber bridge to nowhere." Upon reviewing the debate initiated at the American Enterprise Institute and covered in the *New York Times*, Dee Davis, director of the Center for Rural Strategies in Whitesboro, Kentucky, remarked in a National Public Radio interview that "when they talk about 'cyber bridges to nowhere,' what they're really doing is betraying arrogance. . . . When people think of rural as 'nowhere,' [they're] saying the people who live in those places aren't worth working with, they're not worth helping" (qtd. in Berkes). The National Public Radio interview went on to liken the project of improving rural broadband access to the rural electrification and telephone service projects of the twentieth century. In other words, such projects demonstrate what amounts to a "right of infrastructure" (Berkes) for all Americans, whether rural, urban, or suburban.

The debate over rural broadband access and its historical antecedents is much more complex than we can cover here, but it reflects a typical division in the country over the contributions of rural America. Many Americans think of rural areas as geographically "nowhere," and rural people as quaint, hardworking, and useful as long as they don't require federal resources like urban and suburban Americans do. Then there is the complaint that Katz raised in his American Enterprise Institute speech: rural Americans are a problem because they live energy-inefficient lifestyles, despite the fact they grow food that urban and suburban people eat and produce products that urban and suburban people consume. Even as presidential candidate Barack Obama championed rural broadband access in the federal stimulus package, he represented rural people in Pennsylvania to an urban group of voters in San Francisco as those who are bitter over job losses and then "cling to guns or religion or antipathy to people who aren't like them or anti-immigrant sentiment or anti-trade sentiment as a way to explain their frustrations" (qtd. in Britt). Of course, Obama issued an apology for his statement and said he didn't adequately contextualize his remarks; however, his comments stung many rural voters and allowed his Democratic challenger Hillary Clinton to call him "elitist" and "'out of touch' with everyday Americans" (qtd in Britt).

Such statements about rural people get played out frequently in the press and spark scholars and activists of rural life to try to "reclaim" a more complex understanding of rural life—one not based on stereotypic assumptions about the close-mindedness, insularity, "frontier" mentality, and firearm-obsession of rural residents. We use the word *reclaiming* to signify the effort to see rural places, spaces, and people as deserving equal attention, access, and consideration in matters of economic and public policy such as job creation, education, health care, and technology.

At a more basic level, we use the phrase "reclaiming the rural" to encourage those who are mapping the future in uncertain economic times to *see* the rural at all. Just as the *New York Times* labeled broadband access for rural communities "the cyber bridge to *nowhere*," the rural is routinely absent from the work of futurists such as business professor Richard Florida and the urbanist Jane Jacobs, who influenced him. In his widely read essay "How the Crash Will Reshape America" in the March 2009 *Atlantic*, Florida envisions a future with "a more concentrated geography" in which "great mega-regions will rise farther upward and extend farther outward." Florida describes such geographical configurations as "a landscape that can accommodate and accelerate invention, innovation, and creation—the activities in which the U.S. still holds a big competitive advantage." Similarly, in Jacobs's *Cities and the Wealth of Nations: Principles of Economic Life,* "bypassed places"—rural communities that don't "[serve] city markets or [send] out people to city jobs or [receive] city technology, city transplants, or city money. . . . sink into lives of rural subsistence" (124) and become what Jacobs labels "*morosos,* those without hope" (134). When "invention, innovation, and creation" are seen as only of urban provenance, it is easy to write the rural out of the future—despite the long history of rural invention, innovation, and creation and the fact that predominantly rural states generally fared well during the economic crash of 2008–9.

Additionally, Florida's and Jacobs's discussions about the future development of "mega-regions" do not acknowledge how such growth is based on a reliance on rural areas for the production of food, fiber, and sustainable, renewable energy such as wind power (see Warner). What their futuristic discourses also represent is what historian David Danbom, in *Born in the Country,* characterizes as the trivialization of "the rural past by denying its relevance to the present." Danbom argues that it is all too common for historians and public commentators to portray farms and rural areas as "something left behind by a maturing nation, like a skirt that was no longer in style or shoes that did not fit anymore" (ix).

In the midst of such debates over rural life and the future of rural economies, we situate *Reclaiming the Rural.* The phrase "reclaiming the rural" is hardly unique and has often been used by scholars, rural activists, and educators to demonstrate that rural lives and rural cultures have value, meaning, and complexity. One repeated theme—no surprise here—is the need to reclaim the rural against the tide of urban bias and policies that favor densely populated areas over lesser-populated ones. That the concept of "rural" is often associated with negative qualities—with lack and lag, with "backwardness," "inefficiency," "lack of progress"—is not a new notion, but an ongoing challenge for representing the needs, concerns, and perspectives of rural people and communities.

The phrase "reclaiming the rural" has been used by teachers reclaiming rural schools for rural students, artists reclaiming the cultural role of rural artists, and small farmers reclaiming farming from the throes of corporate agribusiness. "Reclaiming the rural" also has been associated with the "land occupation" movements in Africa, Asia, and South America where displaced peoples have taken back rural lands from governments and corporate interests. What drives much of this effort to "reclaim the rural" is a struggle over resources in rural areas—land, timber, minerals, energy—and a struggle over the terms of representation and access—political, artistic, and legal.

Keeping History in Mind

The history of reclaiming the rural in the United States is complex, tied to the power of the government to claim and then reclaim lands for national purposes whether through the spoils of war, federal land purchases, or acts of Congress. We must remember the Treaty of Guadalupe Hidalgo, which punctuated the end of the 1848 Mexican-American War and "over night reconstituted under the purview of the US state roughly 550,000 [square] miles of land and 60,000 Spanish-speaking residents" (Trujillo). These residents, as Damián Baca demonstrates in his chapter, have lived under three different manifestations of "Western colonial power (Spanish Empire, postcolonial Mexico, US imperial expansion) without moving an inch" (Trujillo). We must also recall the 1862 Homestead Act, which distributed thousands of acres of land occupied by native peoples to white settlers, including thousands of European immigrants ("Homestead Act"). This act, part of the larger genocide of native peoples, including the earlier devastating Indian Removal Act of 1830, ensured the government-mandated "settlement" and agricultural and community development of rural areas by white settlers, including many European immigrants fleeing persecution and seeking improved economic opportunities; yet it also brought the displacement of native peoples onto reservations, consigning thousands of native peoples to death by disease and starvation.

We must remember that government reclamation projects to build dams and dredge rivers to carry water into arid regions for farming and for hydroelectric power benefited agriculture, but exacted serious environmental costs. In 1902, after Congress passed the Reclamation Act, "which required that water users repay construction costs from which they received benefits," the government established the National Reclamation Service as part of the U.S. Geological Survey. The rhetoric of "reclamation," meaning irrigation projects, was that arid land was being "reclaimed" for "homemaking": "Irrigation's supporters believed reclamation programs would encourage Western settlement, making homes for Americans on family farms"—but at the same time drew water from other populations (see chapter 1 in this volume) and remade the Western landscape. Millions of federal dollars were spent on the construction of Hoover Dam beginning in 1928 and later when dozens of hydroelectric projects were launched during the Great Depression and after World War II. A story that received less attention during this time period was the massive upheaval that these projects caused, as white townspeople, settlers, farmers, and native people living on reservations were removed and resettled before the dams flooded their communities. This story of "reclamation" followed by "relocation," a synonym for displacement, is played out globally as hydroelectric power projects in India and China have led to the relocation of millions of rural citizens. On the Columbia River Basin in Washington, when the salmon population declined precipitously due to some four hundred dams on the Columbia River, fish ladders were built to allow migrating salmon the chance to return to their spawning grounds. Such efforts to even further manipulate natural resources have had mixed results ("Fish").

Thus, over the last two centuries, the federal government has first claimed and then reclaimed lands for government purposes, a complex exercise of power that puts the needs and concerns of one group or entity over another. The act of claiming and then "reclaiming" the rural involves an awareness of complicated histories that are inflected by relations of class, race, gender, power, institutional authority, and the environment. Anyone seeking to reclaim the rural must account for what purpose it is being reclaimed, for whom, and what costs and benefits reclamation offers to different constituencies.

Scholars must also be vigilant about not falling into celebratory rhetorics of rural life that rely too much on nostalgia for their power. Doing so risks placing rural areas in the paradigm of mere longing for "days gone by" or places where life is "simpler" and less affected by social and economic changes. We don't intend the term reclamation to mean laying exclusive claim to represent the rural in stereotypical, monolithic ways. Instead, we offer this collection as an attempt to reflect more accurately the continually changing, nuanced, context-dependent realities of rural life while acknowledging the complex histories, power struggles, and governmental actions that have affected and continue to affect the lives of rural citizens. Across this book, authors tap into the myriad ways reclamation can function rhetorically, historically, and pedagogically as we seek to make the realities of rural life more visible.

What Is Rural?

The term *rural* itself has been contested in recent years by scholars seeking to reclaim its demographic definition. As Andrew Isserman, a regional economist at the University of Illinois, notes, "'rural' is used in . . . overlapping and often contradictory ways, always defined by what it is not—not urban, not metropolitan" (466). Isserman explains that under the two most widely used demographic systems in the United States,

> The Grand Canyon is in metropolitan America and so are more than a million farmers. . . . Under the system of the U.S. Census Bureau, we define urban very carefully and precisely and designate as rural that which is not urban. . . . In contrast, integration of town *and* country, urban *and* rural, leads us to define metropolitan areas consisting of urban and rural areas that are functionally related to one another. Under the system of the Office of Management and Budget (OMB), we define metropolitan very carefully and precisely, beginning with an urban area at the core, but then we use the word rural indiscriminately as a widely adopted synonym for places, both urban and rural, that are not within metropolitan areas. (465–66)

The consequences for researchers and for rural residents themselves, as Isserman notes, are significant. He writes that

> we presently have no satisfactory way to measure rural for the study of rural economies or the assessment of rural conditions. Key economic and demographic data are not available for urban and rural areas, and metropolitan and nonmetropolitan commingle urban and rural, leaving us unable to separate them. Yet getting rural right is in the national interest. When we get rural wrong, we reach incorrect research conclusions and fail to reach the people, places, and businesses our governmental programs are meant to serve. (466)

For demographic purposes, Isserman's pragmatic solution uses county data to classify U.S. counties as rural, mixed rural, mixed urban, and urban. A rural county, in Isserman's designation, has fewer than 500 residents per square mile, 90 percent of its population in rural areas, and/or fewer than 10,000 residents in urban areas of the county (Isserman; Isserman, Feser, and Warren). A mixed-rural county in Isserman's schema "meets neither the urban nor the rural county criteria, and . . . its population density is less than 320 people per square mile" (Isserman 475).

Isserman's map of the United States, using these guidelines, shows a stark majority of the landmass as rural or mixed-rural; based on the 2000 census, these counties represent 41 percent of the U.S. population. Rural and mixed-rural areas lie in nearly every state, emphasizing the diversity of rural geographies and cultures. We sought to capture this diversity in selecting chapters for this volume, which focus on most major regions of the United States—the West, Midwest, South, and Northeast—and on Mexico and Canada.

It is important to define rural not only demographically and geographically, but culturally as well. The word *rural* functions for many as a marker of identity, regardless of demographic criteria or current location. People may self-identify as rural or identify others as rural, and by so doing invoke a complex chain of associations and ideologies. Individuals who were raised in areas that meet demographic definitions of rural may explicitly reject that term as an identity marker, only to reclaim it later in life—even if they settle in an urban area.

For example, the contributors to this volume feel strong associations with rurality, even though we are operating in professions—academia, education—that are typically seen as urban, or, at least, as urbane (despite the history of land-grant institutions and their relationships to rural communities). Those of us who began our lives in rural areas and moved to urban areas to seek employment are part of the great outmigration that has seen declining populations in rural communities across the globe from the mid-twentieth century through today. The migratory nature of the academic job market has further uprooted us from even our regions of origin, so that many of us now work on rural issues often at quite a distance from those places that gave us our sense of a rural identity. Still, one need not live continuously in rural areas to have a political grasp and appreciation for the challenges of rural life.

Outmigration is such a pervasive feature of contemporary rural communities that to fully understand rural identity, rural rhetorics, and rural literacies, one might consider them as operating in diaspora. Literacy researchers John Duffy and Victoria Purcell-Gates demonstrate this in their work, respectively, on the Hmong resettled in Wausau, Wisconsin, and on Southern Appalachians relocated to a midwestern city. As Duffy describes, rural out-migration and the cultural accommodations that followed were hardly a matter of pure choice, but something more complex:

> Literacy development is local, situated, and specific, but it is also global, transnational, and profoundly historical. To say this is . . . to recall Eric Wolf's appeal that we consider the interrelated and undeniable totality

of forces—what he called "that wider field of force"—that influence the ways in which human beings make sense of who they are and where they belong in the world. (151)

In the early twenty-first century, one particular transnational movement profoundly contributes to the "wider field of force" that affects the lives and choices of rural peoples: neoliberalism. While the political philosophy of liberalism tends toward capitalism, in it, market-based economies are only justified insofar as they contribute to the larger goal of human rights and freedoms (Weinstein). In neoliberalism, an ideological offshoot, the maintenance of the free market has become the primary goal. Stephanie Mudge describes the "distinctive ideological core" of neoliberalism as "the elevation of the market—understood as a non-political, non-cultural, machinelike entity—over all other modes of organization" (705). Elsewhere, she defines the term as "an ideological system that holds the 'market' sacred" (706) and notes that

> neo-liberalism's expressions in policy and politics are produced at the intersection of the intellectual, political, and bureaucratic realms, generating not one neo-liberalism but many neo-liberalisms. These expressions are not coherent in the sense of producing identical political languages and policies, but they are anchored by the same common sense: the autonomous force of the market; the superiority of market or market-like competition over bureaucracies as a mechanism for the allocation of resources. (724)

Neoliberalisms give markets primacy over people and empower transnational corporations to exercise control over markets with the cooperation of national governments. As a result, under-represented constituencies, such as rural residents who lack lobbying power, have difficulty asserting their needs and values. When rural people and land become seen solely as economic, political, or military resources to be mined and exploited, they become wholly subject to the "wider field of force":

> It was the Hmong presence in Xieng Khouang—with its strategic proximity to North Vietnam, its mountainous terrain so ideal for guerilla activity, and its soil so suitable for profitable opium poppy cultivation—that would eventually ensnare the Hmong in a series of relationships with Western global powers that would forever change their history and culture. (Duffy 26)

This is a telling example of the ways rural landscapes—and the people who inhabit them—can be caught up in potential economic and political forces that can have serious consequences.

To avoid treating rural areas as sites for resource exploitation, sites of cheap labor, or as dumping grounds for toxic substances or institutions that no one else wants in their backyards (prisons, for instance) means identifying with rural life and people. Such identification, regardless of one's location in a rural, urban, or suburban locale, is a key element, we believe, in sustaining rural communities. In *Rural Literacies,* we used an adaptation of Kenneth Burke's term *identification* to describe a relationship we refer to as "mutual identification," a fundamental goal of any rhetoric that works toward rural sustainability. Here Eileen Schell describes how a rhetoric of mutual identification could ameliorate the effects of the farm crisis:

> The rhetoric of mutual identification emphasizes the common interests of farmers and consumers. . . . Instead of identifying farmers as victims and objects of pity, as they are often portrayed in the tragedy narrative, readers/ viewers can begin to see the situation of farmers as interconnected with their own concerns for healthy communities and healthy food. Rhetorics of the farm crisis that practice mutual identification demonstrate how farmers and consumers can be united around common issues of concern such as food safety, E coli outbreaks, use of hormones and pesticides, environmental policies, rural migration and out-migration, immigration policy, corporate control and overdependence on a few large corporations to provide all of our food ("Rethinking"). Arguments about the farm crisis that are based on mutual identification emphasize sustainability—sustainability of not only rural communities, but of urban and suburban communities as well. (98)

It is in these ways that we see the topic of rural literacies, rhetorics, and pedagogies as being of vital concern to all—not only to those of us who work in or for explicitly rural populations. As Isserman notes, the demographic problem of "the rural" arose in part from "the separation of territory into town or country, urban or rural, lead[ing] us to define rural as homogeneous with respect to being not urban" (465). In other words, for a long time we have simply not been able to *see* rural areas as anything other than "other." The very demographic methods used to identify the rural have defined it as monolithically not-us—when "us" defaults to urban. When a rural area is intimately connected to an urban one, creating the possibility for mutual identification, the rural nature of that community is demographically erased as it is folded into the "metropolitan" designation. *Reclaiming the Rural* is an invitation to both "reclaim" and re-see what distinguishes the rural from, and connects it to, the urban and suburban.

Chapter Overviews

This volume is divided into three sections: Land Economies and Rhetorics, Histories, and Pedagogies. We have maintained this division to organize what follows, but as each author works to unpack her or his central topic, there is inevitable crossover into one or more other areas. Section 1, Land Economies and Rhetorics, addresses the struggles rural residents and stakeholders face as they engage in debates over how to sustain themselves in a globalized world. Section 2, Histories, examines how rural individuals and organizations integrate manual and intellectual labor as well as foster the literacy sponsorship needed to sustain rural communities. Section 3, Pedagogies, considers how to involve rural students, schools, teachers, and communities in curricular and pedagogical work that encourages active and aware citizens, ready to meet the challenges of rural life.

The "Land Economies and Rhetorics" section begins with an essay that directly addresses the resource issue that is most associated with "reclamation"—water rights, one of the central environmental and sociopolitical conflicts in the history of the rural American West. Marcia Kmetz examines how two rural groups—native peoples and ranchers in the Wind River area of Wyoming—create an ethos for themselves in the debates over water rights. Next, Cori Brewster documents the struggle over the terms of representation and access in agricultural literacy curricula, focusing on two programs that seek to represent farm issues to a nonfarming public. Brewster demonstrates the ways these curricula rewrite the history of who farms and why, and advance a neoliberal agenda that serves corporate interests. In chapter 3, Cynthia Ryan investigates how farmers respond to the rhetoric of neoliberal economic development whose ethic of "get bigger or get out" pervades agricultural publications. As Ryan shows, this neoliberal dictum exists alongside traditional, romantic representations of farm life, and it is in this complex rhetorical mix that farmers must make real decisions about how to best thrive in the global economy.

While the essays on land economies and rhetorics demonstrate how reclamation is wedded to the struggle over resources and representation, reclamation in the Histories section demands that we uncover rural histories in ways that are not too celebratory or preservationist but reflect the material, social, and economic realities of rural life. Damián Baca examines how a grassroots Indohispana/o educational think tank promoted historical and critical literacies in northern New Mexico as the region moved rapidly from a historically agrarian, preindustrial existence to a postindustrial cradle of the atomic age. Jane Greer reclaims the common depiction of rural women's labor from the stereotype of soul-deadening, intellectually simplistic drudgery. She asserts the "intellectual sophistication, creativity, and resourcefulness" of this work well suits the demands new economies will make on rural areas. Carolyn Ostrander examines the role of the Grange as a rhetorical sponsor that offered rural women orators the rhetorical space to "formulate independent opinions and to address 'mixed' audiences" while still operating within "nineteenth-century claims about the role of virtuous women." I. Moriah McCracken analyzes 4-H, another key sponsor of rural literacy and rhetoric. McCracken breaks down the binary between bureaucratic "knowledge-telling" writing and "higher" forms of "knowledge-transforming" writing, arguing that the hybrid literacy forms 4-H encourages may be one way to help rural people value and integrate the manual and intellectual literacies of rural work life. Rounding out the Histories section, Susan Myers examines how the development of the Mexican public education system engages the tension between intellectual and physical labor. Focusing on one Mexican rural town, Myers demonstrates the ways religious rhetorics and nationalist agendas converged to create an educational system that, despite its efforts, does not serve the local community as intended.

The final section, Pedagogies, explores both challenges and successes as educators negotiate *with* rural populations instead of deciding *for* them. First, Robert Brooke describes the nurturing of young rural activists through a project in which Nebraska high school students created video segments on rural issues for statewide public television. Brooke documents the ways such programs better equip students for rural citizenship and advocacy given the high demands on rural citizens for rhetorical efficacy and political savvy. Then Christian Goering, David Jolliffe, Laine Gates, Kelly Riley, and Hillary Swanton explore a university-community partnership and its effects on University of Arkansas at Fayetteville college students who mentored rural Delta high school students in a place-based literacy project. The project illuminates the potential for mutual identification among urban, suburban, and rural students. Valerie Mulholland examines the possibilities of creating mutual identification in a classroom context, reflecting on her attempts to sensitize her university English methods students to the issues of race and difference they will face teaching in rural Saskatchewan. While Mulholland considers the reductive ways many multicultural curricula engage the "other," Sara Webb-Sunderhaus examines the reductive ways literacy is marketed to rural college students. She contrasts the representations of literacy's benefits in campus bookstore posters with the ways students reshape those messages as part of a rural ethos of reciprocal literacy sponsorship. In the final chapter, Jacqueline Edmondson and Thomas Butler analyze the critical literacy development of practicing K-12 teachers, especially in light of the push toward education as standardized test preparation. The authors propose systemic changes to produce teachers who can truly teach literacy for sustainability in their classrooms, working to reclaim the rural from rhetorics of neoliberalism to move toward sustainability for all.

Finally, in his afterword, rural education expert Paul Theobald historically contextualizes the chapters in the collection, reminding us how rural policies have long been wrapped up in cultural misunderstandings. He challenges readers to productively move toward reclamation in their own work.

As these essays contribute to efforts to "reclaim" rural literacies, they also open new directions for research and pedagogy. We hope readers will further those new directions and push the boundaries of what it means to do research and engage in teaching practices that address rural literacies. In particular, we hope readers will see opportunities for expanding teaching and research about rural literacies beyond the boundaries of North America and into other geographic locations.

Works Cited and Consulted

Berkes, Howard. "Stimulus Stirs Debate over Rural Broadband Access." Morning Edition. *National Public Radio.* 16 Feb. 2009. Web. 16 Feb. 2009.

Britt, Russ. "Obama Remarks Likely to Hurt Pennsylvania Effort: Statements on Rural Americans May Come Back to Haunt Democrat in Fall." *MarketWatch.* Web. 14 April 2008.

Center for Media Justice. "Rural Broadband and the Stimulus Package: Digital Inclusion Is Hardly a 'Cyberbridge to Nowhere.'" Web. 20 May 2009.

Danbom, David. *Born in the Country: A History of Rural America.* Baltimore: Johns Hopkins UP, 1995. Print.

Donehower, Kim, Charlotte Hogg, and Eileen E. Schell. *Rural Literacies.* Carbondale: Southern Illinois UP, 2007. Print.

Duffy, John. *Writing from These Roots: Literacy in a Hmong-American Community.* Honolulu: U of Hawaii P, 2007. Print.

Eboch, Josh. "Keep Digging: Does Rural Internet Access Qualify as Shovel-Ready Economic Stimulus?" *American Enterprise Institute for Public Policy Research.* Web. 20 May 2009.

"Fish Passage at Dams." Columbia River History. Northwest Power and Conservation Council. Web. 13 June 2009.

Florida, Richard. "How the Crash Will Reshape America." *Atlantic* Mar. 2009. Web. 7 June 2009.

Greenwood, M. J. "Internal Migration in Developed Countries." *Handbook of Population and Family Economics.* Ed. M. R. Rosenzweig and O. Stark. New York: Elsevier Science B.V., 1997. Print.

Herszenhorn, David M. "Internet Money in Fiscal Plan: Wise or Waste?" *New York Times.* Web. 2 Feb. 2009.

"The Homestead Act." Library of Congress. *American Memory.* Web. 15 May 2009.

Isserman, Andrew M. "In the National Interest: Defining Rural and Urban Correctly in Research and Public Policy." *International Regional Science Review* 28 (2005): 465–99. Print.

Isserman, Andrew M., Edward Feser, and Drake Warren. "Why Some Rural Communities Prosper While Others Do Not." Report to USDA Rural Development. 23 May 2007. Regional Economics and Public Policy Research Group, University of Illinois at Champaign-Urbana. Web.

Jacobs, Jane. *Cities and the Wealth of Nations: Principles of Economic Life.* New York: Vintage, 1985. Print.

Marre, Alexander. "Rural Out-Migration, Income, and Poverty: Are Those Who Move Truly Better Off?" Agricultural and Applied Economics Association Joint Annual Meeting. Milwaukee. 26–29 July 2009. Print.

Mudge, Stephanie. "What Is Neo-liberalism?" *Socio-Economic Review* 6 (2008): 703–31. Print.

Plane, D. A. "Demographic Influences on Migration." *Regional Studies* 27. 4 (1993): 375–83. Print.

Powell, Douglas Reichert. *Critical Regionalism.* Chapel Hill: U of North Carolina P, 2007. Print.

Purcell-Gates, Victoria. *Other People's Words: The Cycle of Low Literacy.* Cambridge, MA.: Harvard UP, 1995. Print.

"Rethinking 'Save the Family Farm.'" *ActionMedia.* Web. 20 Mar. 2004.

Trujillo, S. "Chicana/Knowledge/Race/History/Chicano." "When History Wakes." Web. 13 June 2009.

U.S. Department of the Interior, Bureau of Reclamation. "The Bureau of Reclamation: A Very Brief History." Web. 13 June 2009.

Warner, Melanie. "Can Wind Power a Rural Renaissance?" Center for Rural Affairs. 15 February 2009. Web. 13 June 2009.

Weinstein, Jack. *Adam Smith's Pluralism: Rationality, Education, and the Moral Sentiments.* New Haven: Yale University Press, forthcoming. Print.

Section I

Land Economies and Rhetorics

1

A River Runs By It: The Performance of Rural Civic Ethos in the Wind River Water Disputes

Marcia Kmetz

What we call man's power over nature turns
out to be a power exercised by some men over
other men with nature as its instrument.
—C. S. Lewis, *The Abolition of Man*

How could we dare do anything other than protect and
honor this last core, the land from which we came, the
land that has marked us, and whose essence, whose
mystery, contains our own essence and mystery?
—Rick Bass, "On Willow Creek"

Nestled in the northeastern portion of Wyoming and tucked between the often snowcapped Wind River mountain range to the west and the Absaroka and Owl Creek ranges to the east, the Wind River valley is said to be "rich with juxtaposition" (Greater Yellowstone): Red Desert badlands compete against blue mountain peaks; "authentic" Old West towns compete against the expansive Wind River Reservation; working ranches compete against open wilderness; an arid landscape competes against nearly two thousand miles of fishing streams. Of all these oppositions, though, it is the water that has come to define the place and to divide it; the water luring early ranchers to the area and setting in motion a battle between agriculture and aridity, native methods and modern technologies.

The story of agriculture in the Wind River valley is nearly a western cliché: easterners looking for new lands and a new chance in the wilds of the West, the American government promising free land to those who could "prove it up" as homesteaders, and dreams built around an idea of settling—civilizing—untamed and uninhabited lands. This is a narrative repeated with ease because of its frequency of use, a narrative that marks new beginnings in the lives of white settlers and a new fate for the American West.

Yet this is a story of dis-ease as well, for the land, as we know, was not uninhabited and not free for the taking; the process of taming the West was a violent one that eradicated the lives and cultures of the Native Americans, in this case the Eastern Shoshone and the Northern Arapaho. The Shoshone, who had once moved freely through parts of Colorado, Utah, and Wyoming, were relocated to the Wind River Reservation by treaty in 1863. The First Treaty of Fort Bridger provided the Shoshones with 44 million acres they had selected in the Wind River valley. This treaty was revised by the Second Treaty of Fort Bridger, executed a mere five years later, which moved the reservation to a new location east of the Wind River range and reduced the size of that reservation to approximately 3 million acres but secured "absolute and undisturbed use of the land." Those absolute rights were revised ten years later, in 1878, when the U.S. government added the Northern Arapaho Indians to the reservation (Bellamore 20). Further reductions in the size of the reservation followed as the tribes relinquished lands surrounding their hot springs and an additional 1.48 million acres in exchange for money and cattle. As Geoffrey O'Gara notes, "It was an opportune moment in history to take advantage of the Indians. An 1894 special report to the U.S. Census indicated that while the Shoshone and Arapaho had made a good-faith effort to become farmers, they were starving, and the government had failed to deliver the food, the seed, or the tools it had promised" (18).

As their tribal lands and food resources were increasingly diminished and as their attempts to become farmers generally failed, as the reservation system intended, the tribes suffered. Coinciding with the succession of land through the first and second McLaughlin Agreements (1897 and 1904/5 respectively) was the passing of the General Allotment Act intended to "promote and accelerate Indian assimilation into white society" (Bellamore 21). This act began a process of divvying up reservation lands based on a model of individual ownership, distributing lands to individual Indians who would own that land outright after 25 years, assuming they could succeed at farming and could afford the remaining fees. Frequently, those fees could not be paid and the lands were sold, generally to white settlers. After the allotment process was completed, "excess" lands were opened to white settlement (Bellamore 21). What this complex narrative of compelled distribution of lands created was a patchwork of ownership within the Wind River valley, the foundation for later debates over water rights to the diminishing Wind River.

This is also a story of dis-ease because settlers carried the eastern cultural ideology that land was forever bountiful, resources forever renewable, water forever flowing. Water is not forever flowing in the landscape of the West. Marc Reisner, author of *Cadillac Desert*, argues that "In the West, lack of water is the central fact of existence, and a whole culture and set of values have grown up around it. In the East, to 'waste' water is to consume it need-lessly or excessively. In the West, to waste water is *not* to consume it—to let it flow unimpeded and undiverted down rivers" (12). Thus the absence of water and the response of local citizens to that absence shaped the character of the American West:

> Aridity, more than anything else, gives the western landscape its character. It is aridity that gives the air its special dry clarity; aridity that puts bril-liance in the light and polishes and enlarges the stars; aridity that leads the grasses to evolve as bunches rather than as turf; aridity that exposes the pigmentations of the raw earth and limits, almost eliminates, the color of chlorophyll; aridity that erodes the earth in cliffs and badlands rather than in softened and vegetated slopes, that has shaped the characteristi-cally nocturnal life of the deserts. (Stegner 46)

Stegner goes to on to argue that "in the attempt to compensate for nature's lacks we have remade whole sections of the western landscape" (47). This is particularly true of the Wind River valley, a landscape not naturally suited to the agriculture it now attempts to sustain, an area of rugged mountains and sagebrush flatlands that requires massive irrigation systems to produce somewhat meager amounts of alfalfa hay and sugar beets, predominantly.

This character of the land, deeply impacted by its aridity, also deeply im-pacts the character of its inhabitants, those who rely on limited supplies of water for agricultural survival. The landscape of the West is felt as a part of the communal character, as part of what it means to be western. As author Mary Clearman Blew articulates, "I am bone deep in landscape. In this dome of sky and river and undeflected sunlight, in this illusion of timelessness, I can almost feel my body, blood, and breath in the broken line of the bluffs and the pervasive scent of ripening sweet clover and dust, almost feel the sagging fence line of ancient cedar posts stapled across my vitals" (7). So deeply felt is the land that it becomes a central part of the community living on it. This connection to the character of the land is clear for the Wind River tribe of the Northern Arapaho, who base it upon a lengthy historical relationship with the land and an enduring future one: "Our magnificent mountains and plains continue to inspire and shape the character of our people, leading us to pro-tect this heritage and use our land wisely" ("Location"). Some local farmers, on the other hand, came late to the valley and thus have a different, but equally powerful, connection to its character: "Many of them had endured years of drought on dryland farms in Nebraska and Oklahoma where, as one said to me, 'all you could do was look at the sky.' Here they had a ditch, and the assurance that water would never be a problem; even when it was still treeless rabbitbrush, it felt like the Promised Land" (O'Gara 34). Whether local landowners came early or late, whether they were most concerned with preserving the land or cultivating it, this western landscape became the "habitual dwelling place"; that is, an *ethos*, a place that has formed local character and consciousness, a character that is as much about the place as it is about the moral character of people.

Ethos as a "Habitual Gathering Place"

Aristotle argued, somewhat reluctantly given his preference for *logos*, that "moral character, so to speak, constitutes the most effective source of persuasion" (*Rhetoric* 1.2.1356a13). Yet this sense of *ethos* is often seen as the property or character of an individual, as a strategy that applies solely to or is constructed solely by the rhetor. That individualistic understanding is a modern interpretation, argues S. Michael Halloran, and not correlative to earlier communal uses of *ethos* in ancient Greece:

> In contrast to modern notions of the person or self, *ethos* emphasizes the conventional rather than the idiosyncratic, the public rather than the private. The most concrete meaning given for the term in the Greek lexicon is "a habitual gathering place," and I suspect that it is upon this image of people gathering together in a public place, sharing experiences and ideas, that its meaning as character rests. To have *ethos* is to manifest the virtues most valued by the culture to and for which one speaks. (Halloran 60)

Understanding ethos as a performance of communal identity rightly locates it back in the community and rightly acknowledges the role of place in that community. "A habitual gathering *place*" indicates that place is a central component of character, that the physical location of the rhetorical act contains a character of its own that shapes communal values and the rhetor's performance of those values.

This meaning of ethos as a "habitual gathering place" predates the "more familiar and related translations as 'moral character' and 'ethics'" of Aristotle, argues Michael Hyde in his introduction to *The Ethos of Rhetoric* (xiii). He notes that our earliest understanding of the concept of ethos dates back to Homer and Hesiod, traveling *rhapsodes* who performed particular communal values related to specific places in the ancient world. This carries forward, too, into the more notable spaces of rhetorical activity in antiquity. The Greek assembly, for example, was a definably different place than the Roman polis, and as such, the performances of ethos in those two spaces were distinct, representing differences in the character of the communities as well as the character of the places. Consider, too, Socrates's favoring of the city in the Platonic dialogue *Phaedrus*, noting that the "rustic sort of wisdom" was paced and performed differently from that of reasoned discourse in the city and arguing that "the country places and the trees won't teach me anything, and the people in the city do" (Plato 140). Thus, place holds a central role in rhetorical performance and in audience perception as it relates to a speaker's ethos.

Scholars in rhetoric have taken notice of this alternative understanding of *ethos* that centers on the role of location or place in character. Nedra Reynolds argues that people "inscribe *who* they are by showing *where* they are" (325). Michael Hyde has also argued that the dwelling places in this definition of ethos "define the grounds, the abodes or habitats, where a person's ethics and moral character take form and develop" (xiii). In this way, we form a connection between the tradition of ethos as a habitual dwelling place and the Aristotelian understanding of moral character. The place shapes character; the land, in part, creates the community.

The places of the rural West have shaped my own ethos, one placed squarely in the landscapes of rural Montana and within the communities that inhabit them. I was raised in Fort Benton, "the birthplace of Montana," a lingering town located on the banks of the Missouri River. This was a town built by travel on those waters; a town facing deep divides over issues of water use and cultural history; a town now caught in the preservationist model, labeled as "retain[ing] much of its 'steamboat days' character" (Chouteau County) and recorded on the National Register of Historic Places; boasting no fewer than four museums, but fewer than 1,600 residents. This is a place defined by outsiders, but one whose fight for survival and self-definition mirrors, in many ways, the fight in the Wind River valley. Both places are building toward a defining ethos, an ethos reminiscent of a rhapsodic, rather than Aristotelian, definition.

Given the power and importance of definitions, their centrality to the water disputes in the Wind River valley and to the construction of character in the region, my analyses will focus on definitions through the recorded texts of this debate in its most active moments. Those texts include interviews gathered in a documentary film, where we will be paying particular attention to how the interviewees construct both their own character and that of their local counterparts, as well as legal documents and local newspaper stories gathered throughout the course of the debate. I have opted to analyze the recorded texts of this debate rather than to conduct personal interviews in order to determine how the participants were constructed in that moment rather than rely upon personal reflections after the fact.

A Defining Character: Beneficial Use and the Purposes of the Reservation

John Wesley Powell, in a report titled "Lands of the Arid Region," detailed the differences between the eastern and western United States by arguing that "the eastern region is supplied with abundant rainfall for agricultural purposes . . . but westward, the amount of aqueous precipitation diminishes in a general way until at last a region is reached where the climate is so arid that agriculture is not successful without irrigation" (1). This report, focused on the region stretching from the midpoint of the Great Plains through the Rocky Mountains and to the Pacific Ocean but excluding the Pacific Northwest, additionally declares that any substantial attempt at agriculture in the region would be fraught with difficulty: "Many droughts will occur; many seasons in a long series will be fruitless; and it may be doubted whether, on the whole, agriculture will prove remunerative" (3). Powell, then in charge of the geographical survey of the Rocky Mountain region, made these predictions in his report submitted to the government in 1879, a study completed during times of radical transformation in the Wind River valley: the numbers of bison in the area were dwindling due to fur traders who came first as a trickle and then *en masse*; the federal government learned of the existence of the lands of Yellowstone and, recognizing their distinct beauty, chose to protect them as designated public lands (an act that required the forced removal of local Indian populations); settlers followed shortly behind, trusting in the governmental promise of a substantial irrigation project.

The consequence of this transformation was a dramatic change in the definition of the place. What had once been open and free, lightly populated by humans and densely populated by wild game, was now earmarked for agriculture. Rather than reading Powell's study as the warning it clearly was, that the land was not suited for a substantial agricultural project and that there would not be water enough to sustain such an endeavor, the government sold western Wyoming as a landscape that could be successfully cultivated by hardworking settlers. The Homestead Act of 1862 not only opened up western lands for individual ownership but also redefined the purpose of those lands: as part of that act, the homesteader and head of family had to live on the land, make improvements, and *farm* the land for five years. The language in the act states that the homestead must be made for the "purpose of actual settlement and cultivation." Such an act required that citizens should remake the land for agricultural purposes, regardless of the initial character of that land. This was less important in areas where soil was suitable and water plentiful. But the Wind River valley is different.

This can be seen in contemporary arguments over the tribes' water rights. The present equation for determining the amount of water due to the tribes, as the holder of the state's first priority, is based on the amount of irrigable land available on the reservation. Yet Wyoming chief justice Thomas has said that "it seems highly unlikely that anybody's going to build dams and irrigation projects to irrigate what sort of are sagebrush flats at the moment. It just doesn't make sense" (*Wind River*).

The requirement of irrigable land was based on governmental perceptions of the character of rural land as agricultural, and the character of the nation as agrarian, rather than a clear understanding of this particular place and its particular inhabitants. These perceptions are clear in the documents relating to the removal of the Shoshone from these lands. The 1863 Fort Bridger Treaty, responsible for the initial reservation, recognized the impact of white culture on the Shoshone, noting that the government was "aware of the inconvenience resulting to the Indians in consequence of the driving away and destruction of game along the routes travelled by whites, and by the formation of agricultural and mining settlements." Perhaps because of that impact, this early treaty allows for the reservation to fulfill whatever purposes the Shoshone "may deem suitable to their wants and condition, either as hunters or herdsmen." Yet because of these impacts, the customary Shoshone ways of living on the land were no longer viable choices. This was recognized in the second Fort Bridger Treaty, which "clearly makes the point that the government wants the Indians to give up any sort of tribal allegiance and transform themselves into independent citizen farmers" ("Fort Bridger Treaty, 1868"). Article VIII, in particular, describes the rewards for Indians who selected a plot of land within the reservation and began "cultivating the soil for a living."

This redefinition of place is crucial in an area where water is scarce and determinations of water rights turn on definitions. Native American water rights were first upheld in the landmark case *Winters v. United States* (1908). That case, initiated by the Gros Ventre and Assiniboine tribes on the Fort Belknap Reservation in eastern Montana, was brought because the tribes were making every effort to become the farmers required by treaty yet were being burnt out by upstream farmers. The justices in the case determined that whenever the government reserves a piece of land (for reservations, military bases, national parks, etc.), it also reserves an appropriate amount of water to fulfill the purpose of that reservation. In this case, the purpose was defined as agricultural and thus the Indians received a substantial senior water right. Still, this decision remained vague enough to create serious conflict in the community and in the courts:

> The decision proved to be one riddled with ambiguities. For example, some authorities have suggested that the purpose of the reservation was agricultural in nature and that the reserved water rights were limited to quantities that could be put to use for irrigated agriculture within the boundaries of the reservation. Others have adopted a broad interpretation, suggesting that the Indian entitlement extends to any use that promotes economic development. The uses encompassed by the reserved right define—albeit loosely—those quantities that the court might deem "sufficient." The writers' opinion, however, falls short of providing a framework for such important and exacting definitions. These and other questions were left unanswered. (Bellamore 23–24)

This leaves room for differences in interpretation by courts and local citizens. And interpretations of "beneficial use," a term drawn from riparian doctrine, which argues that "a person acquires an enforceable right to use water only by actually diverting a quantity of water from its natural sources and applying that quantity of water to a beneficial use" (Mergen and Lui 689), vary widely.

Yet the western ideology has shifted to "first in time, first in right," a doctrine that affirms that those who have the senior water right receive their water first. This ideology is meant to better meet the needs of those cultivating "the living laboratory of yet untamed western lands. It severs the link between land ownership and water rights that form the backbone of the riparian doctrine adopted in the eastern United States. It is imbued with the character of those who forged it—miners, ranchers, homesteaders, and others—who came to settle and exploit the newly acquired territories of the United States" (Bellamore 28). It is important to note that the character ascribed to this ideology, and thus to the land, is founded on the belief that the newcomers, white settlers and miners, "forged" the land, made use of it. The Shoshones, those who predated these newcomers by 3,000 years, were not listed among the participants in the creation of character in this land and in the policies that control its resources. Thus the definition of beneficial use sat squarely and solely with the early white agriculturalists.

Local agriculturists see beneficial use only in the physical distribution of water to cultivate the land. As local farmer Bill Brown argues, "If a person's in agriculture, the water's basically their livelihood because in this country, without the water you could raise absolutely nothing" (*Wind River*). Agriculture could not survive in the region without water, and there is simply not enough to go around. The absence of water then creates a polarized discussion: is water use beneficial only for agriculture or can it be beneficial for other purposes? The simplified debate reads as us-versus-them, a choice between agriculture and fish. As Brown goes on to say, "Water . . . it's pure and simple to me. We developed the arid lands of the west for the people of the nation to produce, to feed people. That's justifiable in my way of thinking. I think it should take precedence over the fishing" (*Wind River*). In this way of conceiving the land and its purposes, the farmer is cast as devoted to the good of the country and thus is performing as a *vir bonus*, the good man model of ancient ethos. Letting the water flow is seen as waste. As Jimmy Hubenka, another local farmer, argues, "If they can use it, fine, I think they should use it. But just running it down the river benefits nobody. That's not putting it to beneficial use" (*Wind River*).

Yet the Shoshone and Arapaho tribes find that working for the good of the people means protecting the environment in a way that preserves it for future generations. Running the river dry in an effort to promote agriculture in arid regions seems nonsensical in their cultural way of conceptualizing the value of land. As such, the tribes have fought since April 1990 to utilize part of their reserved water right for in-stream flow. As part of that argument, the tribes coauthored a joint *Wind River Water Code* that "addresses the importance of interconnections between water and other resources on the landscape, identifies beneficial use of water for both cultural and religious purposes, and emphasizes the role of local indigenous ecological knowledge determining sufficient water for various uses" (Flanagan and Laituri 266). The tribes hoped to expand the state's definitions of beneficial use to better represent the character of the land and better serve the communities living on or making use of that land.

The tribes described bitter resistance to their attempts at redefinition: "In-stream flow is a four-letter word for western water rights, because agriculture—that's the law on western water. And any time any entity—whether as a tribe or even a non-Indian irrigator—if they want to transfer use of water from the beneficial use of agriculture to another beneficial use, that's a tough task" (Wes Martel, qtd. in *Wind River*). It was a tough task, fought all the way to the state supreme court. As Chief Justice Thomas says, "The case came to us because of the desire of the tribes to develop a fishery concept with the maintenance of an in-stream flow, and dealing with that, our court by a majority concluded that the reservation essentially had been established as an agricultural economic environment, and so that the reserved water rights were the rights that would be consistent with agricultural use. In-stream flow to maintain a fishery was not consistent with that sort of right" (*Wind River*). This limited definition of beneficial use focuses attention exclusively on the agricultural definition of the local area and neglects a more complex understanding of the character of the place.

The Shoshone and Arapaho see it differently than the court. For them, this is about a drastically limited definition of beneficial use and a misinterpretation of local conditions: "'Since we restricted them to agriculture, that makes sense that we shouldn't allow them to have in-stream flow because we agreed that it's an agricultural reservation.' That was his rationale pretty much, you know? For them to be convinced that in this day and age the reservation was created for agriculture just kind of blows me away. Especially here in Wyoming and in this part of the country" (Jimmy Hubenka, qtd. in *Wind River*). What the discourse from the tribes represents that the legal discourse does not is an understanding of the character of the land as part of the argument. Note that the tribes' counterargument is not simply that this comment is racist, which would be counterargument enough, but that it neglects the character of Wyoming, and importantly, the character of their rural portion of Wyoming.

For the Shoshone and Northern Arapaho, this place carries a different character. The tribal understanding of the character of Wind River is based on the reservation:

> As an Indian, you're part of a community interminably grounded in a place. For better or worse, it was the land of your parents and will be the land of your children, whether they live there or not. By your lineage, you share in its ownership with thousands of others, share in its responsibilities, its past, its suffering, its future. The minerals, the soils, and the water—that most essential resource in the West—are as mutual as ancestral blood. (O'Gara 5–6)

The farmers in the Wind River valley also conceive of this place as a generational holding, a place they have earned based on their perseverance through doggedly hard times. O'Gara says local farmers "scratched out a living on lands that had defeated others. The altitude was high here, the growing season was short, the soil wasn't great—they had lots of hurdles to overcome. They had stuck with it while neighbors had gone for easy wages in the oil patch, while uranium miners and city folk had bought up country places to be weekend cowboys with the kind of money farmers never expected to see" (35). Both of these competing parties have a deep connection to this place; both of the parties are determined to live in the Wind River valley in a manner that sustains their cultural perceptions and ways of life.

The Character of Cowboys and Indians

Ethos, as a habitual dwelling place, requires that local speakers "manifest the virtues most valued by the culture to and for which one speaks." This can be problematic, however, when the values endorsed by differing cultures vary as dramatically as those between the rural white farmers of the Wind River valley and the Shoshone and Northern Arapaho of the Wind River Reservation. The additional layer of race and racism, of the lived history of genocide borne by the descendents of these cultures now forced to live as neighbors and fight for limited resources, makes ethos in this area particularly complex. The producers of the documentary *Wind River* argue that fights over water are a modern day story of cowboys and Indians; yet the story playing out over the Wind River is far more rhetorically complex than such a simplistic—though not entirely inaccurate—image suggests.

Americans are well versed in the caricature of the westerner, the white rancher riding the range or tilling the soil, living a life centered on faith and family, a character constructed around an ideology of individualism and hard work. This is the bootstraps mentality in action: settlers who came west to build a life with hard work, seeking success through the labors of their own hands. Americans are equally versed in the caricature of Native Americans, viewed through a Hollywood lens, as savage peoples in need of civilization. Yet when these images change from caricatures to the character of neighbors and local citizens, when the faces seen are not John Wayne and Tonto but rather Wind River farmer Bill Brown and Shoshone spokesman Wes Martel, the discourse changes tenor. As O'Gara notes about the Wind River watershed and the debates that swirl around it: "It is the unfinished struggle between Native Americans and the whites who surround and threaten to subsume them—once a military conflict, now a cultural war, complicated after all these years by the fact that neighbors, even antagonistic neighbors, know one another in intimate and sometimes affectionate ways" (6).

Yet what neighbors know, in this valley, is often based more on national policy than on local interaction. O'Gara, having attended numerous town hall meetings and lectures to both groups during his time as a local reporter, notes that "it was obvious . . . that these ranchers had rarely spoken with tribal leaders—perhaps never" (36). Having no personal interaction to draw from, the cultures rely instead on the national definitions of character brought by legislation and literature. For the Native Americans, their national character was defined in 1831, written in the decision of *Cherokee Nation v. Georgia*. In that decision, John Marshall coined the term "domestic dependent nation" for the tribes of the Americas. To justify this definition and positioning, Marshall argued that the tribes "occupy a territory to which we assert a title independent of their will, which must take effect in point of possession when their right of possession ceases. Meanwhile, they are in a state of pupilage. Their relation to the United States resembles that of a ward or guardian" (Prucha 59). This is made worse by the justice's recognition of the Cherokee Nation as "a people once numerous, powerful, and truly independent, found by our ancestors in the quiet and uncontrolled possession of an ample domain, gradually sinking beneath our superior policy, our arts and our arms" (58). Thus our binding definition of native tribes is based upon an assumption of their power and pride in their culture but an equally sure assumption that the culture of the whites was superior, having defeated the Indians on the plains and reduced them to wards of the government.

This discourse of native peoples' deficiency and defeat remains in the water rights disputes. As scholar Patricia Limerick argues, the process of claiming water "is so much easier if you have a cultural understanding that tells you that the other party really does not substantively exist. So as you converge on the resource, if you don't even notice that you're converging or if you are so certain of your own legitimacy and the marginality or peripheralness of the other guy, that really makes the process a lot easier" (*Wind River*). Bill Brown echoes this claim when he states that, "If I would have known how the Indians felt about us farming on the reservation, I would have never considered investing in this country, but I've got a lifetime invested in this project" (Wind River). It would seem a simple conclusion that Native Americans would generally not respond well to whites farming on their lands, but when the character descriptions circulating in the Wind River valley echo the legislative description, grounded in verbiage of victory and cultural superiority, settlers assume the land and resources are available for the taking. That verbiage is similarly seen in the remarks of Chief Justice Thomas of the Wyoming Supreme Court when he argues that, "Here we have indigenous tribes that basically have all of what we now call the United States of America. Two hundred years later, they don't have very much of it [nervous laughter]. And, uh, of course the other side of that coin is . . . well, that's what happens when you lose" (*Wind River*). This is a message heard repeatedly in local discourse surrounding the Shoshone and Arapaho, that the superior race reaps the benefits, including the natural resources, while the dependent race suffers the consequences of defeat.

This discourse moves further into national definitions based on racism in its bemoaning of payments or subsidies provided to the tribes by the federal government. Johnny Hubeka, a local farmer from the LeClair district, argues that "probably part of the thing is that the government has ruined quite a few of the Indians because they've had a lot of handouts for them" (*Wind*

River). There is no recognition in the discourse of this debate that most of the irrigation projects, particularly those benefiting the local white farmers working on the reservation, were paid for in part from Indian funds that were held "in trust" by the government. Those projects were meant to be repaid by the local farmers, but to date the farmers have defaulted:

> It's a subject that makes farmers squirm because they pride themselves on being self-reliant, living off the land and feeding the world while the city dwellers soak up the cheap food and welfare programs. The Bureau of Reclamation released statistics in the 1980s showing that while the government had poured over $70 million into the Riverton Unit, farmers had never repaid a cent of the cost. (O'Gara 37)

This is precisely why ethos is so crucial to these debates. The logical arguments clearly favor the Shoshone/Arapaho water rights; they clearly demonstrate that fortunes meant for the tribes were used to benefit local white citizens; they clearly show the value, ecologically speaking, in the ways the tribes are attempting to use the water in protection of the natural environment and in preservation of their culture. Yet these are summarily disregarded because of the label of deficiency that surrounds the national character of Native Americans.

The farmers have fared little better in the national discourse, despite the fact that their early character was defined in positive terms. The character of the farmer arose in the ancient work of Virgil, a Roman poet who "romanticized the harmony and community of the countryside in implicit contrast to the bustle and impersonality of urban life, emphasizing the nobility of the farmer" (Hanson x). This image of the farmer's romantic nobility was carried forward by Hector St. John de Crèvecoeur, whose *Letters of an American Farmer* helped to create a national American identity. This crafted nobility reached a fevered pitch with Jefferson's idealization of the yeoman farmer, that small landowner who, because of his inherent goodness and sense of duty to his country, best represented the American ideal. This image, like that of the savage Native American, remains frozen in our national consciousness and resists complication. There is a rationale for this kind of consistent and preserved image, a sense that Eileen Schell describes as "a way to maintain an idealized vision of what is essential and vital about a people" (79). Yet while there is purpose, there is danger as well: "preservationist models . . . seek to make of rural places a monolithic symbol of a collective American heritage for those who live in urban and suburban areas, rather than vital and diverse communities that can adapt to economic and demographic shifts" (Donehower, "Rhetorics and Realities," 44). Just as the American consciousness sees the noble savage rather than real and participatory Native Americans, so too does the American consciousness see the noble farmer rather than my uncle, Cliff Young, who is fighting to feed the nation and his family.

Contemporarily, the noble farmer has been defined as "defeated," paralleling the language about Native American cultures, as Jacqueline Edmondson has noted: "We often think of these areas as defeated, indicating at some level that the traditional farm life is no longer sustainable" (7). The danger in this definition is that a defeated place no longer needs civic rhetoric, no longer needs discussion and debate to chart the most effective course for its residents. A definition of defeat also reduces local rhetors' abilities to persuade outside audiences based on their character. They are remnants of a life that no longer works, of a culture that succumbed to the progressive superiority of globalization and corporation. It is true that the American family farm is in trouble and, in western states, part of that trouble is certainly connected to aridity. What this ultimately means is that at the very moment ethos matters most, the communities inhabiting the Wind River valley find their ethos least effective.

Conclusion: After the Fall

Kenneth Burke has argued that rhetoric "is concerned with the state of Babel after the Fall" (23). Babel has fallen in the American West, precipitated in part by neoliberal practices emphasizing the individual. These practices have radically shaped agricultural communities (as Cori Brewster and Cynthia Ryan describe in the following chapters of this section), crafting deep divides between the dominant urban or corporate interests and the marginalized interests of rural agricultural communities. In the Wind River valley, the divide is primarily internal, centered on two marginalized groups further marginalizing one another over local natural resources. This internalization of the debate has done great cultural and ecological harm to its participants, with the Wind River running dry as local farmers attempt to sustain a large-scale agricultural system unchanged in this arid country. National definitions of character, of both person and place, have drowned out any local attempts at redefinition. Deep cultural and political divisions continue to keep those who are physically together ideologically apart.

Now more than ever, rural civic ethos—an ethos centered on the community and the place rather than on the neoliberal individual—matters. Aristotle readily saw the value of character early in the traditions of rhetoric. That value has increased as the stakes have risen, and the stakes couldn't be higher for rural citizens living in the Wind River valley, each group marked as defeated, silenced in larger debates about the policies that so intricately affect their lives. While the challenges between the Native American cultures and those of the white farmers have been difficult and divisive, while a fight over limited resources has widened the gap between cultures at war with one another for centuries, a larger battle with greater consequences is on the horizon; a battle that will require a cooperative effort in order to sustain a rural way of life in the Wind River valley and in the American West.

As *Discover Magazine* recently reported, oil companies have been quietly buying up water rights in the American West in preparation for oil shale mining projects. The environmental law and policy organization Western Resource Advocates recently discovered "more than 200 water rights held by six energy companies, including Shell and ExxonMobil, which, it is estimated, are collectively entitled to divert at least 6.5 billion gallons of water from rivers in western Colorado" ("Oil Companies Buy Rights"). Diverting water for the extraction of oil falls within the broad category of "beneficial use"; as long as the water is there, "legally and physically," as a spokesperson for Shell has said, the oil companies will have first dibs, putting agriculture at risk of extinction and further damaging any argument for in-stream flow.

Oil companies are not the only groups converging on these limited resources. Cities stretched to their seams have also come calling, purchasing water rights from farmers who are struggling under the go-big-or-go-home corporate economy of farming. As the *New York Times* has reported, "The sale of water rights, which allow the owners to take the specified amount of water for their use, was once regarded as unthinkable. But it is becoming increasingly common across the arid West. The demand for water in urban areas is outpacing supplies in mountain rivers and reservoirs while farming, which experts estimate has consumed more than 80 percent of the West's water, is in a crisis" (Knudson). This is happening in many cities in the West including Denver, Colorado, just five hours south of the Wind River valley.

As agricultural and Indian concerns for the Wind River valley come under pressure from the global economy, from the corporate entities and urban interests that have defined rural citizens as defeated and who are now arguing for their own rights to the resource, rural residents in the Wind River valley must find a way to define one another differently and unite in a joint battle to protect their interests. Understanding rural civic ethos as tied to a place that both groups inhabit and both have reason to protect may provide them a point of commonality to begin this process. It may also allow the rural citizens of the Wind River valley to finally and successfully argue for their local expertise, grounded in the experience and knowledge of place, and for their own value in the conversations that are so critical to their lives and livelihood.

Works Cited

Aristotle. *On Rhetoric: A Theory of Civic Discourse*. Trans. George A. Kennedy. New York: Oxford UP, 1991. Print.

Bellamore, Tom. "From Sharing to Strife: A Case Study of the Adjudication of the Big Horn River System and Its Impact on the Wind River Tribes." *Beyond Litigation: Case Studies in the Water Rights Disputes*. Ed. Craig Anthony Arnold and Leigh A. Jewell. Washington, D.C.: Environmental Law Institute, 2002. 15–78. Print.

Blew, Mary Clearman. *All but the Waltz*. Norman: U of Oklahoma P, 1991. Print.

Burke, Kenneth. *A Rhetoric of Motives*. Berkeley: U of California P, 1969. Print.

Donehower, Kim. "Rhetorics and Realities: The History and Effects of Stereotypes about Rural Literacies." Donehower, Hogg, and Schell 37–76. Print.

Donehower, Kim, Charlotte Hogg, and Eileen Schell. *Rural Literacies*. Carbondale: Southern Illinois UP, 2007. Print.

Edmondson, Jacqueline. *Prairie Town: Redefining Rural Life in the Age of Globalization*. New York: Rowman and Littlefield, 2003. Print.

Flanagan, Cathleen, and Melinda Laituri. "Local Cultural Knowledge and Water Resource Management: The Wind River Indian Reservation." *Environmental Management* 33.2 (2004): 262–70. Print.

"Fort Bridger Treaty, 1863." *Wind River Indian Reservation*. Eastern Shoshone Tribe. Web. 17 June 2008.

"Fort Bridger Treaty, 1868." *Wind River Indian Reservation*. Eastern Shoshone Tribe. Web. 17 June 2008.

"Greater Yellowstone Resource Guide." Wyoming's Wind River Valley. Web. 8 Jan 2009.

Halloran, S. Michael. "Aristotle's Concept of Ethos, or If Not His, Somebody Else's." *Rhetoric Review* 1.1 (Sept. 1982): 58–63. Print.

Hanson, Victor Davis. *The Land Was Everything: Letters from an American Farmer*. New York: Free Press, 2000. Print.

"Homestead Act of 1862." *The Our Documents Initiative*. Web. 12 Jan 2009.

Hyde, Michael J. "Rhetorically, We Dwell." *The Ethos of Rhetoric*. Ed. Michael J. Hyde. Columbia: U of South Carolina P, 2004. xii–xxviii. Print.

Johnson, Nan. "Ethos." *Encyclopedia of Rhetoric and Composition*. Ed. Theresa Enos. New York: Routledge, 1996. Print.

Knudson, Thomas J. "Dry Cities of West Buy up Farm Water Rights." *New York Times* 10 Feb. 1987: A1. Print.

Lamberton, Robert. Introduction to *Hesiod: Works and Days and Theogony*. Trans. Stanley Lombardo. Indianapolis: Hackett, 1993. 1–16. Print.

"Location." *Northern Arapaho Tribe*. 25 Jan 2007. Web. 22 Dec 2008.

Mergen, Andrew C., and Sylvia F. Lui. "A Misplaced Sensitivity: The Draft Opinions in *Wyoming v. United States*." *University of Colorado Law Review* 68 (Summer 1997): 683. Print.

O'Gara, Geoffrey. *What You See in Clear Water: Life on the Wind River Reservation*. New York: Alfred A. Knopf, 2000. Print.

"Oil Companies Buy Rights to Access Water before Communities and Farmers." *Discover: Science, Technology, and the Future*. 20 March 2009. Web. 4 April 2009.

Plato. "Phaedrus." *The Rhetorical Tradition: Readings from Classical Times to the Present*. Ed. Patricia Bizzell and Bruce Herzberg. New York: Bedford/St. Martin's, 2001. 138–68. Print.

Powell, John Wesley. *Report on the Lands of the Arid Region of the United States*. Washington: GPO, 1879. Web.

Prucha, Francis Paul, ed. "*Cherokee Nation v. Georgia*." *Documents of United States Indian Policy*, 3rd ed. Lincoln: University of Nebraska Press, 2000. Print.

Reisner, Marc. *Cadillac Desert: The American West and Its Disappearing Water*. New York: Penguin, 1993. Print.

Reynolds, Nedra. "Ethos as Location: New Sites for Understanding Discursive Authority." *Rhetoric Review* 11.2 (Spring 1993): 325–38. Print.

Schell, Eileen E. "The Rhetorics of the Farm Crisis: Toward Alternative Agrarian Literacies in a Globalized World." Donehower, Hogg, and Schell 77–119. Print.

Stegner, Wallace. *Where the Bluebird Sings to the Lemonade Springs: Living and Writing in the West.* New York: Penguin, 1992. Print.

U.S. Fish and Wildlife Service. "Water Rights Definitions." Web. 4 April 2009.

"Welcome to Choteau County." Web. 4 April 2009.

Western Resource Advocates. "Water on the Rocks: Oil Shale Water Rights in Colorado." 2009. Web. 4 April 2009.

Wind River. Dir. Drury Gunn Carr and John Dillon. High Plains Films, 2006. DVD.

"Wind River Water Code." U.S. Environmental Protection Agency. Web. 3 Jan 2009.

2

Toward a Critical Agricultural Literacy

Cori Brewster

> Let every man study political economy. Let him teach it to his
> children, expound it to his neighbors and proclaim it to the
> world. Let the sword of justice fall. The arm is already lifted to
> deal the blow. The bright blade gleams in the sunshine of Liberty,
> Equality and Justice. Its dazzling brightness is felt flashing in the
> face of monopoly. The minions of Mammon are trembling behind
> their strong entrenchments. "Justice is mine, saith the Lord."
> —W. Scott Morgan, *History of the Wheel and
> Alliance, and the Impending Revolution* (1891)

> Science education is fundamental in preparing the future
> generations of consumers and opinion leaders. The leadership of
> those recognized is an example for all of us in helping students
> understand the contribution agriculture makes to our society.
> —Kerry Preete, vice president of Monsanto,
> U.S. Crop Production, "Monsanto Gift Benefits
> Agriculture in the Classroom" (9 June 2005)

For more than a century, "agricultural literacy" campaigns have exerted a profound if often unnoticed influence over Americans' understanding of political, social, and economic concerns, particularly in rural communities. From the schools for rural adults operated by the Farmers' Alliance in the late 1880s and 1890s, to agricultural clubs for young people such as 4-H and Future Farmers of America, to the myriad print publications, radio broadcasts, social events, fairs, conventions, advertisements, public lectures, school curricula, television programs, and now websites and other electronic "educational" media developed and paid for by shifting configurations of public and private sector interests, efforts to shape public understanding of agriculture and the social and political contexts in which it is practiced have been both far-reaching and wide in scope. Indeed, Americans of all ages both within and outside rural communities have been subject to (and often participants in) increasingly sophisticated and well-calculated ideological battles between competing agricultural interests in the United States since at least Reconstruction. Directly or indirectly, all of these campaigns have sought to shape voter and consumer understanding of the political economy of agriculture and relationships between capital and democracy in the face of highly unequal distributions of land, power, and wealth. How Americans should understand matters of race, nation, gender, family, and religion have necessarily been central if not always explicit elements of these campaigns as well.

Following a brief history of early agricultural literacy efforts in the United States, I turn in this chapter to an analysis of two contemporary curricula and the rhetorics of identity and economy they work to interweave. The first, "Growing a Nation," is the centerpiece of an interactive, multimedia agricultural history curriculum developed for middle and high school students that is available to teachers free online and through Agriculture in the Classroom programs across the country. Initially a state-level project created by Extension Service faculty at Utah State University, the program was extended to all fifty states and aligned with national history standards for 5th- through 11th-grade students at the request of the U.S. Department of Agriculture's undersecretary for research, education and economics, Joseph Jen ("USDA, USU Team Up"). The second "curriculum," *America's Heartland,* is a weekly half-hour program aired on public television that is produced and funded primarily by Monsanto and the American Farm Bureau Federation, with added support from the American Soybean Association, the National Corn Growers Association, the Cotton Council, the United Soybean Board, the U.S. Grains Council, and the National FFA Organization ("About the Show").

Like many earlier agricultural literacy efforts, these contemporary curricula attempt to direct public understanding of the political economy of agriculture in ways that support (and sometimes mask) sponsors' ends. In doing so, they illustrate two different but equally concerning rhetorical trends: attempts to dehumanize and ostensibly depoliticize agriculture, on the one hand, and on the other, attempts to appropriate and redeploy long-standing agrarian tropes. Both strategies can be understood as part of a longer-term, increasingly sophisticated effort on the part of national and multinational corporate interests to undermine historically galvanizing symbols and storylines of more progressive agricultural movements.

More specifically, "Growing a Nation" and *America's Heartland* illustrate two ways in which agriculture literacy curricula are being used today to rationalize neoliberal policies and the free market approach to human relations upon which those policies depend. Neoliberalism, as Stephanie Mudge explains, is an "ideological system" with intellectual, bureaucratic, and political dimensions that is "built on a single, fundamental principle: the superiority of individualized, market-based competition over other modes of organization" (706–7). Though actual reforms may vary across contexts, neoliberal policies generally emphasize "liberalization, deregulation, privatization, depoliticization and monetarism," aiming to promote "unfettered competition by getting the state out of the business of ownership and getting politicians out of the business of *dirigiste*-style economic management. Neoliberal policies also aim to 'desacralize' institutions that had formerly been protected from the forces of private market competition, such as education and health care" (704).[1] Neoliberal initiatives in U.S. agriculture include, among other things, efforts to eliminate crop subsidies, lift environmental regulations, privatize federal crop insurance programs, and promote free trade.[2]

It is important that "Growing a Nation," *America's Heartland,* and like "curricula" be understood in this context, as part of a broad and shifting "ensemble of economic, political, and ideological strategies" (Hennessy 75) that help to advance neoliberal policies and supporting worldviews. Read together against a wider historical and ideological backdrop, they underscore the need for teachers and community organizers alike to pay closer attention to how and in whose interests "agricultural literacies" are currently being crafted in the United States and how we might help students of all ages negotiate agricultural messaging in more critical and responsive ways.

Cultivating Agricultural Literacies, 1860s to the Present

The term "agricultural literacy" is a relatively new one, coined in the 1980s by educators and others interested in extending the study of agriculture beyond vocational clubs and classrooms.[3] In public educational settings, it typically refers to "education *about* agriculture," and is distinguished from the more hands-on "education *in* agriculture" provided to students preparing (or being prepared) to work in the field. "Agriculture is too important a topic to be taught only to the relatively small percentage of students considering careers in agriculture and pursuing vocational agricultural studies," as the Committee on Agricultural Education in Secondary Schools argued in 1988:

> The committee envisions that an agriculturally literate person's understanding of the food and fiber system includes its history and current economic, social, and environmental significance to all Americans. This definition encompasses some knowledge of food and fiber production, processing, and domestic and international marketing. . . .

Achieving the goal of agricultural literacy will produce informed citizens able to participate in establishing the policies that will support a competitive agricultural industry in this country and abroad. (1–2)

Although the definition has been refined somewhat over the past two decades, agricultural literacy is typically framed in much the same way today: as a functional literacy characterized by the acquisition of knowledge and skills required to perform in particular contexts or to assist sponsoring agencies in achieving particular aims (see Barton 10–32, 189–96; Brandt 17–21).[4]

Efforts to promote agricultural literacy in the United States date back well before the term itself came into use, however, at times reflecting far more critical and liberatory approaches than current school-based definitions might suggest. In fact, carefully orchestrated "agricultural literacy" campaigns can be traced at least as far back as nineteenth-century farmers' organizations such as the Agricultural Wheel, the Farmers' Alliance, and the Patrons of Husbandry, more commonly known as the Grange.[5] Many such groups served not only as cooperative organizations through which farm families could exert greater power in negotiations with railroads, banks, and merchants, but also as civic, social, political, and educational "clubs" through which members exchanged and acted upon a wide range of practical and political information. Under the direction of Farmers' Alliance president Charles Macune in the 1890s, for example, "many suballiances developed adult education programs in which children and literate adults helped teach Alliance men and women," according to Theodore Mitchell. Mitchell says the mathematics curriculum developed by Macune and delivered to more than one hundred thousand subscribers through the Alliance newspaper the *National Economist* was grounded in the computation of interest rates, crop shares, and such figures as the per capita wealth of the nation (the latter providing a basis for comparison of elite wealth versus their own wealth). Reading and writing focused on studying forms of exploitation around the globe, unified by the "warning" that the "centralization of wealth and power, a reciprocal process, always leads to repression by the rich and powerful of the poor and powerless." (qtd. in Mooney and Majka 46)

The goal of such curricula, according to Theodore Mitchell, was to combat the political "miseducation" of farmers under Gilded Age capitalism that Alliance leaders believed limited class consciousness and kept farmers from identifying with organized labor as exploited fellow "producers" (Mitchell 70–71)—the "real people," as it were, who deserved the full fruits of their own sacrifice and hard work (see Berlet and Lyons; Canovan; Kazin).[6]

Even as economic conditions began to improve somewhat at the start of the twentieth century, U.S. farmers continued to develop new membership-based organizations that drew on the "more progressive elements of nine-teenth-century agrarian populism" (Mooney and Majka 55; see also Reyn-olds). Of these, the National Farmers' Educational and Cooperative Union grew to be one of the largest and most influential. Though the organization's positions became markedly less "radical" during the Cold War era, early teachings centered around four main themes:

> First, a sense of "disadvantage" portrays the farmer as a victim of both nature and the political economy of capitalism. . . . Second, a pacifism sees war as tied to the interests of the wealthy. . . . Third is cooperativism, which as an economic principle was meant to combat capitalism by replac-ing the "profit system" with a "cooperative commonwealth" in which "all business is cooperatively owned." . . . Fourth is the farm family ideal. . . . While cooperativism was the economic means of defending the family farm, the ideal of the family farm, grounded in Jeffersonian democratic ideology, was the basis on which political appeals were made as a means of defending this ideological objective. (John Crampton, qtd. in Mooney and Majka 58–59)

Although groups differed from community to community and region to re-gion, a constant theme well into the 1940s was that protection of agriculture from monopoly capitalism and of participatory democracy from "moneyed interests" depended upon the organization, education, and political partici-pation of farmers.[7] This message was communicated to members and the broader public through newspapers, speakers' bureaus, meetings, conven-tions, educational programs, children's clubs, and fairs. In addition, as Mary Neth explains, women often

> created social occasions that gave these groups deeper meaning and made commitments stronger. . . . Women's activities, such as picnics, plays, and pageants, helped recruit new members and raised money. For example, a combination of cooperative sales, money from basket socials, and coop-erative labor funded the creation of a Farmers' Union education camp in Wisconsin in the late 1930s. (141)

It was in direct response to such groups' influence that the federal gov-ernment, corporate agribusiness, and the Chamber of Commerce joined forces in the late 1910s to establish the American Farm Bureau Federation, an organization that has represented itself rather disingenuously as "of farmers, by farmers, and for farmers" ever since (see Berger 5–6; Mooney 221–26; and Neth).[8] As Patrick Mooney explains, "the reason the state (with agribusiness) stepped in to organize the Farm Bureau was precisely because farmers were organizing themselves. Not only were smallholders organizing, but they were organizing around socialist agendas":

> To a great extent the Farm Bureau was, in fact, an effort by capital and the state to co-opt any grass-roots movement of farmers themselves. . . . Born in a Chamber of Commerce office, the Farm Bureau was nursed by the USDA, the Extension Service, Sears Roebuck, International Harvester, the Chicago Board of Trade, the railroads, and finance capital. . . . In the process the Farm Bureau succeeded in transforming most of those forces, which farmers had for years identified as the enemy, into the alleged political representative of the farm population. (221)

From the start, the ideological tactics employed by the Farm Bureau directly reflected an interest in containing farmers' critiques of capitalism and subverting potential alliances between farm groups and organized labor. Key to the bureau's efforts were two main strategies: first, to link cooperativism to communism, and second, to disarm the "farmer as producer" rhetoric at the heart of more progressive agricultural movements.

Despite significant changes in agricultural technology and world politics over the past century, these rhetorical strategies and the intent behind them have remained largely the same: by recasting farmers not as "producers" but as "managers," "experts," and "entrepreneurs," small farmers' successes can be used to celebrate free enterprise while their failures can be blamed on poor individual choices—not on oligopoly, corporate greed, or national and international farm, tax, and trade policies, as before.[9] In focusing on farming as an industry, moreover, rather than as a way of life with implications for family and community well-being, notions of agricultural "progress" can be linked more easily to economic and technological "advances" that benefit large corporate interests regardless of the effects they might have on individual farmers, consumers, families, or communities. Through the Farm Bureau's close ties to the Extension Service and other state and federal agencies, agricultural programs for children and teens like 4-H and Future Farmers of America have often served as direct funnels for Farm Bureau politics and views of agricultural practice—positions informed primarily by large corporate interests and rationalized through the free market ideologies of the far Right (see Berger; Kile; Mooney; and Neth; and see chapters 5 and 7 in this volume).[10]

This historical backdrop is critical to understanding both the rhetorical complexity and the rhetorical implications of agricultural literacy campaigns today. Indeed, it would be difficult to appreciate the particular hands contemporary curricula play without at least some understanding of the ideological reverberations of earlier educational campaigns. Like many current efforts to shape public understanding of agriculture, "Growing a Nation" and *America's Heartland* both advance neoliberal agendas. In doing so, however, they respond to the residual power of producerist rhetoric in markedly different ways.

Storying American Agriculture

The first approach to agricultural literacy that demands closer critical attention is represented in programming like "Growing a Nation: The Story of American Agriculture"—namely, the effort to dehumanize and depoliticize farming by pitting "objective science" and the profit imperative against all possible objections to corporate agricultural practice.[11] Fairly transparent politically, this secondary agricultural history curriculum is peppered with the god terms one might expect: *progress, technology, science, freedom*, and so on. The dramatic loss of small farms in the United States is explained blandly as the result of global market forces, while small farmers who remain are represented either as "hobby farmers" or as "good managers," with those forced out of farming blamed indirectly for their failure to keep up. Smaller farmers increasingly "choose" to go organic, sell locally, and work additional jobs off the farm, according to this story, as these things make them more competitive in the current economic situation.[12] Farmers' markets have "become popular," similarly, not because farmers increasingly need to cut out middlemen in order to sell food crops at cost or because of growing consumer concerns about commercial agricultural practice, but because good farmers are adaptable ones, able to market "niche" products to higher-income consumers who likewise "choose" to spend their extra dollars on specialty products.

Along the same lines, the "Better Times" of the 1990s are marked in "Growing a Nation" by "innovative" technologies, lower interest rates, and free trade, with the elimination of trade barriers through the North American Free Trade Agreement highlighted in particular (Lesson 4, screen 8). As "Lesson 4: 1970–Present, Into a New Millennium" concludes,

> Today, significant changes are happening for every aspect of American society. Advances in science and technology are fueling a global economy. The pace of scientific research is accelerating. International trade, with 96 percent of the world's population living outside of our nation's borders, is expanding.
>
> These changes bring American farmers fresh and complex challenges. . . .
>
> To address these challenges agricultural scientists and American farmers need to continue using the latest tools and technologies and to work closely together to keep agriculture competitive and to ensure that all

Americans have access to a wide variety of safe, healthy and plentiful food. (Spielmaker)

Nothing in the curriculum is necessarily untrue: farming today is highly capital dependent, and "efficiency" in the use of water, chemicals, seed, fuel, labor, and other farm processes does play a critical role in determining which farms make it and which don't, particularly as smaller farms try to compete with very large family and nonfamily operations better able to negotiate contracts and make long-term investments in land and equipment.[13] But the perspectives foregrounded and the information eclipsed in "Growing a Nation" nonetheless contribute to a fairly limited view of agriculture in America, one tilted firmly in favor of multinational seed and chemical corporations with a huge stake in manufacturing the consent of future workers, voters, and consumers.

More insidiously, the program's industry-centered, rather than "producer"-centered, introduction to agricultural history is matched by the laissez-faire approach to racial and gender inequity students are offered in the curriculum as well. The cover of "Growing a Nation" provides one clear example. In the black and white background of the program's cover image, viewers move from Abraham Lincoln, to farmers plowing with horses, to an aproned George Washington Carver at work in his laboratory. In the green foreground are a woman scientist, a strand of DNA, and a single plant. The metonymic string of specific human subjects here and throughout the curriculum is telling: students move from "honest Abe," popular symbol of democracy, abolition, and national unity; to Carver, black agricultural scientist deployed tokenistically both in his time and ours; to an unknown white woman in a lab coat, also arguably a token and a friendlier representation of biotechnology and scientific "progress" than a picture of corporate headquarters or a university science building might have been.

If on the one hand this "diverse" collection of human symbols presents a more inclusive agricultural history than students in the United States have traditionally been offered, on the other, its transparency would seem to give it away. In the final lesson, for instance, we learn that Ann Veneman was the first woman ever to be appointed to head the U.S. Department of Agriculture—a marker of progress for women, ostensibly, for which George W. Bush is given credit. Veneman, incidentally, also helped engineer the North American Free Trade Agreement and served on the board of Calgene, the first U.S. company to market a genetically engineered food product, the FlavrSavr tomato ("Secretary of Agriculture"). Carver is used in "Growing a Nation" in much the same way, credited in the timeline with "find[ing] new uses for peanuts, sweet potatoes, and soybeans, [and] helping to diversify southern agriculture." But as Barry Mackintosh points out, it was Carver's utility as a symbol of "appropriate" accomplished black behavior that most contributed to his fame and to the popular myths built up around him (see also McMurry). By populating the multiculturalized scene with a series of women and people of color representing those who have "risen to the top," and without challenging relations of power in any significant way and who apparently speak happily for the policies and practices of corporate capitalism, "Growing a Nation" and like efforts effectively bolster sponsors' ethos as "inclusive," even "progressive." At the same time, they reassure students that the "invisible hand of the market" will ultimately rectify all.[14]

Even more sophisticated, however, are recent efforts by corporations and organizations such as Monsanto and the American Farm Bureau Federation to redeploy historically galvanizing agrarian tropes largely as is—in effect, to depart from past strategies to deflate populist tropes and wed them to beneficent corporate images instead. As Kenneth Burke argues in "Revolutionary Symbolism in America," "We convince a man by reason of the values which we and he hold *in common.* . . . As a propagandizer, it is not his work to convince the convinced, but to plead with the unconvinced, which requires him to use *their* vocabulary, *their* values, *their* symbols, insofar as this is possible" (271–72, italics in the original). Ethical or not, using stories and symbols that already resonate powerfully with an audience is a much easier way to "disarm" them and get new ideas in the door, as Burke put it, than presenting "over-simplified, literal, explicit . . . lawyer's briefs" that conflict with what a reader or listener currently believes 273). "After getting these people into your party, you can give them a more accurate sense of what you are aiming at," Burke reiterated in a later discussion of his speech. "But in the first stage, the propagandist must use certain terms which have a certain ambiguity, and which for that very reason give him entrance into other areas" (280). While it is unlikely that Monsanto and the American Farm Bureau Federation plan to give viewers "a more accurate sense of what [they] are aiming at" down the road, *America's Heartland* clearly reflects this rhetorical strategy. Much more effective than attempting to distance non-farmers from farmers, or to construct agriculture as an industry governed largely by faceless hero-scientists and their innovative new technologies, Monsanto, the American Farm Bureau Federation, and like organizations are instead calling up agrarian symbols and storylines that already resonate powerfully with viewers to get a positive image of themselves in the door. This appropriation is effective primarily because it is subtle, because it does not immediately appear to be political, and because it allows the "propagandizers" to wed their image to ones their audience is more likely to trust. Airing programs like *America's Heartland* on public television, moreover, gives the appearance that the program is more or less nonpartisan, education rather than advertisement, and developed in the interest of the public good.

Each week, the thirty-minute program is divided into five segments, each dedicated, as narrator Paul Ryan tells us, to "great farms, families, and their fascinating stories." The program is both deliberative and epideictic—or, more accurately, deliberative masked as epideictic—a means of urging support indirectly for particular policies, practices, corporations, and industry-related groups through celebratory stories of people and ways of life that the program's sponsors ostensibly cherish, too. As Ryan tells us at the beginning of the first episode of the first season, "We would like to think of this as a unique opportunity, a chance for you to join us in celebrating Americans who work so hard to provide food and fabric, who love the earth and coax its bounty from soil and water. As we begin our journey through America's heartland, one of the most interesting things I think is just how fascinating these folks are—how many great stories they have to tell."

In each episode, viewers are introduced to a series of American farmers, ranchers, and "entrepreneurs" who not only represent the agrarian values of stewardship and cooperation but speak to the trinity of progress, profit, and hard work, as well. Mike Johanns, U.S. secretary of agriculture, stitches this farm ethos together in the opening to the first episode: "It is those values of honesty, family, faith, commitment to purpose, dedication, self-discipline, all of those things. It's part of what you see in rural America today." Accordingly, a segment on Colonel Sanders in episode 104 describes the "elderly Horatio Alger" figure as "someone whose life embodies some of our best values, a courtly white-suited gentlemen who combined hard work, perseverance, a sense of fairness, and a little Kentucky charm to find success in his golden years." To be sure, a visitor to the Sanders museum tells us, the "Colonel" represents "the right type of attitude": "instead of sitting around after he retired," he went on to "greater things."

The narrator and other guest voices emphasize this combination of values repeatedly throughout the series, stressing the entrepreneurial aspects of agriculture alongside its producerist worth. "It took a certain level of character, commitment, hard work, patience, endurance, entrepreneurialism to make a small farm work," says historian Kevin Starr, for example. "Part of what it is to be an American can be defined by the virtues and success of the small farmer." Or, as Ryan tells it, "The American farmer, the rancher, any American that grows the products that feed us, that feed the world, their stories mirror the larger tale of us as a nation. It's a story of struggle, setbacks, courage and success. A myth and an image based on fact." This last quote is particularly noteworthy, as it works a long-standing Monsanto public relations slogan word-for-word into the rural, agricultural identity being spun in the show. Monsanto's pat answer to public concern about agricultural chemicals since the 1962 publication of Rachel Carson's *Silent Spring* has been that synthetic pesticides and fertilizers are necessary "to feed the world"—a rhetoric of compromise designed to put a noble face on the company and the farmers who use its products in spite of well-documented health and environmental costs (see Forrestal 193–202). It's fitting, then, that Iowa farmer Lee Faris is featured in the segment "Going Green in Iowa" in the show's tenth episode: "Faris is an environmentalist," viewers are told. "Not the kind that chain themselves to trees—he's the kind who makes a living off the land. For him, the preservation of natural resources also preserves his family's future." Read through the logic of neoliberalism, Faris's voluntary environmentalism simply reflects good business sense. Unhampered by restrictive environmental regulations, we are to understand, "noble farmers," like Faris, and the companies that supply them should simply be trusted to do what's best.[15]

Perhaps the most notable strategy *America's Heartland* exploits in appropriating populist tropes, however, is focusing segments on people and programs designed to parallel popular figures in contemporary progressive agricultural movements and media. These range from the see-through to the more subtle: running a segment called "A Cowboy's Conscience" on singer/songwriter/farmer Michael Martin Murphey, for instance, who "celebrates the heartland in both his music and in the way he lives his life," but, unlike the better known Willie Nelson, keeps himself and his family out of politics. The friendly farm faces we see in Deborah Koons Garcia's film *The Future of Food*, which examines Monsanto and other corporations' marketing of genetically modified seeds, are answered in *America's Heartland* likewise with faces just as friendly and ostensibly just as interested in the well-being of the planet. These characters don't seem at all concerned, however, about terminator genes, cross-pollination by GM crops, the patenting of indigenous seeds by biotechnology firms, or other issues currently on the corporation's public relations radar.

Clearly one of the most troubling examples of this strategy in *America's Heartland* is the segment in episode 111 on Jubilation, a planned Florida community home to Harvest for Humanity. In place of farmworkers who have successfully unionized or become cooperative owners of farms on which they work, we have in this story instead an affluent white Christian family who moved into an agricultural area to "develop" the community and its people, the majority of whom are poor and working-class people of color. As the synopsis of the program on the *Heartland* website explains,

They are the backbone of American agriculture—the men and women who toil in the fields to put food on our tables. It's not an easy life. And that's what Dick and Florence Nogaj . . . discovered during a vacation to southwest Florida and the little town of Immokalee. . . .

The poverty in this small town was similar to what Dick and Florence had seen on their travels to third-world countries. They found that to be politically, socially, and spiritually unacceptable. So they decided to take action. The couple felt that the only way to improve wages and conditions for farm workers was to come up with a new kind of farming operation. They moved to Immokalee and established a foundation and a venture they call "Harvest for Humanity." . . .

Whether you're a picker or a packer, everyone who works at the farm starts at $8.50 per hour, which is about three dollars above the local minimum wage.

The higher wage allows farm workers to support their families without public assistance. . . .

The Nogajs also set their sights on affordable housing. In 2002 the doors opened on Jubilation, a community development where the workers of Immokalee or people who never owned a home could enjoy the American dream.

Although the assumptions behind Jubilation and Harvest for Humanity are downplayed somewhat on *America's Heartland*, the organization's website is frank: "Partnering with God's People for a Better Life," Harvest for Humanity aims to provide "unique opportunities for a hand-up experience for farmworkers that they otherwise would never have" ("The Harvest Farm: Introduction").

While the Nogajs' politics might appear at first to run contrary to those of the Farm Bureau and other *Heartland* sponsors—and while much of what they have done is clearly commendable—Harvest for Humanity is an entirely appropriate choice for the show: private, charitable, and "faith based" rather than worker-organized, government-directed or publicly funded, the program exemplifies neoliberal goals. Far from pointing to the inequities inherent in capitalism, the Nogajs' philanthropic efforts help rationalize it instead. As Andrew Carnegie argued in "Wealth,"

In bestowing charity, the main consideration [is] to help those who will help themselves; to provide part of the means by which those who desire to improve may do so; to give those who desire to rise the aids by which they may rise; to assist, but rarely or never to do all. . . .
[. . .]
Thus is the problem of the Rich and Poor to be solved. The laws of accumulation will be left free; the laws of distribution free. Individualism will

continue, but the millionaire will be but a trustee for the poor; intrusted for a season with a great part of the increased wealth of the community, but administering it for the community far better than it could or would have done for itself.

Whether the Nogajs themselves subscribe to Carnegie's version of "aid to the worthy," they are presented in this way, and they offer a far safer image of people working to address the exploitation of agricultural laborers than a segment on the Coalition of Immokalee Workers, the United Farm Workers, or similar organizations might have. Still, the segment retains the caveat: "Like any experiment, it may be too early to tell if Harvest for Humanity remains successful in the long run. Consumers may balk at paying a higher price for Fair Food products. And it's not certain other farmers will be able to afford to replicate this model." As far as the show's sponsors are concerned, what seems to matter most is that the viewing public learn to associate Monsanto, the American Farm Bureau Federation, and other supporters with caring about the well-being of farmworkers, as represented by the Nogajs and their private-sector philanthropic work.

In episode after episode, *America's Heartland* capitalizes on agrarian symbols and storylines that a wide segment of their viewing public already views positively in order to create identification between the values and lifestyles of the show's "characters" and its corporate sponsors. If the American Farm Bureau Federation is celebrating small farmers on the program, in other words, they must represent such farmers' interests in Washington, D.C.; if Lee Faris is looking out for the environment, so must Monsanto be. I oversimplify, of course, but the agenda is clear: to brand, to "prepare voters," and to stave off potential challenges to present and future corporate agricultural practice. In this spirit, *America's Heartland* offers folksy stories about noble producers that are at once romantic, reassuring, and accommodating, and that ostensibly provide evidence once again that individualism, democracy, meritocracy, and unregulated corporate capitalism are simply natural parts of a distinctly American whole.

In sum, "Growing a Nation" and *America's Heartland* provide important insights into the rhetoric and ideological objectives of much industry-centered agricultural literacy curricula today. Both advance neoliberal agendas, illustrating as they do so the range of recuperative rhetorical moves currently being employed to diffuse the progressive potential of populist tropes. In the process, they bring the limitations of functional and skills-based approaches to agricultural literacy into even sharper relief.

Toward a Critical Agricultural Literacy

"Since we all have a stake in agriculture," Kim Donehower, Charlotte Hogg, and Eileen Schell argue in *Rural Literacies*, "we also have a vested interest in better informing ourselves and helping others become better informed about where our food comes from and how its production and consumption affect us and our environment" (170). Given the ideological contexts within which agricultural literacy curricula continue to be developed, I would add that we have a vested interest as well in better informing ourselves about how and why agriculture is currently being communicated to nonfarm publics and in developing models of agricultural literacy that better prepare students to enter the rhetorical fray.

If critical literacy entails "learning to read and write in order to become conscious of one's experience as constructed within specific power structures," as Deborah Adelman and Shamili Sandiford put it, a critical agricultural literacy might easily be described the same way. For writing teachers, perhaps the simplest place to start is with rhetorical analysis of agriculture-related texts, asking students to compare how similar tropes and storylines are used by different authors for different purposes across contexts and at different moments in time. It would be instructive, for instance, to analyze how Jeffersonian imagery is currently being deployed by agricultural organizations across the political spectrum, including farmworker advocacy groups to whom the "noble farmer" ethos has historically been denied. The offices of rhetoric might provide fruitful starting points for analysis as well, as students consider ways in which contemporary multimedia and mixed genre texts blur classical divisions between the epideictic, forensic, and deliberative, and how arguments about food and farm politics are made in sites that audiences are less likely to read as attempts to persuade.

Another approach would be to begin with students' own agricultural literacy narratives, asking students to reflect on the experiences, institutions, and media through which they have come to understand their own and others' relationships to agricultural production and distribution. As Schell has observed, the "dominant narratives of the farm crisis"—including those attempting to rationalize the unprecedented centralization of global food systems—"foster an 'agricultural illiteracy' among the general public whereby the conditions under which our nation's food is grown, harvested, distributed, and marketed are made opaque and inaccessible" (81). Identifying the direct and indirect sponsors of our own agricultural literacies would seem an important step not only in beginning to problematize agricultural policies and practices, but also in casting a more critical eye on the storylines through which those policies and practices have been obscured, rationalized, and/or explained.

Both directly and indirectly, food production and distribution systems structure our relationships to people and institutions within our communities and around the globe. Helping students read and respond to the agricultural world requires that we pose problems about where our food comes from and why, and about how we continue to be raced, gendered, faithed, and classed by agricultural policies, practices, and groups. In doing so, however, we must be prepared to help students read and respond critically to agricultural "words" as well, directing explicit attention to the powerful roles rhetoric plays in mediating our relationships to one another, farm owners, farm workers, farming communities, and food.

Notes

I owe many thanks to Victor Villanueva, Patricia Ericsson, and Joan Burbick for their comments on early drafts of this essay.

1. See also discussions of neoliberalism by Harvey; McChesney; Chomsky; Hennessy; and Bourdieu. As McChesney explains, "Neoliberalism is the defining political economic paradigm of our time—it refers to the processes and policies whereby a relative handful of private interests are permitted to control as much as possible of social life in order to maximize their personal profit" (7). In public forums,

> neoliberal initiatives are characterized as free market policies that encourage private enterprise and consumer choice, reward personal responsibility and entrepreneurial initiative, and undermine the dead hand of the incompetent, bureaucratic and parasitic government, that can never do good even if well intended, which it rarely is. . . . At their most eloquent, proponents of neoliberalism sound as if they are doing poor people, the environment, and everybody else a tremendous service as they enact policies on behalf of the wealthy few. (7–8)

2. See for example reforms advocated in two 1995 American Enterprise Institute publications, Sumner, *Agricultural Trade Policy*, and Sumner (ed.), *Agricultural Policy Reform*. As many scholars have noted, it is difficult to make precise distinctions at the policy level between "liberal" and "neoliberal" reforms, in part because this ideological shift has occurred over time as differently oriented think tanks and industry groups have come to exert greater influence over U.S. agriculture policy, and in part because any particular policy is multiheaded, and tracing paths of influence and intent is tricky at best. But perhaps the larger problem, as I illustrate indirectly in this chapter, is that it takes time for any ideological movement to sufficiently disentangle itself from its predecessors and take coherent enough form across contexts to be recognized as a distinct phenomenon of its own.

3. For other early efforts to define agricultural literacy for use in educational settings, see Douglass; and Frick, Kahler, and Miller.

4. As Deborah Brandt might point out, such programs "pursue students" far more actively than targeted student populations tend to "pursue" them (5). "To treat [print] literacy as a resource is to appreciate the lengths that families and individuals will go to secure (or resecure) literacy for themselves and their children," Brandt writes. "But it also takes into account how the resources of literacy skill are exploited in competitions for profit or advantage that go on within the larger communities in which people live and work and in which their literacy learning takes place" (5). This final point applies directly to neoliberal agricultural literacy campaigns of the kind I examine in this chapter.

5. See for example Morgan; and Dunning, both published in 1891; McMath, *American Populism*; Mitchell, *Political Education*; and Mooney and Majka. See also chapter 6 in this volume for a discussion of the Grange.

6. This history warrants far more detailed analysis than I have space for here, particularly in regard to race, region, religion, and gender. See for example Ochiai; Reid; and Reynolds for more in-depth studies of agrarianism and populism among African American farmers from the mid-nineteenth through early twentieth centuries. See Neth for fuller analysis of gender in rural and agricultural organizations.

7. See for example "Response to Monopoly Capitalism, 1860–1900" and "Prosperity and Depression, 1900–1939" in Mooney and Majka.

8. Although there has certainly been wide participation of farmers in the Farm Bureau from the beginning, as Mary Neth writes, "equating membership with full acceptance of their agricultural policies [is] somewhat questionable" (134):

> Despite the significant number of farmers who were members of the AFBF, large landowners who had little sympathy for small family farms and agricultural professionals [have] dominated the AFBF leadership. The Farm Bureaus ultimately contained a broad-based membership, but the AFBF leadership and structure firmly linked the organization to the goals of production-oriented, centralized agriculture. (135)

9. See also Eileen Schell's discussion of "smart diversification" rhetoric. As Schell points out, this rhetoric generally "has two components: one focused on individual adaptability and innovation and the other on a collective embrace of neoliberalism" (79).

10. I don't mean to suggest that 4-H and FFA brainwash participants, or that members and leaders lack the ability to engage curricula critically or adapt it according to their own needs. Rather, I would point to the active roles interested sponsors like the Farm Bureau have played in guiding such organizations' curricula, using youth "outreach" efforts of this sort to advance their own ideological goals. See for example Kile; and Berger.

11. I want to thank curriculum designer Debra Spielmaker for sharing the history and educational objectives of "Growing a Nation" with me over the phone in summer 2008.

12. As Schell points out, "the rhetoric of smart diversification emphasizes how farmers can survive by 'thinking outside the box' through strategies such as niche farming, farm tourism, and technological methods like precision farming" (79); what it generally fails to do is help "the reader or viewer to understand how we arrived at the demise of the family farm through international trade policies, federal agricultural policies, and the globalization of capital" (81).

13. See "America's Diverse Family Farms" for standard USDA definitions of farm type and recent data on profits and government payments according to farm size and ownership.

14. See San Juan's discussion of similar tactics: "In spite of the resistance to the gains made by the women's liberation movement in the last four decades, Americanization is undeterred in deploying symbols of white women's 'liberation' to project the liberal capaciousness of the state. Such symbols are, of course, incorporated in a co-optive or recuperative way and harnessed to promote the interests of transnational corporations" (79).

15. There are a number of things going on in the story of Faris as an environmentalist: On one hand, Faris fits the romantic mold of yeoman farmer: his farming practices reflect his love for family and country, and his version of stewardship clearly echoes the agrarian values historically advocated by organizations such as the Farmers' Alliance and the Grange. In this regard, Faris offers an easily marketable (if deeply misleading) image of contemporary agricultural practice with which Monsanto can "get in the door." On the other hand, Faris is a businessman, and his environmentalism can be explained rationally: he doesn't "chain himself to trees" for no good reason like the "extremists" to which he is contrasted; he makes good environmental choices because it's part of remaining profitable and sustaining his business over the long term. Viewers need not support environmental restrictions on farmers and agricultural corporations, in other words, because the profit imperative and environmental stewardship ultimately go hand in hand.

Works Cited and Consulted

Adelman, Deborah, and Shamili Sandiford. "Reflections from the Garden: Developing a Critical Literacy of Food Practices." *Radical Teacher* 78 (Spring 2007): 5–10. Print.

"America's Diverse Family Farms: Assorted Sizes, Types, and Situations." Economic Research Service. Washington, DC: USDA, 2001. Print.

America's Heartland. American Public Television. KVIE, Sacramento. 2005.

America's Heartland. 2008. Web. 11 July 2008.

Barton, David. *Literacy: An Introduction to the Ecology of Written Language*. 2nd ed. Malden, MA: Blackwell, 2007. Print.

Berger, Samuel. *Dollar Harvest: The Story of the Farm Bureau*. Lexington, MA: Heath Lexington Books, 1971. Print.

Berlet, Chip, and Matthew Lyons. *Right-Wing Populism in America: Too Close for Comfort*. New York: Guilford, 2000. Print.

Bourdieu, Pierre. "The Essence of Neoliberalism." *Le Monde Diplomatique* Dec. 1998. Web. 4 Jan. 2009.

Brandt, Deborah. *Literacy in American Lives*. New York: Cambridge UP, 2001.

Burke, Kenneth. "Revolutionary Symbolism in America." *The Legacy of Kenneth Burke*. Ed. Herbert Simons and Trevor Melia. Madison: U of Wisconsin P, 1989. 267–73. Print.

Canovan, Margaret. *Populism*. New York: Harcourt Brace Jovanovich, 1981. Print.

Carnegie, Andrew. "Wealth." *North American Review* (June 1889): 653–64. Print.

Carson, Rachel. *Silent Spring*. Greenwich, CT: Fawcett, 1962. Print.

Chomsky, Noam. *Profit over People: Neoliberalism and Global Order*. New York: Seven Stories, 2003. Print.

Committee on Agricultural Education in Secondary Schools. National Research Council. "Understanding Agriculture: New Directions for Education." Washington, DC: National Academy, 1988. Print.

Degler, Carl N. "Beyond Rhetoric." *American Populism*. Ed. William F. Holmes. Lexington, MA: D. C. Heath, 1994. 125–34. Print.

Donehower, Kim, Charlotte Hogg, and Eileen E. Schell. *Rural Literacies*. Carbondale: Southern Illinois UP, 2007. Print.

Douglass, Gordon K., ed. *Cultivating Agricultural Literacy: Challenge for the Liberal Arts*. Battle Creek, MI: W. K. Kellogg Foundation, 1984. Print.

Dunning, Nelson A., ed. *The Farmers' Alliance History and Agricultural Digest*. 1891. New York: Arno, 1975. Print.

Forrestal, Dan J. *Faith, Hope and $5,000: The Story of Monsanto*. New York: Simon and Schuster, 1977. Print.

Frick, Martin J., Alan A. Kahler, and W. Wade Miller. "A Definition and the Concepts of Agricultural Literacy." *Journal of Agricultural Education* (Summer 1991): 49–57. Print.

The Future of Food. Dir. Deborah Koons Garcia. Cinema Libre, 2005. Film.

Harvest for Humanity. "About." 2006. Web. 11 July 2008.

Harvey, David. *A Brief History of Neoliberalism*. Oxford: Oxford UP, 2005. Print.

Hennessy, Rosemary. *Profit and Pleasure: Sexual Identities in Late Capitalism*. New York: Routledge, 2000. Print.

Holmes, William F. "The Leflore County Massacre and the Demise of the Colored Farmers' Alliance." *Freedom's Odyssey: African American History Essays from Phylon*. Ed. Alexa Benson Henderson and Janice Sumler-Edmond. Atlanta: Clark Atlanta UP, 1999. 239–48. Print.

Kazin, Michael. *The Populist Persuasion: An American History*. New York: Basic Books, 1995. Print.

Kile, Orville Merton. *The Farm Bureau through Three Decades*. Baltimore: Waverly, 1948. Print.

Lentricchia, Frank. "Analysis of Burke's Speech." *The Legacy of Kenneth Burke*. Ed. Herbert Simons and Trevor Melia. Madison: U of Wisconsin P, 1989. 281–96. Print.

Mackintosh, Barry. "George Washington Carver: The Making of a Myth." *Journal of Southern History* 62.4 (Nov. 1976): 507–28. Print.

Macune, Charles. "Purposes of the Farmers' Alliance." *The Farmers' Alliance History and Agricultural Digest.* 1891. Ed. Nelson A. Dunning. New York: Arno, 1975. 258. Print.

McChesney, Robert. Introduction. *Profit over People: Neoliberalism and Global Order.* By Noam Chomsky. New York: Seven Stories, 2003. Print.

McMath, Robert C. *American Populism: A Social History, 1877–1898.* New York: Hill and Wang, 1993. Print.

———. *Populist Vanguard: A History of the Southern Farmers' Alliance.* Chapel Hill: U of North Carolina P, 1975. Print.

McMurry, Linda O. *George Washington Carver: Scientist and Symbol.* New York: Oxford UP, 1982. Print.

Mitchell, Theodore R. *Political Education in the Southern Farmers' Alliance, 1887–1900.* Madison: U of Wisconsin P, 1987. Print.

"Monsanto Gift Benefits Agriculture in the Classroom." Monsanto. 9 June 2005. Web. 11 July 2008.

Mooney, Patrick H. *My Own Boss? Class, Rationality, and the Family Farm.* Boulder, CO: Westview, 1988. Print.

Mooney, Patrick H., and Theo J. Majka. *Farmers' and Farmworkers' Movements: Social Protest in American Agriculture.* New York: Twayne, 1995. Print.

Morgan, W. Scott. *History of the Wheel and Alliance, and the Impending Revolution.* 1891. New York: Burt Franklin, 1968. Print.

Mudge, Stephanie Lee. "The State of the Art: What Is Neo-Liberalism?" *Socio-Economic Review* 6 (2008): 703–31.

Neth, Mary. *Preserving the Family Farm: Women, Community, and the Foundation of Agribusiness in the Midwest, 1900–1940.* Baltimore: Johns Hopkins UP, 1995. Print.

Ochiai, Akiko. *Harvesting Freedom: African American Agrarianism in Civil War Era South Carolina.* Westport, CT: Praeger, 2004. Print.

Reid, Debra. "Rural African Americans and Progressive Reform." *Agricultural History* 74.2 (2000): 322–39. Print.

Reynolds, Bruce. "Black Farmers in America, 1865–2000: The Pursuit of Independent Farming and the Role of Cooperatives." Rural Business-Cooperative Service Research Report 194. Washington, DC: USDA, 2002. Print.

San Juan, E., Jr. *Racism and Cultural Studies: Critiques of Multiculturalist Ideology and the Politics of Difference.* Durham, NC: Duke UP, 2002. Print.

Schell, Eileen E. "The Rhetorics of the Farm Crisis: Toward Alternative Agrarian Literacies in a Globalized World." *Rural Literacies.* By Kim Donehower, Charlotte Hogg, and Eileen E. Schell. Carbondale: Southern Illinois UP, 2007. 77–119. Print.

"Secretary of Agriculture Ann M. Veneman." Office of the White House. Washington, DC: United States Government. Print. Web. 11 July 2008.

Spielmaker, Debra. *Growing a Nation: The Story of American Agriculture.* 2005. Web. 11 July 2008.

Sumner, Daniel. *Agricultural Trade Policy: Letting Markets Work.* Washington, DC: American Enterprise Institute, 1995. Print.

Sumner, Daniel, ed. *Agricultural Policy Reform in the United States.* Washington, DC: American Enterprise Institute, 1995. Print.

Tweeten, Luther. *Terrorism, Radicalism, and Populism in Agriculture.* Ames: Iowa State UP, 2003. Print.

"USDA, USU Team Up to Produce Multimedia History of American Ag." LetterPress Software. 2005. Web. 11 July 2008.

3

"Get More from Your Life on the Land": Negotiating Rhetorics of Progress and Tradition in a Neoliberal Environment

Cynthia Ryan

As Dad and I settle in to talk about the farming life, the rain pours down. Across the dirt road that runs on the west side of my parents' house, a "lake" that should be a field is once again replenished. It's June. The rain has been falling in record amounts since the middle of March. Some corn has been planted. No soybeans yet. Since I've arrived from Alabama with my girls for a visit with Grandma and Papa in Illinois, I am reminded of the daily information-seeking rituals that drive a farmer's choices—planning a day's, week's, or hour's work around weather forecasts, rain gauges, soil conditions, market updates. Each generation gathers data through newer and more sophisticated technologies, but the understanding that knowledge is crucial to successful farming is handed down by example from one generation to the next.

The landscape constantly changes due to factors that have more to do with politics and economics or technology than with what a given acre of land is best suited to produce. Adjustments are coming, just like they always have, and will continue to change the face of agriculture.

—Owen Taylor, "Holding On to Farm Life," *Progressive Farmer*, February 2008

As the passages that begin this chapter illustrate, the business of farming is fraught with unpredictability. During the summer in which I conducted a study of six Illinois farmers, the familiar challenges of uncooperative weather and poor soil conditions hung over the heads of men who yearned to "get in the field and finish their planting." But once the rains subsided and crops were planted, these farmers still faced other challenges that had less to do with "what a given acre is best suited to produce" (65) and more to do with the political environment that defines American agriculture in a global context in the twenty-first century. Farmers like my father, the fourth generation of Ryans to work acres of rich, midwestern soil, routinely weather environmental conditions (rain, drought, wind, and hail) alongside an industrial climate that privileges large commercial operations over small to midsize family farms.

In a society that increasingly supports an ideology of neoliberalism that places the interests of individuals ahead of collective goals, the values and practices that have sustained multigenerational farming communities throughout the country are becoming more difficult, if not impossible, to negotiate.[1] This chapter offers a look at the challenges of surviving in the current agricultural climate from two industry standpoints: the perspectives of a group of multigenerational farmers who operate small to mid-size farms in central Illinois, and the views of the editor-in-chief of one of the industry's longest running publications, the *Progressive Farmer*, based in my current "hometown" of Birmingham, Alabama.[2] Though interviewed separately, participants' comments reveal components of a complex, and necessary, conversation about the possibilities for and limitations to "progressive" practices in the agricultural industry. As the collected data illustrate, farm "progress" can be interpreted diversely: as the welcome adoption of bigger and better technologies built for increasingly larger and more commercially powerful operations and/or as the sustenance of farming families and communities whose lives are literally embedded in the soil. Following an overview of the ways in which these dual definitions of "progressive" have been portrayed historically in representations of farm life, I provide evidence that participants in this study reveal strategies for addressing these definitions discretely and in tandem—whether through their philosophies for running a sound farming operation or for covering the industry for readers with a stake in how progress is understood and enacted. My findings also support a sustainable model of "progressive farming" in the twenty-first century that recognizes and incorporates functional and critical literacy practices that have contributed to farming success for several generations.[3]

Limiting Ideologies of Successful Farming

Introducing the scope of their project in *Rural Literacies*, Donehower, Hogg, and Schell ask readers to consider their initial reactions to the pairing of *rural* and *literacy* in the book's title. The authors reference images rooted in media past and present, from "visions of a nineteenth-century farm wife reading by candlelight in her claim shanty" to "the bigotry of the Ku Klux Klan in the rural South" to perceived "insufficiencies of rural education." One of the central goals of *Rural Literacies* is to "move beyond" what are often "highly impressionistic, ahistorical, and seriously out of synch" understandings of the "economic realities of rural life" (1). In the introduction to this book, *Reclaiming the Rural*, Donehower, Hogg, and Schell discuss the frequency with which *rural* is defined, oftentimes dismissively, against the backdrop of its assumed opposite, *urban* or *metropolitan*, a definitional fallacy noted by regional economist Andrew Isserman. Such portraits are not only frustrating to those of us who have experienced very different versions of rural life, experiences grounded more often in what we "have" and "do" as opposed to what we "lack," but also damaging as they fuel marginalizing farm policies that ultimately rob communities of both their "idyllic" charm and the opportunity to participate fully in an evolving farming industry. In this section, I present some of the existing research on predominant images and ideologies associated with successful farming. This research leads to my own study while substantiating the claim that tensions between conflicting perspectives on "successful farming" place an untenable burden on farm families striving to sustain their livelihood in rural communities that are losing ground daily to commercial interests. The juggling of sometimes quite contradictory images of industry success can prove equally difficult to manage from an editor's standpoint.

Numerous scholars have questioned the dichotomous lenses through which farming is viewed: the lens of "romanticized agrarianism" positioning farmers in an imaginary landscape of wholesome values and simple lifestyles juxtaposed to the lens of "industrialized business" lumping family farms into the same category as all other representatives of corporate America (Cochrane). In chapter 2 of this book, Cori Brewster's discussion of agricultural literacy campaigns that attempt "to dehumanize and ostensibly depoliticize agriculture" on one hand while they "appropriate and redeploy long-standing agrarian tropes" on the other offers concrete evidence of the strategic rhetorical messages that carry clout in contemporary portrayals of farm life. Brewster notes that current displays of agricultural reality tend to celebrate only those stories that uphold politically preferred visions of rural life while claiming a wholesome commitment to non-partisan values, an assessment echoing Schell's discussion of the contradictions in farm policies since the 1980s purporting to capture the spirit of unlimited prosperity for farmers while stripping hardworking communities of the resources and

incentives to compete in a global market. Industry stereotypes contribute
to oppositional rhetoric, a struggle between "backwardness" as a form of
naïve idealism and "progressiveness" as a necessary sound-minded approach
to succeeding in the current agricultural climate. Examinations of the discourse "pushing and pulling" the industry further demonstrate the political
undercurrents that urge those assessing the state of agriculture to operate
within an either-or mentality—to apply what Schell terms "tragedy rhetoric"
to small farms believed to rely on outdated, traditional practices and values
and to associate a "rhetoric of smart diversification" with the greater profits
realized by individuals who embrace a corporate vision portrayed as inevitable and preferred (94–96).

Gerry Walter's research on images of success and the ideologies they
support among farmers and in farming publications establishes the staples
of "successful-farming rhetoric" that addresses one, or sometimes both, of
these dual perspectives ("Images"; "Ideology"), in the process suggesting the
correlation between historicized political realities and agricultural values. In
three major farming magazines published during 1944–45 and 1990–91, the
latter years emerging on the heels of early efforts by Farm Aid, Walter finds
that widespread "noncommercial images of stewardship and community,
family, and religious orientation" ("Ideology" 601) exist alongside messages
stressing productivity as a marker of success—a negotiation of perspectives
that renders commercial success in a context of shared priorities. By contrast, in the 1950s and 1960s era of "rapid industrialization and technological
change" (602), the same publications present a "successful-farmer image" that
privileges business savvy and aggressive management skills over commitment to romantic agrarian values. Associating the dominance of particular
ideological perspectives on farming with the socioeconomic realities of agriculture, researchers have substantiated the discursive shifts that occur in
industry ideals and advice presented to farmers (Bruce; Farrell; Fry; Marti),
as well as in farmers' own representations of success (Ford and Babb; Walter,
"Ideology"). Contrasting values once presented as compatible can be risky
from a publisher's perspective, though. Jack Odle notes that his experiences
working for the *Progressive Farmer*—as a writer, editor, and eventually editor-
in-chief—have taught him that "what's important is not the shifts that you
make, it's how you make them." By "understanding the magazine's core audience" and paying attention to "changes occurring" among this population,
a magazine can maintain readership through a clear and consistent voice.

In industry publications, a moderate position that balances a continuum of
successful farming values in flux might be the sensible response to the ever-
changing landscape (and reader demographics) characterizing American

agriculture. Schell's argument for a Burkean model of "mutual identification" to replace individualist constructs of blame and shame (94–98) is one such alternative. An understanding of progressive farming that acknowledges overlaps between the needs and values of multiple constituencies is arguably a more rational, nuanced approach than the impulse to define "progress" as either profit-driven *or* family-focused. Drawing on study data, I suggest that dichotomous thinking can also be the result of falsely severing "functional" and "critical" perspectives on literacy in a farming context. A sustainable model reconciles functional knowledge of successful farming practices with critical assessments of emerging agricultural literacies linked to technologies, markets, and other components of farming in the twenty-first century.

· From the Field

The six farming participants who took part in this study are all members of multigenerational farming families, and all own and/or rent acreage used primarily for growing corn and soybeans in central Illinois. Participants range from fifty to eighty years of age, and half of the interviewees have retired from farming while continuing to be actively involved in decision-making about the operations taken on by younger family members or neighboring farmers. Interviews were conducted individually in participants' homes, in most cases while sitting around a kitchen table. My interview with Jack Odle, editor-in-chief of the *Progressive Farmer* since 1991, took place in the Birmingham, Alabama, corporate offices for the magazine. Launched in 1876, this industry publication has a long history that is recognized by many American farmers, who may have observed members of previous generations reading the *Progressive Farmer* for agricultural news and advice. While the magazine initially focused solely on readers in the southern United States, by the latter half of the 1900s, issues targeted readers in the Midwest and other regions as well. Numerous books and articles have been written about the publication's history, including the sponsoring company's launch of a range of popular periodicals including *Southern Living, Health,* and *Coastal Living* (Johnson; Lauder; Logue and McCalla).

Data are organized around two emerging principles that demonstrate, first, participants' take on a polarized characterization of farming practices as *either* forward-thinking *or* outdated and unsophisticated; and second, the implications for reconciling this false dichotomy through a model of progress that converges the priorities and tenets associated with functional and critical literacies. While several critics have pointed to misperceptions perpetuated by images of farm life as romanticized and somewhat backwards or as highly industrialized and profit-driven, my study reveals that participants on both sides of the discursive fence—as working farmers and as producers of trade publications—can (and perhaps must) have a foot firmly planted in both worlds. Most of the farmers that I interviewed connected their own experiences as well as the experiences of members of previous generations to current portrayals of the knowledge and tools required to succeed in the industry. And while the technologies that farmers are witnessing are arguably bigger, better, and certainly less economically attainable, they insisted that adoption of promising technologies must follow critical assessment of the immediate and future impact on farming communities. Thumbing through the pages of the *Progressive Farmer*, Jack Odle also points to many messages that simultaneously reflect traditional values of farming as a business and a lifestyle as well as the quickly changing environment to which American farmers are expected to adapt. As Odle's comments reveal, the purchase of the *Progressive Farmer* in 2007 by DTN Industries, a company marketing "real-time commodity and option prices, weather and [other industry] information right on [a farmer's] Blackberry™ device" ("My DTN" B-19) predominantly to farmers of large operations, was also accompanied by a need to reframe many of the magazine's messages about successful farming. All participants, then, seem to be at a crossroads of sorts, making them an effective population for study.

"Good Judgment": Competing Discourses and the American Farmer

In an agricultural scene where "bigger is better," farm participants attribute many of the purchasing decisions they make today to advice communicated and enacted by previous generations. The *Progressive Farmer* similarly evokes handed-down wisdom as one key to survival for a new generation of farmers who face their own kinds of challenges (see Woolsholh). Innovations in machinery, genetically modified seed, diverse tilling techniques, and computer-driven technologies are compared to the development of practices and equipment realized by parents or grandparents. Jerry, a recently retired farmer who owns approximately 750 acres, shared that his father, who farmed during the Great Depression and often relied on the sale of a few eggs or fresh milk to feed his family, would likely be "bewildered by the capital [needed] for farming today."[4] "In my dad's lifetime," Jerry says, "2-row and 4-row planters were used" and "we [Jerry and his partner/brother] had an 8-row planter." Now, "they [manufacturers] are making 16- and 24-row planters" which can do the job in a fraction of the time. Other "surprises in farming," he notes, include the shift from "wagons to single-axle trucks to semis" for loading corn and soybeans, and combines that "pick 12 rows" as opposed to two. On the other hand, Jerry notes that his "dad started out plowing a field with horses" and eventually switched to a plow pulled by a tractor: "He knew how things [could] change in a lifetime."

Participants resisted simplified assessments of new technologies that have dramatically transformed the work of farmers, noting both the contributions and costs associated with adopting the latest "toys" for farming. A reliance on "good judgment" was presented as pivotal to participating in an industry that touts increasingly more advanced (and expensive) tools for successful farming. "Good judgment," I concluded from farm participants' comments, involves a process of weighing factors that may counter the principles for success in a commercial environment focusing primarily on profits. One lesson that he learned from previous generations, Jerry offers, was that "to get ahead, you can't buy everything that's supposed to make your farming better." Farmers "can't bury their heads in the sand" and ignore the potential for "hybrid crops, fertilizers, [or] GPS systems," all commodities regularly improved on and promoted in the *Progressive Farmer*, but they have to be selective when deciding which technologies will pay off and then "scrimp" to afford them.

Jerry's belief that the value of a new approach or device is determined over a period of time and not simply by the immediate gain it appears to provide was also echoed by Bob, who owns 30 acres and cash rents from numerous landowners. Bob agrees that farmers demonstrate good judgment by "paying attention to their neighbors' fields and seeing what's working for them." While Bob's comments circle back to an individual farmer's decision-making process, the notion that information is gathered from within a working community of farmers implies identification with, and possibly responsibility to, a wider group.

In most issues of the *Progressive Farmer*, the "rhetoric of smart diversification" (Schell) is couched at least partially in the context of specific farming operations. By following the particular circumstances experienced by select farmers in one region of the country, for instance, editors acknowledge that not all farmers or farming communities maintain identical histories or priorities. Some stories suggesting the importance of situated knowledge, for example a cover story on results of a "farm country" poll examining what's important to a diverse population of rural Americans (Miller), are highlighted in ways that both affirm a larger community with shared values and isolate the self-interests of individual farmers. Clay Rightmer, a cattle farmer in Schulenburg, Texas, says that "Dad [Harold Rightmer] and I are trying to preserve a heritage and a lifestyle that has been passed down through generations. . . . It defines who we are and how we live" (Miller 24). Embedded in an overarching discourse of neoliberalism, an ideological system privileging the impulse to grow a farm operation and hence fuel individual profit, editorial support for sound decision-making strategies that will benefit "farm country" as a united, albeit varied, population is frequently overshadowed by an emphasis on survival of the individual farm and the lifestyle it supports.

The contradictions inherent in a notion of "good judgment" as making yourself, and by extension, the industry, successful are evident throughout the publication and are reinforced in farm interviewees' handling of the difficult obstacles today's farmers face. In a cover story entitled "Losing Two Acres, Every Minute," Link introduces the problem of urban sprawl with the statement "It is sometimes called a farmer's last crop." After years of earning a livelihood from the land in the form of "hay, soybeans, wheat and corn," a farmer (read "any" farmer) discovers that selling his land for commercial purposes or to city dwellers who have always wanted a home in the country can be quite lucrative. After acknowledging that "it's his [the farmer's] right to sell his land," Link asks, "But is it right?" (47). Subsequent human interest stories focusing on farmers living in Pennsylvania, Wisconsin, and Michigan provide answers to the question by revealing the cost to neighbors who are forced through land sales to look out on subdivisions or strip malls. In this story, the *Progressive Farmer* provides editorial support for farmers who resist urban sprawl, even though large landowners are a target audience for the magazine, and their offspring may be among those who benefit from regulations like Section 1031 allowing a deferral of taxes for sellers who use money earned to purchase another plot of land.

Evidence of conflicting values can also be seen in an advertisement for Farm Plan, a service provided by FPC Financial, printed in the same issue as Link's story. Picturing a man swinging a golf club in the middle of an open pasture populated sporadically by cattle, the caption reads "Your Course. Your Rules." The advertisement focuses on "stay[ing] in control of your cash flow" and urges the reader to visit the company's web site to learn how to "farm on your terms" (21). In this instance, the reader's attainability of a workable farm plan might interfere with the interests of a larger community of farmers—a community that is neither addressed nor implied in the ad. The apparent contradiction between community-based decision-making (as suggested by the call to unite against urban sprawl) and individual choice (as revealed in the ad for Farm Plan) can be attributed to the maintenance of polarized images of romantic and commercial agrarianism in the magazine and the population it represents. Language focusing on the sole golfer's space and his right to make decisions that work best for him on his course abruptly dismisses the need to negotiate one farmer's use of land and pursuit of personal happiness with others.' Unacknowledged is the argument that the sustainability of rural areas and comfortable agrarian lifestyles—including the possibility of golfing freely in an open pasture—depends on resistance to a neoliberal implication that "Your Course. Your Rules." can co-exist peacefully with community interests. The contrast between the message conveyed in the Farm Plan advertisement and the article on uniting against urban sprawl demonstrates the push and pull of rhetorics that are represented as oppositional rather than as working in tandem. At the same time, the juxtaposing of contradictory messages begs for an integrated editorial philosophy on making "good" business decisions—choices that may be supported superficially by a functionalist perspective on literacy as the knowledge and skills deemed necessary for survival while critically assessing the effects on other farmers striving to hold on to their own farmland, an attention to mutual, rather than individual, survival.

Within the rural Illinois community where farming participants live and work, regular interactions between farmers appear to counter some of the problems of neoliberal dismissal of rural sustainability. Tom, an eighty-year-old retired farmer whose son now works his family's land, reflected on how a specific set of values focusing on community, family, and work passed down by his grandmother has guided how he thinks about farming and the actions that he believes support this perspective. In her role as a primary "literacy sponsor" (Brandt), Tom's grandmother "raised [him] on sayings" that he eventually wrote down. While on the surface, many of Tom's grandmother's sayings may be interpreted as trite clichés, on closer examination, these nuggets of advice reveal features of functional literacy alongside critical literacy. For instance, Tom shared one of his grandmother's most memorable sayings—"Seed time and harvest time shall not cease as long as the earth remains"—which he interpreted to mean that even a disappointing harvest provided "something" of value, "maybe not what you were hoping for, but something." Against an ideology of neoliberalism that promotes values of individual competition, where "something" that may not measure up to what you "hope[d] for" is deemed a failure, this saying reveals a more complex, community-based notion not only of sustainable farming, but also of sustainable living. "There was always someone who would ask me if I wanted to help them out [with their crops or livestock] when times got hard," he told me. "They asked me to help so I could earn enough for a few groceries." Edmondson's critique of neoliberal ideologies that purposefully position hope and success in a global economy outside the purview of rural communities is poignantly revealed in Tom's statement that he "used to have a neighbor on every corner, [but] now they just want what you've got." Like others in the study, however, Tom's reliance on a community of friends and farmers with whom he has been acquainted for most of his life is an important source of support for resisting and responding to the draw of neoliberal values.

In my interviews with Illinois farmers and with Editor-in-Chief Jack Odle, it became evident that while all seven participants recognize and contend with the changing expectations and requirements for surviving in the agricultural industry in the twenty-first century, their perspectives on this change make all the difference. The farmers I spoke with remain embedded in a community of people whose relationships reach back several generations in many cases. In contrast, Odle no longer lives in the Kansas farming community where he was raised. His adult working life has been spent in the field of agricultural journalism, and like most magazine editors, Odle's stance on the industry he covers requires a somewhat removed perspective that acknowledges current trends of interest both to advertisers and to the audience of larger farm operators and managers who are targeted more aggressively since the purchase of the *Progressive Farmer* by DTN. And while Odle's editorial style encourages writers to "get out in the field and visit with people" (Odle) to find out what they are thinking about and dealing with, the day-to-day interactions that support a more complex, sustainable model of "progressive farming" integrating functional and critical literacy practices is possibly too locally concentrated to address adequately in a publication with a wide and varied industry audience.

One example of a national story that garnered the attention of farmers as well as the farm industry press illustrates the influence participants' perspectives may have on their negotiation of a neoliberal emphasis on a profit-driven definition of successful farming and a community-based privileging of other indicators of success. During the week that I conducted interviews in Illinois, a farmer in Purdy, Missouri, was being hailed the "soybean guru" in the agricultural press (Campbell). With "over 12,000 acres in production" and 700 acres committed to soybeans, Kip Cullers is described as "scout[ing] his fields every day" by driving from field to field, "put[ting] over 11,000 miles on his pick-up in just three months" during the spring season. Purdy's high soybean yield, "139 bushels an acre in 2006," which "crushed the previous . . . record of 118 bushels per acre" and "159 bushels per acre in 2007," is attributed to choosing seed with the "right genetics." While the *Progressive Farmer* did not feature the story in the issues that I examined for this study, the magazine's regular inclusion of stories on how individual farmers can make their operations more efficient and more profitable relates the story of Cullers's achievement to an ideology familiar to readers.

I asked Don, one of the study participants who returned to the family business of farming after a short stint in banking, for his thoughts on recent coverage of Cullers's accomplishment. Don acknowledged that while perspectives on successful farming vary, he questions two aspects of Cullers's story. First, Don notes that with more than 12,000 acres to tend, Cullers would be physically unable to "walk his fields," feasibly a farmer who never "get[s] his feet muddy." Second, while the agricultural media applauds Cullers's record soybean yield, Don wonders whether a large farm owned by one man prevents others from farming smaller plots of land. This participant's statements suggest a fundamental belief that those who tend to the soil should be "in" the soil. Smiling, Don says that he doubts Cullers has time to "listen to the birds" since he probably spends most of his time on the computer. He's living "a corporate life on the farm," Don concludes with a smirk.

Don's comments reflect the disempowerment that occurs when large landowners preclude the development of smaller operations. Though not explicitly stated, Don's argument that farmers need to be able to maintain personal oversight of their fields is tied to his contention that spreading acreage among several farmers is preferable to monopolizing the industry in a particular region, an argument that conflicts directly with the *Progressive Farmer's* focus on empowering larger farm owners. While a prosperous landowner may have the tools to produce an amazing yield, the sign of success from a corporate perspective, the industry loses something significant according to this participant. The extent of this loss is perhaps most evident in Don's reference to "an old farmer" who told Don in the late 1970s that "one of these days, [he would] have to run through a lot of fields to find a *good* farmer"—one who understands the land and how to care for it properly. A yield deemed successful from a marketing standpoint looks quite different from within the community, a tenet that explicitly critiques the limitations of a neoliberal paradigm. For farmers situated in close-knit communities where handed-down guidelines for success remain firmly planted in the collective memory of its members (Kitch), the teasing apart of individual endeavors and community effects is perhaps more difficult to sustain.

A "Good Farmer": Living and Working In a Rural Community

In the pages of the *Progressive Farmer*, an agrarian lifestyle continues to be promoted not only as attainable, but also as highly desirable for raising a family. Several stories explicitly draw on the past, reasserting the assumed values and traditions of farming families conveyed throughout the magazine's history (see Johnson). For example, the cover story "Growing Great Kids" traces the success of 4-H in shaping farm kids who possess the "five C's" of "confidence, competence, connection, character, and caring" (Myers 51). The article celebrates the differences and similarities between the organization then and now, offering, for instance, that "today only about 8 percent of 4-H members live on a farm" (53), while noting that current and future leaders of our nation, including an "Iowa farm girl [who went] from showing cattle to running the space station" (Vath 55), can trace their roots to 4-H. While the *Progressive Farmer's* rendition of the purposes and current state of 4-H varies somewhat from the account offered by I. Moriah McCracken in chapter 7 of this book, in which she states that 4-H was never intended to be a club focusing solely on rural kids and that the organization currently boasts a slightly higher percentage of members still living in rural areas (12 percent), both McCracken and Myers note the prioritization of "doing" and "thinking" that distinguishes 4-H. In the *Progressive Farmer*, "Growing Great Kids" directly follows the issue's DTN Business Extra section including advertorials on "Harvesting the Future" (Davidson) and "Deere's 'Electrifying' New Tractor" (Patrico), placement that could be read as an attempt to merge the image of romantic agrarianism (for city kids, too) alongside a commercial imperative.

While this cover story acknowledges a changing landscape in rural America and addresses how the organization has "adapt[ed]" its mission in the twenty-first century by introducing aspects of farm life in innovative ways (for example, by setting up a hydroponics lab for one club in lower Manhattan) (Myers 53), it fails to acknowledge the limitations of such adaptation. The statement that a mere "8 percent of 4-H members live on a farm" reflects more than a natural movement away from rural America. Scholars have noted that while the migration of younger generations of rural families to urban centers to pursue other professions has been rationalized through the rhetoric of progress, such migration is typically devastating to the communities left behind (Edmondson). By extension, the "five C's" are communicated and contextualized by a decidedly different population of 4-H members described in the story, a change that the magazine reports on while reinforcing the continued value of the organization for today's generation of youth living on farms.

Both farm participants' comments and the pages of the *Progressive Farmer* convey the sense of privilege of belonging to a farming community. Approaches to characterizing the lifestyles that are experienced in rural communities differ, however, in interviewees' comments reflecting divergent industry perspectives. Participants situated in an Illinois farming community emphasized that networks are crucial for maintaining a continuum of values that have existed for generations. An example of such an enacted network is the environment at the local grain elevator, where several of the participants begin their days to talk about "grain prices, machinery, events in the news, family, [and] gossip" with "regulars" who have lived in the community for anywhere from five to fifty years (Jerry). Bob says that outsiders who "don't know anything about farming" can "learn more at the elevator" than by reading all of the industry magazines published. Conversations between farmers are a constant in the community, Bob says: "It's almost like a party line . . . Terry will call me, then Chuck, then Don . . . 'What do you think? Is it too wet to plant? Did you see the price of corn this morning?'" Functional know-how and decision-making skills that address both local and far-reaching contexts are intricately tied to a lifestyle that balances discourse on community and industry. Donny, a third-generation retired farmer, confirms the critical community component of such conversations, saying that an outsider who tries to "learn about farming by only reading a magazine won't know enough to be a successful farmer."

In the *Progressive Farmer*, reported networks tend to concentrate on participation in a family-owned farming operation. A cover story entitled "Holding On To Farm Life" reinforces an image of an agrarian lifestyle changing predictably and naturally alongside an industry decision requiring "smart diversification" (Schell). The inside of a fold-out cover photo pictures Mississippi farmer Chuck King holding his infant daughter Kirby against a background of a cotton field, while the front cover displays the pair nine years later in front of a corn field. These contrastive scenes are contextualized by verbal text: "Little girls grow up, dads get older, crops shift."

Portrayed as an inevitable, and smart, evolution, the shift from cotton to corn for the Kings is a response to "water-use issues, a farm labor shortage and weed resistance" as well as "global competition" from cotton growers in China and India (Taylor, 62, 64). And while the magazine story reports primarily on the economic and environmental conditions influencing the crop shift, this narrative is framed by the story of a dad and his daughter. Vast differences between these overlapping stories of growth are left unacknowledged, however. Readers would expect dad and daughter to age over nine years, but many of the environmental changes that have influenced the King's diversification strategy are impacted by a global economy stressing profit over the practices that have sustained both this family and their community over several generations. So, while the story and accompanying photo suggest a model of "progressive farming" that merges an example of functional literacy—the Kings made changes that were necessary for maintaining their business and their family in a current climate—alongside evidence of assumed critical literacy on Chuck King's part as he evaluated the shifting economy and environment and made a wise and lucrative choice, the specific negative effects (the cost of adopting a new crop or the added labor likely entailed in making the shift, for instance) on King's operation and on his neighbors' operations is not thoroughly addressed. The story provides a snapshot of yesterday and today, but the requirements for a model of "progressive farming" that acknowledges the overlapping considerations of self-survival and community-survival remain unexplored.

Both farming subjects' comments and magazine stories focusing on families like the Kings emphasize the people who are at the heart of the industry and the lifestyles that are available to them. The scope of this attention to people varies, however, in the stories of those situated in close-knit communities and the *Progressive Farmer's* coverage of individual farm families as examples of national trends in the industry. For example, Lawrence, a fourth-generation Illinois farmer, acknowledged the rapid growth of larger family farms (some managing up to "20,000 acres") and the transformation in farming techniques during his own lifetime. While he believes that new methods of farming—for instance, "computers [for everything from] keeping records to hooking up a planter"—are pivotal advancements in the business of farming, Lawrence's focus rests on the people who help to make the farming life more successful. Like many other participants, Lawrence links farming decisions and even specific crops to the family members connected to them—his father, brother, son, nephew—and is reflective about his own choices over the years: "We [Lawrence and his brother, Pete] were a little slow using Roundup* for soybeans, [but once we saw] how well it worked we kept using it" and "I never played the market again [after having to] buy out a contract for selling corn ahead of time." These comments suggest ownership over decisions. But Lawrence's references to the people who have played prominent roles throughout his career as a farmer, encompassing both good and bad decisions, extend beyond immediate family members. This participant shared stories of neighbors, in many instances generations of the same family, whose lives have influenced more than the successes and failures he has experienced in his business. They have also been central characters in the story of his community as he recalls specific incidents occurring in the context of weddings, baptisms, and funerals. Lawrence's portrayal of the dynamics between his family's legacy of farming and the history of the surrounding community reveals the crucial perspective that multigenerational farming families might bring to a model of progress that values the needs of individuals within a dynamic community context.

An Integrative Model of "Progressive Farming"

Based on data gathered from participants on each side of the industry fence, I'd like to conclude with some components of an integrative model of "progressive farming" involving the conscious negotiation of functional and

The cover story "Holding On to Farm Life" depicts two potentially competing narratives of progressive farming. Photography by Deborah L. Ferguson, http://www.southern-images.com.

Little girls grow up, dads get older, crops shift.

In the first nine years of Kirby King's life, pressure on agriculture has intensified. For farmers like Chuck King, a switch from cotton to corn made sense.

critical literacy perspectives. The impulse to *either* hold onto traditional practices enacted through farming as a business and a lifestyle *or* move toward a more commercialized vision of agriculture in the twenty-first century is clearly unproductive. As the participants in this study reveal, farmers who have worked the same land for generations and who have strong alliances within their communities are understandably resistant to forfeiting elements of "good judgment" that have long guided their beliefs about farming, family, and community. At the same time, a magazine like the *Progressive Farmer* cannot embrace only those practices that support an ideology of profit over people without the "risk [of] losing [its] audience" (Odle). And though all participants recognize the value of the "opposing side"—farmers are well aware of the need to know about and carefully adopt promising technologies, while Odle recognizes that his readers (and the publication's owners) expect the magazine to capture some of the romanticism of farm life alongside the "biggest and the best"—there is a tendency to view these positions as contradictory as opposed to potentially mutually empowering. [5]

In fact, farmers and journalists covering the industry display many of the same values and concerns: the right to own land and to earn a living on the land, the ability to remain competitive in a complex and fast-moving global marketplace, and the desire to adapt without sacrificing the institutions that uphold rural life as many of us know it. The farmers whom I interviewed are actively engaged in communities where the requirement to be self-sustaining and to watch out for the needs of neighboring farmers is a daily struggle, while editors of leading industry publications are tasked with representing news of widespread trends, many attainable only by an elite segment of farming professionals, alongside individual stories of living in rural America that at times echo back to a distant era and at other times reveal a shifting picture of what constitutes a "good life" for today's farm family.

A brief rundown of current business arrangements described by Illinois farmers participating in this study reveals just some of the alternatives members of the community have embraced for surviving in the industry, options that demonstrate both a keen understanding of the nuts and bolts needed to maintain an operation and a critical assessment of obstacles to sustainability. Now retired, Jerry cash rents his land to two local farmers who lack sufficient start-up funds. Both of Tom's sons farmed his land before his oldest son was injured and had to get out of the family business. Tom's younger son now farms all but 50 acres of his dad's land. Lawrence's son and nephew farm 750 acres of family-owned property and manage more than 4,000 additional acres owned by other farmers in the area. Don has followed in his father's footsteps, but his business is now comprised of land inherited by his wife as well as his own. Though his son currently farms one field while holding down a full-time job in town, Don is uncertain about his son's future in agriculture. Bob continues to grow his operation by farming for more and more retiring farmers whose children have left to seek work elsewhere. Donny's son farms in a neighboring community, and his daughter married a farmer who lives nearby. He anticipates that they will be the last generation of his family to farm. These stories-in-progress illustrate the crucial choices that farmers, who are well-versed in the examples set by parents, grandparents, and great-grandparents who survived challenges of their own, have made in an attempt to "adjust"—at least temporarily—to the "changing face of agriculture" (Taylor 65). At the same time, reported stories of the gains and losses characterizing farming in the twenty-first century show both the real and rhetorical contradictions that have emerged and will continue to emerge under the present paradigm, in the struggle over whose interests will prevail in an industry rooted firmly in tradition and the hope of progress.

Notes

"Get More from Your Life on the Land" is one of many subtitles presented on the cover of the *Progressive Farmer* through the years. I chose to include this particular tag line because it reflects a central question that underlies the study presented in this chapter: how "get[ting] more from your life on the land" is defined in an ever-shifting industrial climate.

1. The term *neoliberalism*, as I am using it, relies on the definition offered by Stephanie Lee Mudge in *Socio-Economic Review*. Drawing on the "three faces" of neoliberalism—the intellectual, bureaucratic, and political—Mudge argues for a historically grounded understanding of a movement that has created "an unadulterated emphasis on the (disembedded) market as the source and arbiter of human freedoms" accompanied by a central belief in "the elevation of the market—understood as a non-political, non-cultural, machine-like entity—over all other modes of organization" (704–5). As a result, the priorities of select, empowered private interests supplant the needs, values, and voices of less powerful parties seeking a place at the table. Since neoliberalism as an ideology and an implemented practice has become "the defining political economic paradigm of our time" (McChesney 7), it behooves us to ask in what ways we can reconcile the divide between private interests and the interests of the many who are disempowered, both economically and rhetorically.

2. The methodology on which this study is based was approved by the Institutional Review Board at the University of Alabama at Birmingham. Six farmers from central Illinois were interviewed, as was the editor-in-chief of the *Progressive Farmer*. I thank Bob, Don, Donny, Jerry, Lawrence, and Tom for taking the time to talk with me during a busy and trying planting season, and Jack Odle for welcoming me into the offices where the *Progressive Farmer* is created and answering my many questions about this long-standing publication.

3. C. H. Knoblauch associates the "functionalist perspective" on literacy with a "pragmatic emphasis on readying people for the necessities of everyday life . . . as well as for the professional tasks of a complex technological society" (76). Drawing on Giroux and Freire, Knoblauch notes that a "critical literacy" perspective acknowledges that language practices both "objectify" and "rationalize" social conditions that perpetuate a dominant authoritative structure (79). In the context of this study, *functional literacy* refers to participants' descriptions of basic kinds of knowledge needed to maintain a farming business (for example, awareness of the most suitable soil conditions for planting a particular crop), while *critical literacy* is applied to data that

reveal an understanding of the political influences behind messages about successful farming (for instance, skepticism about the "need" for bigger and better farm machinery that perhaps benefits manufacturers more than farmers).

4. All of the farmers who participated in this study asked to be identified by their first names.

5. The example provided earlier in this chapter juxtaposing an advertisement for "Farm Plan" ("Your Course") with an article on urban sprawl (Link) is evidence of the tendency to oppose rather than mediate positions. An alternative editorial strategy might be to answer Link's question about whether a farmer's legal "right" to do with his land as "he" chooses is ethically "right" for the surrounding agricultural community. See, for example, an article by Singleton published in a later issue of the magazine that engages both perspectives.

Works Cited

Bob. Personal interview. 16 June 2008.

Brandt, Deborah. "Remembering Writing, Remembering Reading." *College Composition and Communication* 45.4 (1994): 459–79. Print.

Brewster, Cori. "Toward a Critical Agricultural Literacy." *Reclaiming the Rural*. Ed. Kim Donehower, Charlotte Hogg, and Eileen Schell. Carbondale: Southern Illinois UP, 2011. Print.

Bruce, Norma J. "Serials for the Farm Family of 80 Years Ago." *Serials Review* 21.3 (Fall 1995): 1–22. Print.

Campbell, Jeannie. "Soybean King Kip Cullers." *Market to Market*. Iowa Public Television transcript. Web. 29 Aug. 2008.

Cochrane, William W. "American Agricultural Development, Rural Values and Societal Valuation Conflicts." *Agriculture, Change and Human Values*. Ed. Richard Haynes and Richard Lanier. Gainesville: U of Florida P, 1982. 1–13. Print.

Davidson, Daniel. "Harvesting the Future." DTN Business Extra. *Progressive Farmer* Apr. 2008: S6–8. Print.

Don. Personal interview. 11 June 2008.

Donehower, Kim, Charlotte Hogg, and Eileen E. Schell. "Constructing Rural Literacies: Moving Beyond the Rhetorics of Lack, Lag, and the Rosy Past." *Rural Literacies*. By Donehower, Hogg, and Schell. Carbondale: Southern Illinois UP, 2007. 1–36. Print.

Donny. Personal interview. 16 June 2008.

Edmondson, Jacqueline. *Prairie Town: Redefining Rural Life in the Age of Globalization*. Lanham, MD: Rowman and Littlefield, 2003. Print.

Farrell, Richard T. "Advice to Farmers: The Content of Agricultural Newspapers, 1860–1910." *Agricultural History* 51.1 (1977): 209–17. Print.

Ford, Stephen A., and Emerson M. Babb. "Farmer Sources and Uses of Information." *Agribusiness* 5.5 (1989): 465–76. Print.

Fry, John J. "'Good Farming—Clear Thinking—Right Living': Midwestern Farm Newspapers, Social Reform, and Rural Readers in the Early Twentieth Century." *Agricultural History* 78.1 (2004): 34–49. Print.

Isserman, Andrew M. "In the National Interest: Defining Rural and Urban Correctly in Research and Public Policy." *International Regional Science Review* 28 (2005): 465–99. Print.

Jerry. Personal interview. 10 June 2008.

Johnson, Mary Elizabeth, ed. *Times Down Home: 75 Years with* Progressive Farmer. Birmingham, AL: Oxmoor House, 1978. Print.

Kitch, Carolyn. *Pages from the Past: History and Memory in American Magazines*. Chapel Hill: U of North Carolina P, 2005. Print.

Knoblauch, C. H. "Literacy and the Politics of Education." *The Right to Literacy*. Ed. Andrea A. Lunsford, Helene Moglen, and James Slevin. New York: MLA, 1990. 74–80. Print.

Lauder, Tracy. "The *Southern Living* Solution: How *The Progressive Farmer* Launched a Magazine and a Legacy." *Alabama Review* July 2007, 186–221. Print.

Lawrence. Personal interview. 17 June 2008.

Link, Joe. "Losing Two Acres, Every Minute." *Progressive Farmer* Mar. 2008, 46–51. Print.

Logue, John, and Gary McCalla. *Life at* Southern Living: *A Sort of Memoir.* Baton Rouge: Louisiana State UP, 2000. Print.

Marti, Donald B. "Agricultural Journalism and the Diffusion of Knowledge: The First Half-Century in America." *Agricultural History* 54.1 (1980): 28–37. Print.

McChesney, Robert. Introduction to *Profit over People: Neoliberalism and Global Order* by Noam Chomsky. New York: Seven Stories, 2003. Print.

McCracken, I. Moriah. "'I Pledge My Head to Clearer Thinking': The Hybrid Literacy of 4-H Record Books." *Reclaiming the Rural.* Ed. Kim Donehower, Charlotte Hogg, and Eileen Schell. Carbondale: Southern Illinois UP, 2011. Print.

Miller, Dan. "Farm Country Speaks Out." *Progressive Farmer* Aug. 2008, 17+. Print.

Mudge, Stephanie Lee. "What Is Neo-liberalism?" *Socio-Economic Review* 6 (2008): 703–31. Print.

"My DTN, My Way." DTN advertisement. *Progressive Farmer* June/July 2008. B-19. Print.

Myers, Victoria G. "Growing Great Kids." *Progressive Farmer* Apr. 2008. 50–55. Print.

Odle, Jack. Personal interview. 12 Aug. 2008.

Patrico, Jim. "Deere's 'Electrifying' New Tractor." DTN Business Extra. *Progressive Farmer* Apr. 2008. S4–5. Print.

Schell, Eileen E. "The Rhetorics of the Farm Crisis: Toward Alternative Agrarian Literacies in a Globalized World." *Rural Literacies.* By Kim Donehower, Charlotte Hogg, and Eileen E. Schell. Carbondale: Southern Illinois UP, 2007. 77–119. Print.

Singleton, Natalee. "Mending Those Neighborly Fences." *Progressive Farmer* Sept. 2009, 62–63. Print.

Taylor, Owen. "Holding On to Farm Life." *Progressive Farmer* Feb. 2008, 62–65. Print.

Tom. Personal interview. 11 June 2008.

Vath, Claire. "The 4-H Astronaut." *Progressive Farmer* Apr. 2008, 55. Print.

Walter, Gerry. "The Ideology of Success in Major American Farm Magazines, 1934–1991." *Journalism and Mass Communication Quarterly* 73.3 (1996): 594–608. Print.

——— . "Images of Success: How Illinois Farmers Define the Successful Farmer." *Rural Sociology* 62.1 (1997): 48–68. Print.

Woolsholh, Karl. "Farm for a Lifetime." *Progressive Farmer* 2 Jan. 2008. Web.

"Your Course. Your Rules." Farm Plan Advertisement. *Progressive Farmer* Mar. 2008, 21. Print.

Section II
Histories

4

Rural Literacies, Postindustrial Countrysides: *Resolana,*
Entre Seco y Verde, and the Shadow of the Atomic Age

Damián Baca

> We are experiencing a personal, global identity crisis in a
> disintegrating social order that possesses little heart and
> functions to oppress people by organizing the hierarchies of
> commerce and power—a collusion of government, transnational
> industry, business, and the military all linked by a pragmatic
> technology and science voracious for money and control. This
> system and its hierarchies impact people's lives in concrete
> and devastating ways and justify a sliding scale of human
> worth used to keep humankind divided. It condones the mind
> theft, spirit murder, exploitation and genocide de los otros.
>
> —Gloria Anzaldúa, 2002

> The future of New Mexico is not technology;
> it is Ohkay Owingeh/Gente.
>
> —"Manita del Norte," 2006[1]

By the closing of the twelfth century, the Ohkay Owingeh and their fellow Tewa-speaking sisters and brothers, of what is currently known as northern New Mexico, had established complex agrarian systems and trade routes across Pajarito Plateau and the northern Rio Grande countryside. While the Spanish Conquest[2] of the sixteenth century wrought violence and brutality upon these indigenous communities, the cultures of the "Old" and "New" Worlds eventually formed an extensive, interdependent rural economy across the region. Spanish settlers and friars brought metal tools, horses, fruits and other crops to the Rio Grande valley, resulting in profound changes to indigenous ways of life. Simon Ortiz of the Acoma Pueblo[3] recalls that eventually a cultural mosaic evolved, one that made it obvious that Spanish and Pueblo peoples came to embody valued and indispensable aspects of one another's culture. Emerging Indohispana/o[4] literacies, for example, began to include sacred knowledge about how to live in accord with the earth and the rhythm of the land.[5] The current northern New Mexico landscape is inextricably entwined with the past and present literacies of these local communities.

The carefully negotiated ties between tribalized Pueblos and their Indohispana/o relatives would become almost completely severed after the United States declared war on Mexico, with the hopes of expanding its slave plantation economy into the province. Additionally, Anglo-European hierarchies of commerce and power kept Indohispana/o and Pueblo rural communities from the burgeoning urban hubs of commerce and education; these new power relations instead imposed ideological dichotomies that distorted local people's cultural distinctiveness into subordination. Several decades after the U.S. war and occupation, second-generation German American physicist Robert Oppenheimer chose the Manhattan Project "Site Y" at Los Alamos New Mexico, the landscape formerly known as Pajarito Plateau, as the site for constructing the atomic bomb.

While much has been written about the Manhattan Project, Oppenheimer, and the deployment of atomic weaponry, the conditions and responses of Pueblo and Indohispana/o rural communities within and around Los Alamos have been neglected or ignored altogether. And while some agrarian cultures of dominant U.S. ethnic identities are beginning to gain recognition by rhetoric and composition specialists, virtually no research on northern New Mexican Indohispana/o rural literacies has emerged until now. This chapter initiates a conversation in our field about Indohispana/o rural literacies in what is now the U.S. southwest.

In contrast to most other North American provinces, northern New Mexico went from a historically agrarian, preindustrial existence to a postindustrial cradle of the atomic age, thereby passing over an entire period of Western colonial and economic development. Los Alamos was a boon to subsistence farmers since they had plots where they could build their homes and continue farming while enjoying relatively well-paying jobs (see Chambers and Aldrich). This created an illusion that one could succeed and become affluent without much formal, institutional education. While the surrounding rural economy became engulfed in the collusion of transnational industry, business, military science, and advanced technology, rural Indohispana/o literacies across the local countryside eventually flowered in response. The grassroots formation of an Indohispana/o educational think tank known as *Academia de la Nueva Raza* (Academy of the New Humanity) in the 1970s as part of the Chicano Movement is one example of the kinds of literacies being formulated and practiced by Indohispano/a peoples. *La Academia* published a number of periodicals and bulletins as philosophical treatises on the ancestral nature and communal spirit of Indohispana/o rurality in northern New Mexico. *La Academia's* publication of its first volume, *Entre Seco y Verde*, sparked multiple decades of further work documenting Indohispanic knowledge drawn from life experiences in cities such as San Antonio, Texas, and also in oral history projects with Mexican farmworkers in Brawley and El Centro, California (see Montiel, Atencio, and Mares).

In this chapter, I argue that local publications from *La Academia*, in particular *Entre Seco y Verde*, a collection of oral history narratives, promote historical and critical literacies as answers to rapid postindustrial governmentality, the latest stage of global colonialism and Western triumphalism. Specifically, these Indohispana/o publications help local populations negotiate, accommodate, debate, and resist succumbing to dominant political powers while also affirming their rural resourcefulness and strength against seemingly insurmountable challenges. Before analyzing *La Academia's* key volume *Entre Seco y Verde*, I first offer a brief history of the Pajarito Plateau/ Los Alamos landscape.

Pajarito Plateau/Los Alamos: A Brief History

While the earliest evidence of human existence in New Mexico is attributed to the Sandia people around 25,000 B.C.E., the Clovis were plausibly the first to settle along the region's eastern plains and river valleys about 10,000 B.C.E. Clovis inhabitants, and later the Folsom and Cochise, crossed the area in search of mammoth, bison, and other game. Eventually, these cultures began cultivating corn, squash, and beans, thereby providing the earliest evidence of agricultural life in the southwestern United States. Centuries later, approximately 1130 C.E., the Anasazi people migrated from the north to settle along the river valley.

By 1175, cultures of the Keres linguistic group would settle on Pajarito Plateau, west of the Rio Grande. Some inhabitants constructed dwelling places with volcanic rock, while others lived in natural caves along the canyon walls. Not long thereafter, a second migration from the north would reach the plateau, bringing the Tewa language into the area. Large community dwellings were built upon the mesa tops, and the people carved artificial caves from the canyon walls to create multiple cliff dwellings. Within fifty years of their arrival, the Tewas eventually relocated due to drought, food shortages, and multiple raids by neighboring Navajos, Utes, Apaches, and Comanches. By 1550, indigenous settlers had abandoned the Pajarito Plateau for pueblos along the Rio Grande, where warmer temperatures and irrigation made for easier farming. In addition to their dwellings, indigenous settlers left behind thousands of petroglyphs, carvings into rocks, which can still be found throughout the canyons of the Pajarito Plateau.

Academia de la Nueva Raza

In *The Contested Homeland: A Chicano History of New Mexico,* Erlinda Gonzales-Berry and David Maciel note that

> Nuevomexicanos entered the twentieth century with a strong sense of place and cultural identity. The Spanish-language newspaper industry continued to thrive and was instrumental in fostering the cultural scene by providing a space for the publication of creative literature. More important, newspapers provided a forum for projecting political agendas that promoted the interests of the Nuevomexicano community. Certain dominant themes, among them politics, class contradictions, labor conflict and organization, demographic changes, cultural perseverance, and the pursuit of civil rights stand out. (84)

Despite significant land loss, violence, and discrimination directed at Pueblo and Indohispana/o cultures, their knowledge and experience of rural living remained politically influential; however, Indohispanic and Pueblo farming cultures cannot be properly understood through the patriarchal rhetorical lenses of the Athenian agora or Plato's Academy. They are better understood as webbed networks as opposed to cultural and intellectual hierarchies.

As the Indohispanic community sought practical avenues to confront the challenges of a postindustrial age, they also held on to their spiritual ideals. The community deployed the vision of a networked learning society composed of learning communities as an overarching concept for responding to the requirements of techno-globalism. The learning society is a strategy for uncovering and building on knowledge ubiquitous in everyday life; its two fundamental goals are cognitive learning and consciousness-raising. The first entails learning how to use the mind critically to acquire knowledge and practical skills appropriate for everyday life, especially to meet the technological requirements of the cyber age. The principal skill demanded by the cyber age is literacy that extends beyond alphabetic literacy to include technology, information, health, law, economics, media, ecology, and globalization.[6] It takes into account not only the cognitive aspects of learning, but also the total experience and field within which the individual lives and moves. Consciousness-raising, on the other hand, provides a new awareness of the challenges of the cyber age. These two components of the learning society bear the fruit of a "new" awareness with "respond-ability."

In *La Academia de la Nueva Raza*, the idea of a learning society grew out of the examination of and reflection on living experiences in New Mexican rural communities. From traditional narratives, "new" literacies and consciousness-raising began to emerge. Community members understood that one learns through the material realities of doing. Thus, younger generations traditionally learned how to butcher animals under the supervision of elders. Young women and men learned animal anatomy as they prepared the animal parts. As the young carried out these tasks, elders gave instruction on the meaning and importance of certain procedures: "Mucho cuidado con la hiel, si quebras la viejiga se contamina la carne. Cortale el nervio en la pierna pa' que se ablande la carne" [Be very careful with the bile, if you puncture the gallbladder, you'll spoil the meat. Cut the nerve in the thigh so that the muscles relax and the meat softens]" (Atencio, "Resolana" 3).

Young women, primarily, learned to deliver babies by apprenticing under experienced midwives. They learned to plaster with mud, make *hornos* (adobe ovens), and weave cloth through observation and practice. Beliefs, ceremonies, and rituals were passed on to the young through the Penitente society, a lay religious brotherhood. They learned doctrinal commitments by actively participating in prayers, hymns, rituals, and service to the Penitente brotherhood and their families. Young women learned the rites, rituals, prayers, and hymns through participation in women's religious societies. They got their practical knowledge about the use of herbs for health and well-being as well as cooking skills from mentors.

The telling of traditional narratives was the primary way of transmitting life lessons, knowledge, norms, and moral guideposts. There is a strong parallel between this traditional educational model of apprenticeship and new models arising in response to a postindustrial society. The young learned to understand their everyday life experiences and their culture while incorporating a body of knowledge and traditional values and norms. If one were to place a canopy over a traditional New Mexican village, one would have a school, a learning community where the skills and knowledge necessary to sustain and give meaning to life in that particular society were taught through experience and hands-on learning. Learning and doing were inseparable: one did and thereby one learned. Conversation and reflection would occur between activities, and the next time the same task was performed, an opportunity to apply compounded knowledge from the first experience was created. A growing body of knowledge and skill emerged from these experiences.

This hands-on learning through doing and reflection is perhaps analogous to Paulo Freire's notion of praxis learning (71–86). In the educational institutions of industrial society, learning, though, has largely become separated from practice. Once knowledge has been severed from practice, learning becomes the mere transference of information from those who have it to those who do not. Learning and knowledge have thus become isolated from each other and from action, yet they mesh with each other, like cogs in the industrial wheel.

The idea of a learning society took a leap into the policy arena during the Clinton administration as many began to ponder the fate of the welfare state in postindustrial society. Many compassionate and rational individuals in the United States would agree that some form of the welfare state, or at least its safety net aspects, should endure for those who fall through the cracks in a market economy. The right to an income accompanied by a single-payer comprehensive healthcare system would offer all an equal chance at a sustainable life. In addition, a move toward a learning society would allow the government to make a full commitment to ensure its citizenry would have the opportunity to become technologically literate, especially in media technology. It would also prepare the populace in the use of appropriate (low-tech) and affordable technology that sustains a healthy environment. Such a learning society would also emphasize the arts and humanities. Learning processes such as dialogue would be used to uncover and reclaim subjugated autochthonous and historical knowledge. In addition, the arts and humanities would inspire the psyche and open pathways to creativity and innovation, the driving forces in a knowledge-based society. Ultimately, this would contribute toward a taking up of "new literacies." Such policies, if implemented, would foster distributed literacies across rural populations.

Recognizing that political economy is not part of the market equation, the idea of a state-supported learning society is somewhat utopian. Nevertheless, the idea of a learning society driven by experiential learning seems like a logical approach for reclaiming aspects of the self-reliance of preindustrial society, thus filling the gap left by the welfare state. In the case of *La Academia de la Nueva Raza,* experiential learning was encouraged by way of storytelling. *La Academia's* members conducted dialogues with people, asking them to talk about their childhood experiences and their lives as adults and recorded these stories using audiotape. These conversations were framed by the participants' perceptions and interpretations of changes they had witnessed from their childhood to the present. The dialogues proceeded through imagined spirals of thought and action. Tomás Atencio describes the process in a 1988 lecture titled "Resolana: A Chicano Pathway to Knowledge."

The dialogue between a tutor, or collector, and a contributor engaged both individuals in a creative process of thought and action. This dynamic relationship begins by reflecting on a deed, or action, under discussion in the personal history, oral history, or folklore that is being documented. I assumed the content of an oral history or folklore was based on an actual or imagined occurrence—something that happened in the head or in action— that may have been generalized or embellished by subsequent reporters of the event. Whether the story was factual or not was not important. Our concern was to reflect critically on the individual's perceptions, whether these were mental images or sensory experiences. Upon reflection, the meaning of that account, within a historical context, was revealed and led to subsequent action by the participants in the dialogue. That action could be manifested externally or remain within the mind as an intended or conceived action. In either case, it is action that results from reflection on a previous action. This creative process gives birth to a dynamic spiral of thought and action.

As more was uncovered, the collector and contributor became dynamically linked in a closer understanding of each other's information and knowledge. Language diminished in importance as a tool for understanding as the individuals moved from a rational to a more intuitive mode. In street language, it was *maliciandola*. It was communication with full integrity in the message occurring in a reciprocal exchange of words and meaning; and as understanding is fully achieved "the sun is shining on everything and everybody is seeing everything as it is at the same time."[7]

After reviewing the recorded material, the narratives were transcribed verbatim. As recordings were reviewed, community members noted particular themes, and those were pulled out of the transcription and entered in a separate text. Estevan Arellano, publications editor at *La Academia de la Nueva Raza*, suggested a scriptwriting/filmmaking approach for the transcription; narratives that fit a particular theme were entered in the text in the left-hand column and labeled by theme. Next, they identified the stories that addressed a particular theme and compiled them. These were shared with the contributors, who then learned what others had said about the identified theme. The participants were brought together to talk about their stories and came to a consensual validation and understanding of the meanings of their experiences. This dialogue process, called a "macro-spiral of thought and action," became the "new *resolana*," a process and place for all participants to discover new knowledge, gain understanding, and learn from their collective experiences. As challenges emerged in the community, the community of action would come together for specific discussion and action.

What comes out of the group dialogue—that is, *resolana* or the macro-spiral—becomes knowledge that is committed to print or adapted to other media for dissemination. The micro dimensions produce self-knowledge; the macro dimensions create consensually validated knowledge and meaning. The macro process was truly the contemporary reconceptualization of *resolana*.

Resolana is a pathway to knowledge that derives from a dialectical relation between thought and action in the everyday lives of rural Indohispana/o people. To distribute the *resolana* dialogue to the community in printed form, stories were published in a booklet entitled *Entre Seco y Verde*. The title symbolizes a life cognizant of death, a life of imagination and reason, one filled with both *green* and *dry* periods. In *Entre Seco y Verde*, thematic vignettes join in a dialectical relationship; one vignette addresses the green of life, the other deals with its dry, wilted aspects. The dialectic of vignettes illustrates life's contradictions. For example, one vignette tells of the forest and the community's harmony with nature. Another vignette tells of the coming of lawyers to adjudicate the land, who, in payment for their services, got the land itself. In this way, readers were to learn about history and simultaneously raise their consciousnesses. Although they could not alter the past, they worked toward attaining new literacies that they could apply when facing similar circumstances in the future. *Entre Seco y Verde* was another way of expressing the spiral of thought and action.

La Academia published three thousand copies of *Entre Verde y Seco* in 1972, many of which were purchased by the Home Education Livelihood Program (HELP) in northeastern New Mexico to use as the textbook for adult literacy education. As part of its classes, HELP participants gathered in the West Las Vegas School cafeteria one evening a month to discuss the book's narratives and themes. Called the "Chicano Town and Gown" in order to lure professors and students from the nearby New Mexico Highlands University to listen to their grandparents tell of their life experiences, the evenings fostered a true *resolana*, as people delved into the themes in the book and deepened their understanding through more stories and folktales.

Entre Verde y Seco, edited by Tomás Atencio, illustrates the richness of experiential literacy narratives. The presentation of information in the book follows a rural life cycle, from birth to death. Additionally, the summary reveals an emerging body of knowledge from the lived experiences of a traditional, rural society. I quote from *Entre Verde y Seco* at length to demonstrate how it sets forth the life and literacy narratives of Indohispanic people:

> A woman in her early seventies, mother of four, explains: "I never knew a doctor in my childbearing years—for any of my children. *La partera*, the midwife, *una viejita*, a little old woman, would deliver us; she nursed us to health by holding us to a strict forty-day *dieta*, a period of time when

we did nothing. We were kept still and undisturbed, quiet as brooding hens. She nurtured us with lots of *atole, piloncillo, chaqueque* with milk, and boiled eggs."

. . . The sanctity of life was seen not only in humans but also in all of nature. In describing how she raised her own food, an elderly woman recounts in a detailed description her relationship with the land: "When the days get longer and warmer in the early spring," she said, "I pay someone to plow and to clean the ditches and make the furrows. Then, with my hoe I level the beds so that they look neat and clean, make straight rows, where I dig small holes and there lay the seeds. Then I irrigate until the sprouts show. If the plants of *chile* or tomatoes grow in little heaps and bunched up, I thin them. The tomatoes and cabbage I transplant far from their little brothers so they may thrive and grow beautifully. Then all summer long I spend my days hoeing, weeding, irrigating, and building little earthen mounds to fortify the growing plants until they are ready to yield their fruits."

. . . But the weather and the destiny of the crops were not all left to chance As in childbirth, where San Ramon is the intercessor, in the toil of the land for subsistence other *santos* were summoned to intercede on the farmer's behalf. "In the summer," another person said, "we would celebrate the Feast of the Virgin Mary. Early in the morning, all together, young and old, we would take the Virgin in procession trampling through the fields, without even causing any damage to the wheat." When times were dry, "we would take the *santos* [San Ysidro, the patron saint of agriculture] in procession through the fields, praying for rain."

This was a life of innocence and simple faith, a reflection of the openness to myth, to primal energy. Fulfillment and freedom were harmonious relationships with nature and an acceptance of destiny.

In the social world there were good times and bad times as well. "People in years past," another woman said, "would help each other. In the summer, neighbors would join to mud-plaster each other's houses. They would invite themselves to hoe and irrigate the neighbors' plots. In the fall, they harvested their crops together and at night would shuck piles of corn and tie *ristras* of red *chile* while they told stories, jokes, and shared the news of the day." That was the green of human experience. But reciprocity was gradually replaced with a formal exchange of goods and services. That was the dry.

"In earlier days," reflected a ninety-year-old man, "we had men of honor. Today I don't think we have any. In those days one man would ask another, '*Allligo*, lend me two dollars and I will pay you when the sun sets.' At dusk the man would return the two dollars, because the word was honored.

Not so today. The word of honor is useless. Instead we have complicated documents. People no longer trust." Reflecting more profoundly about these changes, this man offers an explanation: "The true value of things has been exchanged for a promise—an anticipated life in the future. Our communities and the activities of everyday life have become alienated because our sustenance and our possessions have been purchased and have not derived from an intimate relationship among each other and with nature. We no longer pay for the harvest that sustains us with the sweat of our brows; hence we no longer feel the satisfaction of having done something useful and meaningful. We do not feel the soul of the earth because it has become a disgrace to soil ourselves with its dust. We no longer recognize the miracle—the *milagro*—of food, because we have not bent our bodies over a plant to care for it or to pluck its fruits. Neither do we feel the humility nor the nobility of being human because we neither do the most sublime nor the most base of things. We are satisfied with a life of leisure; with a life of no pain."

"Why has life changed?" we ask. "Strangers—foreigners—have come to our lands with their own styles and manners of being. We have believed what they said because we still have some faith in people." In an ironic twist this observer concludes, *"Semos tan buenos que pa' nada semos buenos."* We are so good that we are good for nothing. Another way of saying it is: virtues as moral values are useless as instrumental values.

But, "what else do you want?" he ponders. *"Tenemos corazón bueno y sano."* We have a sense of well-being and wholeness in our hearts. (6-8)

These narratives of birth, agrarian cycles, and communal cultural values convey the concept of *resolana*, of knowledge embedded in communal and agrarian production processes. These processes involve collective literacy practices that include plural voices, perspectives, and new discursive models. The root word of *resolana* is *resol*, which refers to reflection and light, where the sun brings radiance and clarity. *Resolana* departs from the ancient Socratic idea of dialogue to post-Western models, thus inviting possibilities for leveling social hierarchies. Literacy is generated by communities from life experience and reflection rather than transferred in from elsewhere.

In the second segment to follow from *Entre Seco y Verde*, the dialogue *Café y el Atole* narrates the intrusion of Western economic advancement into the rural community. In the central exchange, *café* or coffee advances his argument of superiority and arrogance against *atole*, the indigenous food derived from corn and rooted in Pueblo creation myths. In this narrative, *atole* becomes entwined into a sparring debate with Western commerce.

Café y el Atole, then, is not a communal dialogue but a hierarchical dispute lead by the arrogance and superiority of Western commerce. Yet in the debate, subjugated Indohispanic knowledge critically responds to the expanse of urban commerce and postindustrial economics. The local production of *atole* addresses the colonial tension between the two in order to reenvision "new" cultural and economic possibilities beyond these dynamic tensions:

> Despite this fundamental commitment to virtues as moral values, struggle for fulfillment in the social and political domains persisted. The native confronted the intruder. In *El Trovo del Café y el Atole*, a debate in verse commonly used in New Mexican *pláticas* and declamations of years past, Coffee advances his argument of superiority arrogantly:

> > Yo soy el Café
> > Con azúcar soy sabroso
> > También con carnes fritas
> > Y con sopapilla generoso
> > Con bollitos victorioso
> > Y en puntos bien arreglados
> > Bien parezco en las mesas
> > Con huevos estrellados.
> > > [I am coffee
> > > With sugar I am delightful
> > > When served with meat and fried bread
> > > I'm in great demand by all
> > > And alongside little bread rolls on elegant tables
> > > > displayed
> > > I look distinguished next to colorful fried eggs.]

Atole, the indigenous food derived from corn, significantly rooted in the Indian creation myth, answers assertively:

> > Yo también soy el Atole
> > Desciendo de maíz
> > Y te pondré mis paradas
> > Que bien mantengo a mi gente
> > Con tortillas enchiladas
> > Con esquite bien tostado
> > Ahora te daré noticias
> > Café por comprarte a ti
> > Ya no se alcanzan pa' camisas.
> > > [And I am gruel

A proud descendant of corn
Ready to declare war on you
For I nourish and sustain my people
With tortillas soaked in chili
With popped corn well toasted
Now, let the whole world know
That my people squander their money just to buy you
And hence have no money left to buy shirts.]

Atole triumphs.

The journey, full of conflicts and contradictions, joy and pain, must come to an end. The storyteller, the listener, all must die as many who told these stories have already died. Death is our shadow—*la doña Sebastiana*—the *seco* of life, but we must confront her, and as another man in Santa Fe said, "think about her at least three times a day," lest we miss living an authentic life.

In the tradition of the Pious Fraternity of the Brotherhood of Light—the Penitente—the departed brother bids farewell through the voices of his surviving brothers, who sing:

De la nada fui formado
La tierra me ha producido
La tierra me ha sustentado
A la tierra estoy rendido
Adios por ultima vez
Que me ven sobre la tierra
Ya me echan en el sepulcro
Que es mi casa verdadera.

[I was formed from no substance
Earth gave me my life
Earth has nourished my life
And to earth I am forever bound.
This is my last farewell
For no longer will I upon the earth be seen
I am going to the grave
My true home and final resting place.]

The images of the Virgin Mary, of the crucified Christ, of San Ysidro that people took in procession through the fields, and San Ramon to whom an anxious husband danced during his wife's labor, were carved from wood by men who were known as *santeros*. They were the community's artists who expressed through the *santo* sentiments of suffering and meaning of an isolated community in a harsh environment. *Santos* were the social mediators among people and the symbols of the religious and mythical dimensions that opened the way for humans to communicate with the supernatural. These men gave the community the sacred objects for its rites and rituals. (Atencio 10–13)

Café y el Atole is innovative in that it is precisely a critical response to our current stage of postindustrialism and Western triumphalism—globalization—which maintains the premise that there is one sole epistemic tradition from which to achieve "development," intellectual maturity, and universality. Additionally, *Café y el Atole* makes an intervention into the 500-year-old myth that the accumulation of wealth is the final destination in the "development" of human civilization. Our latest domestic financial failure of 2008–9 further suggests that the dominant economic incentive model *produce>accumulate>consume>consume again* is unsustainable.

Rethinking literacy and knowledge production through *resolana* may invite a larger dialogue and questioning of a plurality of economic possibilities rather than a unilateral, overarching one. What other cultural and economic possibilities might we consider at this moment in time? How are natural resources to be used, and to whose benefit? How might local communities attain representation for their own regional and agricultural interests? How might we develop a humane economy that accounts for the everyday needs of others? Is it possible to rethink the very concept of property and ownership? How can preindustrial, rural literacy bring us to economic models of the accumulation of knowledge where citizenship is not necessarily transformed into consumership?

Conclusion

The publication of *Entre Verde y Seco* provided rural communities with a collective text they could consult when issues and disputes arose in the community. In one sense, the bulletin functioned as a wake-up call, alerting its readership to contemporary regional problems and linking them to a folkloric literacy such as *Café y el Atole* that provided historical context and connected current concerns with earlier struggles during Spanish colonization.

The dual concepts of *resolana* and *Café y el Atole* emerge from Indo-hispana/o rural roots to their application in urban settings and on to a holistic view and critique of globalization. It is noteworthy that *Entre Verde y Seco* has potential for university-based learning as well as nonacademic and community-based learning. The humanities and social sciences as an intellectual project are historically intertwined with global colonialism and Western triumphalism, represented by *café*, a symbol of shifting economy and commerce. The cultural provinces of *atole*, however, involve a broader horizon of knowledge production, that is, the act of thinking, learning, and teaching *with* the rural literacies of Indohispanic communities in the colonial periphery.

In one sense, it could be argued that thinking through *resolana* and *atole* creates a parallel with Plato's dialogues. Yet *resolana* offers a significant counternarrative: discourse is no longer limited to exchanges between two privileged intellectuals geographically and rationally situated in Athens, the metropolis of ancient Greek culture. *Resolana* affirms Indohispana/o rural communities as sources of knowledge, even though they are not grounded in the humanities, social sciences, or any other particular disciplinary tradition that is only known through an academic elite. *Resolana* is an opening for another way of looking at education coming *from* the community, humanizing knowledge rather than creating yet another ideology such as Marxism, Postmodernism, or Western feminism. In opposition to the vanguard history of the West and the expanse of global capitalism, *resolana* invites us to create new literacies, new learning models, new pedagogies, new histories, which, in the best of possible futures, might bring about an end to Western triumphalism. As the Zapatistas say, "luchar por un mundo donde otros mundos sean possibles," or in English, "fight for a world where other worlds are possible."

Thus a pedagogical shift could occur from didactic lecture approaches to *resolana*—a practical approach of interactivity in learning environments. A pedagogy for democratizing knowledge might reenvision the western university as interactive network, interconnected through the web and guided by regional rather than state-level degree-granting boards. Yet *resolana* is profoundly non-ideological and calls for others to think through their own community circumstances, to open communication for future inquiries, education reform, and new economic possibilities.

Notes

This chapter is part of an ongoing collaboration with Yvonne Montiel, Miguel Montiel, Tomás Atencio, and E. A. "Tony" Mares.

1. See New Mexico Office of the State Historian, Digital History Project .

2. The term *Spanish* is inaccurate, historically. The people who came with Oñate were not all directly from Spain. Many were *mestizos* (mixed blood) from Mexico; there were people from the Canary Islands, and there were some from France.

3. The Castilian word *pueblo* evolves from the Latin word *populus* ("people"), and literally means "village." Spanish combatants first used the term to identify the various indigenous agrarian settlements of what was then considered northern Nueva España. Today, there are twenty-one federally recognized Pueblo nations in New Mexico.

4. The expression *Indohispana/o* consists of a dynamic spectrum of shifting and contested subjectivity. At one extreme of this continuum are people who understand their individual and communal identity as primarily indigenous. At the other extreme are those who deny indigenous affiliation as part of their lineage and instead see themselves within a largely isolated Spanish-Iberian inheritance of the past 400 years in the Americas. See Baca; Lamadrid; and Montiel, Atencio, and Mares on Indohispana/o cultures.

5. See Anaya and Ortiz.

6. See Kist.

7. Atencio, "Resolana." *Snapeando*, a cognate deriving from the Anglo colloquialism "snap," means to see the essence of something by way of insight. *Maliciandola* likely derives from *malicia*, the loss of innocence. The concept of "the sun shining on everything" was used by O'Odham elders to describe full integrity in communication, wherein the sender of a message, the message itself, the receiver of the message, and the feedback to the sender, are clear.

Works Cited and Consulted

Anaya, Rudolfo, and Simon Ortiz. *A Ceremony of Brotherhood, 1680–1980.* Albuquerque: Academic, 1981. Print.

Anzaldúa, Gloria, and Analouise Keating. *This Bridge We Call Home: Radical Visions for Transformation.* New York: Routledge, 2002. Print.

Atencio, Tomás. "La Academia de la Nueva Raza: El Oro del Barrio." *El Cuaderno (de Vez en Cuando)* 3.1 (Winter 1973): 4–61.

——. "Resolana: A Chicano Pathway to Knowledge," revised version. Personal collection, Albuquerque, NM, 2003. Print.

Baca, Damián. *Mestiz@ Scripts, Digital Migrations, and the Territories of Writing.* New York: Palgrave Macmillan, 2008. Print.

Chambers, Marjorie, and Linda Aldrich. *Los Alamos, New Mexico: A Survey to 1949.* Los Alamos, NM: Los Alamos Historical Society, 1999. Print.

Freire, Paulo. *Pedagogy of the Oppressed.* New York: Continuum, 2006. Print.

Gonzales-Berry, Erlinda, and David Maciel. *The Contested Homeland: A Chicano History of New Mexico.* Albuquerque: U of New Mexico P, 2000. Print.

Kist, William. *New Literacies in Action: Teaching and Learning in Multiple Media.* New York: Teachers College, 2004. Print.

Lamadrid, Enrique. *Hermanitos Comanchitos: Indo-Hispano Rituals of Captivity and Redemption.* Albuquerque: U of New Mexico P, 2003. Print.

Mares, E. A. "The Fiesta of Life: Impressions of Paulo Freire." *El Cuaderbo (de Vez en Cuando)* 3.2 (Spring 1974): 4–16. Print.

Montiel, Miguel, Tomás Atencio, and E. A. Mares. *Emerging Chicano Dialogues on Community and Globalization.* Tucson: U of Arizona P, 2009. Print.

Oppenheimer, Robert. *Physics in the Contemporary World*, Arthur D. Little Memorial Lecture at M.I.T. 25 Nov. 1947. Print.

Reinhold, Robert. "Agrarian New Mexico Seeks a Silicon Harvest." *New York Times* 12 June 1984. Print.

Schwartz, Peter. *The Art of the Long View: Planning for the Future in an Uncertain World.* New York: Double Day/Currency, 1991. Print.

5

Women's Words, Women's Work: Rural Literacy and Labor

Jane Greer

In *The Mind at Work*, Mike Rose laments that "labor, as a political and social force, has diminished in power and has less immediate grab on the national imagination," and he urges scholars in literacy studies to attend to how "work gets defined and the attributions we make about it" because "these attributions color the kind of social and civic life we can imagine" (xxii). To counter the erasure of labor from the public sphere, Rose documents the analytic and rhetorical skills of waitresses, welders, hair stylists, plumbers, and electricians living in the urban and suburban areas of California and Arizona. Mathematical calculations, aesthetic judgments, feats of memory, time management, relationship building, the interpretation of a wide range of visual and verbal texts, and sophisticated rhetorical performances—all these intellectual maneuverings Rose observed as he watched people at work. Tracking the ingenuity that workers bring to daily tasks allows Rose to offer a nuanced portrait of labor that is neither "ennobling or dehumanizing" but that instead captures the complex meanings of work in people's lives across the economic and occupational spectrum (25).

This essay builds upon Rose's important project in two ways. By examining the literacy practices of rural women as they have documented their own lives and labors, I aim both to extend conversations about the place of work in people's lives still further across the geographic and occupational spectrum and to put workers' own writing at the center of study. Listening carefully to how workers deploy the literacy resources available to them to describe their daily activities creates opportunities to appreciate the social value they ascribe to their labor and can expand how we understand civic participation. To this end, I undertake a close reading of how Myrtle Tenney Booth (1906–1999), a longtime resident of Randolph County, West Virginia, depicts women's labor in an autobiography she penned in 1985.[1]

Beginning in 1825 with her great-grandparents' marriage, Booth's auto-biography catalogues how Appalachian farmwomen approached their daily chores. The tasks undertaken by farm women across the 160 years and four generations chronicled by Booth—tending livestock, maintaining vegetable gardens, weaving cloth, preserving fruits, making butter and cheese, sewing clothes, preparing meals, raising children, and nursing the sick—required technical expertise, reasoning skills, intellectual flexibility, and rhetorical sophistication, just as the urban-dwelling welders, waitresses, and electricians observed by Rose drew upon their cognitive and linguistic skills to accomplish their work. Booth's narrative also reveals her understanding of labor not necessarily as a marketplace commodity but as a communal resource. Composing an autobiography near the end of her life allowed Booth to neatly suture women's work into a model of civic engagement that made sense for her rural community.

To be sure, Booth's autobiography is not unique in offering a glimpse into the labors and literacy practices of rural women in the nineteenth and twentieth centuries. In recounting the agricultural practices in her Hidatsa community in the mid-nineteenth century, Buffalobird-woman (Maxi'-diwac) documents the ingenuity of women as they crafted tools, laid out fields, and planted corn while also giving voice to the values of her community—reverence for the land and recognition of intergenerational bonds—that informed their labor. Adele "Doaty" Orpen's memoir of homesteading in Kansas in the 1860s details her expertise in animal husbandry. She explains how she kept track of cattle on the vast prairie and notes that with her skills in tracking livestock she was "in great request among settlers around us" (86–90). Iowan Ada Mae Brinton's diaries map not only how the structural features of her farmhouse (e.g., cook stove, well, cistern) affected her approach to laundry and meal preparation but also the complex relationships among neighbors that allowed them to survive the "rough years in the 1930's" (186). And Bessie Jones recounts how she learned "to be a jack-of-all-trades" in the semi-desert of New Mexico—grinding corn, shearing sheep, and doing other "outside chores" along with her domestic responsibilities. As Jones explains, "ranch life is different you see, you all work together for the same purpose" (43). Irrespective of the diverse reasons that prompted them to write their life stories, these rural women devoted significant linguistic resources to describing the details of mundane chores, and like Booth, they emphasized the public value of their work rather than any private gains.

A project that strives to amplify the voices of rural women from decades long past—seeking to understand how they accomplished their daily tasks and to appreciate how they ascribed value to their labor—risks appearing sentimental. But the place of rural women within the economy remains an ongoing concern in the twenty-first century. In the United States, agribusinesses have overwhelmed family-owned farms; Wal-Marts have sprouted up in counties across the nation and forced local retailers to close; and more rural residents are commuting to urban/suburban areas to find work. Stretching beyond the United States, a global food network unequally absorbs and distributes resources so that many residents of wealthy nations can consume any food in any season while malnutrition and starvation are common in other locales. To remedy such inequities, international policymakers have promoted development programs that impose market-based identities on rural women from Nepal to Sri Lanka to Chile as a way to achieve economic growth, social justice, and political freedom (Rankin; Dingo). I believe, though, that attending to the literacy performances of rural women from the past and tracing how they constructed themselves as workers and writers can serve as a starting point for expanding the possibilities available to rural women today. Rather than embracing economic and educational models that reflect an urban, industrial mindset, rural women have presented public arguments on behalf of alternative forms of economic behavior, civic engagement, and literate activity. Penning her autobiography was for Myrtle Booth an attempt to represent her life for future generations and reflected her investment in a view of both literacy and labor as more than assets that acquire value when circulated in the marketplace. For Booth, both words and work enrich the lives of others. I will first situate Booth within the geographic and historical context in which she worked and wrote and then offer a close reading of her autobiography as a literacy performance that links rural labor to civic participation.

The "Workingest" and Most "Capablest" Women: Rural Lives in Need of Reform?

Though Appalachia is a complex region whose diversity should not be overlooked, a general sketch of how the farm women living in the Allegheny and Blue Ridge mountains have historically been figured in the public consciousness provides a useful backdrop for understanding rural women and how they have represented their labor as a contribution to their communities. As historian Henry D. Shapiro has observed in his landmark study, Appalachia first emerged as a distinctive geographic and cultural region in the late nineteenth century. Stories about "peculiar" folks who inhabited the hills and hollows of Kentucky, West Virginia, Tennessee, Virginia, North Carolina, Georgia, and Alabama began appearing in periodicals between 1870 and 1900.[2] Lacking good roads, adequate schools, prosperous churches, and civic organizations, Appalachia was presumably inhabited by lawless moonshiners, feuding families, and ignorant hillbillies. Protestant missionaries flocked to the region to minister to their impoverished brethren, and the Euro-American heritage of white mountaineer families made them seem more worthy of benevolent attention than newly arrived immigrants or recently emancipated African Americans (Shapiro 32–58). Social workers, folklorists, educators, and industrialists soon followed, seeking variously to explore, exploit, and uplift a people who seemed resistant to the nation's vision of itself as boldly progressive (Shapiro; Whisnant; Pudup, Billings, and Waller; Thomas; Billings and Blee; Salstrom; Powell).

Not surprisingly, Appalachian women received their share of attention. Literary artists, social workers, and educators created vivid portraits of mountain farm women in the early twentieth century, too often relying upon two hastily figured, often coexisting, caricatures: the heroic, pioneering woman (or her descendent) who maintains a charmingly rustic home and raises a large, loving family unencumbered by the trappings of urban life; and the slatternly bumpkin whose willful ignorance concerning issues of sanitation and nutrition require remediation by specialists who bring technical solutions and a metropolitan vision of civic life to bear upon the supposed deficiencies of country living. The fiction of Lucy Furman serves as a useful example. Furman's *Sight to the Blind* (1914) focuses on Aunt Dalmanutha, who has a small farm on the Clinch River and initially describes herself with pride as

> the workingest and most capablest woman up and down Clinch; I that not only could weave my fourteen yard,' or hoe my acre of corn, or clear my man's stint of new ground, a day, but likewise had such faculty in my head-piece that I were able to manage and contrive and bring to pass; I that rejoiced in the work of my hands and the pyeertness of my mind and the fruits of my industry, and when my man died were able to run the farm and take keer of the children as good as before.

But Aunt Dalmanutha has been incapacitated by cataracts and must be convinced by a visiting nurse to travel to the city to consult with a physician who is able to restore her vision. After recovering from surgery, being fitted for dentures, learning to read, and seeing the material comforts enjoyed by those living in less rugged areas, Aunt Dalmanutha is a changed woman. She realizes that there is a "rising tide of helpfulness manifest in the human heart everywhere" and decides to spend her savings on "some fine store clothes for to match my teeth and my innard feelings." The newly literate and finely dressed Aunt Dalmanutha returns to her home, announcing that she will "git my loom sot up and running so's to have a-plenty of kivers and linsey for sale come cold weather." The story concludes with Aunt Dalmanutha and her family rejoicing in the knowledge that "prosperity wa'n't no further from us than yan side of the mountain."

The argument of Furman's narrative is clear. Hard-working rural women lead admirable but benighted lives. Under the tutelage of experts, rural women can be made to recognize the value of new technologies and new literacy practices. Appalachian farm women thus gain access to prosperity and to civic identities derived from marketplace interactions—in this case, Aunt Dalmanutha will be a seller of "kivers and linsey" and consumer of mass-produced "fine store clothes." Not only has this rural woman had her physical sight restored—her way of seeing herself, her labor, and her world has also been corrected.

Similar arguments about rural women and their labor can be traced in educational texts, like the *Country Life Readers*, which Cora Wilson Stewart authored for the Moonlight Schools that she founded in 1911 to provide educational opportunities to farm families. Providing literacy instruction for adult learners, this series of three textbooks ostensibly celebrates agrarian life. A closer look at the *Country Life Readers* reveals, though, that farm women attending the Moonlight Schools would have been taught not only to read and write but also to follow in Aunt Dalmanutha's footsteps, acquiring new literacy skills, taking advantage of new technologies, and entering into new civic relationships. Rather than relying upon their own experiential knowledge and the accumulated wisdom of family and friends, women were encouraged to consult books and other printed materials as they provided for their families. For example, in a lesson from the second reader a physician chastises a woman for not preparing nutritious food for her sick husband. In the next lesson, the distraught woman hurries to a neighbor's house to learn to make a restorative beef tea. Rather than drawing upon her own expertise, the neighbor instead responds "Let me get my cookbook. I cook most things by recipe, and then I know that I am making them right" (91). Other lessons in the *Country Life Readers* describe the latest "cold-pack" method of canning and encourage women to use sterile methods to process milk and make cheese. In still other lessons, rural residents were urged to organize formal community institutions. For example, a lesson in the second of the *Country Life Readers* exhorts students to support a local Sunday school so that people can "read and study the Bible together!" According to the lesson, "the Sunday school is a 'get together' affair, and the country needs more of such things" (131). Like Furman's *Sight to the Blind*, Stewart's textbooks invoke the noble image of the hard-working farm woman only to refigure her as inadequate, in need of remediation by professionals who would introduce new technologies and social organizations into rural communities.

Rarely, though, were rural women the mute objects described by literary artists or passive recipients of the educational programs that sought to reform their lives. They rescripted the agendas of the programs offered by educators and appropriated classes and workshops to suit their own ends.[3] They sent letters to popular farm journals disputing their representations of rural life.[4] And they authored community histories, diaries, and autobiographies that speak to the rich diversity of rural women's interests, ambitions, and life experiences. Such texts are often extraordinary literacy performances that offer intriguing glimpses into the place of work in rural women's lives and the place of rural women's lives in their communities.

The autobiography of Myrtle Tenney Booth is one such text. At the age of seventy-nine, Booth decided to document the history of her life and the lives of her ancestors. The death of her husband of fifty-five years and her own poor health had prompted her to leave the mountains of West Virginia that she loved so well and take up residence with her daughter in Ohio. Unsteady on her feet and tethered to an oxygen machine, Booth found her world contracted to a small bedroom/sitting room. With her days no longer filled with chores, writing helped her pass time, and producing a family history that she could give to each of her eight children and twenty-four grandchildren became an important goal. The rhetorical exigence of Booth's narrative thus lies in both process and product. She felt compelled to keep herself busy, and she wanted to create a textual gift for her descendents. Authoring her own story promised her some measure of control over how she would be remembered, and by deploying the literacy resources at hand, she could fix the meaning ascribed to her lifetime of labor.

At 126 pages, "The Life Story of Myrtle A. Booth" was the most extensive textual production of her life. As a child, she sporadically attended a one-room schoolhouse for grades K–8. As an adult, she exchanged newsy letters with relatives, read from the Bible daily, and subscribed to *Reader's Digest* and *Wonderful West Virginia*, a magazine filled with beautiful photographs from the state's Division of Natural Resources. Reading and writing, though, did not dominate Booth's life, and the textual features of her autobiography suggest that the pen was not a ready tool in her hand. She structured sentences idiosyncratically, shifted among verb tenses, and referred to herself both in the first- and third-person, sometimes all in the same paragraph. Despite its rough surface features, Booth's autobiography provides valuable insights into the mental agility that rural women bring to their daily chores and how they articulated their sense of themselves as workers and civic participants.

In theorizing about autobiographical genres, Sidonie Smith and others have called attention to the "mess and clutter" of life writing—how women and other marginalized people "engage dialogically with the cacophonous voices of cultural discourses" as they challenge hegemonic narratives of the self (Smith 21). To be sure, Booth's autobiography is not a tidy or transparent text. I opt, though, to follow the lead of Martha Watson, who has studied the rhetorical dimensions of autobiographies composed by women activists, such as Emma Goldman, Frances Willard, and Mary Church Terrell. For Watson, the life writings of these women are a form of public moral argument, and she suggests the persuasive affordances of such autobiographies lie in the author's position as both central character and narrator and in the generally chronological nature of the genre (6). Autobiographical writing fosters a particularly intimate relationship between writer and reader as the author signals her desire to share her life with others while the reader must be "predisposed to attend to her voice, to try at least to understand her behaviors and decisions" (11). Moreover, through the selection and arrangement of particular life experiences within a chronological framework, an autobiographer explains how her convictions have developed over time and leads readers to appreciate if not adopt those convictions as well. Though the farmwomen like Myrtle Booth who produced autobiographies that can be found in local libraries, historical societies, and the attics of family members may have intended their texts for much smaller audiences than the activists studied by Watson, they too were astute rhetors, seeking to gain purchase on how their rural lives would be remembered.

"I Did Try to Plan My Work": The Intellectual Labor of a Rural Woman

Booth's working life began at a young age. Writing of her eighth birthday and referring to herself in the third person, Booth notes "She was now big enough to help work some. Mostly, she just helped with baby Lovera or maybe she'd dry a few dishes or something like that" (46). By the next year, though, Booth had taken on what she referred to as her first job—"to go of an evening and spend the night with Grandma Samantha and then come home in the morning." While Booth "missed playing with the other brothers and sisters in the evening," she noted with resignation that tending to her elderly relative "was my job, and I went when they told me it was time to go" (47).

Booth would spend the next eighty-five years of her life as a working woman. At the age of twelve, she left school to care for her mother, Agnes, who was badly injured when the family home burned down. As a fifteen-year-old, she worked as a cook in a camp for railroad workers, and four years later, she was sorting tin plate in the Weirton Steel Mill in Clarksburg. At the age of twenty-one, she married Harry Booth, a sawmill worker who had saved enough money to buy a sixty-seven acre farm up the road from Pickens. While raising eight children, Myrtle made cheese, chopped wood, butchered hogs, canned peaches, nursed sick children, pieced quilts, and coped with the unending cycle of chores that are part of life on a small farm.

Like narratives of other rural women (e.g., Buffalobird-woman; Orpen; Brinton; Jones), Booth's autobiography does more than simply catalogue endless chores. Her descriptions of juggling both household and barnyard tasks reveal the cognitive skills and mental flexibility involved in such labor. Take, for example, Booth's description of her mother's textile work:

> Mother Agnes had a large loom. She wove what they called rag carpet. It was beautiful. People would cut rug strings out of old clothes. She had a catalogue where she bought her warp, a heavy string, with all the colors it came in. She would tell the people how many pounds of rags they would need for each yard of carpet. She didn't like to put less than 25 yards in the loom. It would take a day to pull the warp through the rugs, and it usually took two. I have sat more than one day and handed her the warp through the gears with a hook with a catch on it; then after you got ready, you put the cut rags on a shuttle then you would throw that through the warp. The loom had a lever with gears. Then you had a treadle you worked with your feet. Every time you put the shuttle through, you had to step on the treadle. That made the carpet. (44–45)

The range of Mother Agnes's mathematical, mechanical, spatial, and kinesthetic competencies as well as aesthetic judgments emerge from this description, and her work requires the same complex intellectual maneuvering that Rose observed in workers he studied. Establishing the equivalency between pounds of rags (mass) and yards of carpet (area) is a complex mathematical calculation. Having the capacity to manipulate the mechanical relationship between the gears and the warp and the kinesthetic skill to coordinate the movement of shuttle and treadle reveals the disciplined visualization, the application of abstract principles to tangible materials, and problem-solving that are a necessary part of weaving. Moreover, Mother Agnes, like the hair stylists studied by Mike Rose, brought aesthetic values to her task (Rose 52). Choosing from the colors of warp in the catalog allowed Mother Agnes to produce the rag carpets her daughter remembered as "beautiful."

The intellectual capabilities of mountain farm women continue to be apparent as Booth's autobiography progresses. In the months after she gave birth to twins Albert and Alberta in 1934, Booth's workload seemed overwhelming. She would rise at 4:00 A.M. to work while the children slept, then breastfeed the babies and put them back to bed before her four older sons were awake and ready for breakfast. The rest of day would involve shuttling between meal preparation, laundry, tending to farm animals, and more breastfeeding (84). Her workload was further complicated by the fact that her husband often had to take jobs off the farm to earn cash. While Harry worked variously as a strip miner, logger, and road builder, Myrtle assumed responsibility for overseeing the farm, which provided for the family's most basic needs. The ability to function effectively and move efficiently between the dynamic environments of the barnyard and the kitchen demanded not only the physical hardiness of the stereotypical farm woman but also feats of memory, careful attention to the details of physical space, the ability to set priorities, coordinate processes, and combine tasks that were not often credited to rural women in Appalachia during the first half of the twentieth century.[5] Booth offers a succinct explanation of how she was able to juggle so many demands on her time and attention: "I did try to plan my work. I kept things in place and didn't spend a lot of time looking for things" (84).

The ability to plan work and organize tools concretely demonstrates the application of one's mind to the tasks at hand, but Booth's autobiography also reveals the creativity of mountain farmwomen. For example, when Booth's third son, Harley, won a high school state history contest, she brought her ingenuity to bear upon providing him with proper attire for the awards ceremony. This is how she described the dilemma she faced and her solution:

> Five days to come up with a suit is all I had after I got the teacher's note that Harley had won and was supposed to go to Pickens. He would be called up on the stage and Mrs. Opal would pin it [a golden horseshoe] on him. Harley had a good pair of blue woven dress pants, but he wore a zipper jacket with them, so Myrtle didn't know what to do. Then she remembered that he had a good gray suit. It had been through three boys and the pants had a hole in the seat. Myrtle came up with the idea that maybe she could take the coat and dye it blue to match his pants. The next morning she tried the coat on Harley and it was a perfect fit, but how was she to get it the same shade of blue as his pants? After everyone was ready for bed, Myrtle got out her blue dye and at 11:00 she decided she had the exact shade, so she hung the coat on a hanger and said a little prayer and went to bed, hoping that when morning came it would be the right shade of blue, and it was blue. She pressed it and no one ever knew but that the pants and coat had been bought together. (95–96)

During a few uninterrupted hours at the end of the day, Booth turns her full attention to the creative task of repurposing existing resources to serve new ends. She taps into her practical knowledge of pigments and fabrics as she experiments with various proportions of blue dye and water, assessing the impact of her formulations on the gray suit. Like the hair stylists Rose describes, Booth is engaged in a task that requires visual acuity, analytic skills, and astute decision-making based on the accumulated wisdom of past experience, and she must be able to project how wet fabric will look when dry.

Booth's narrative also validates how rural women's ingenuity gives rise to various ways to accomplish daily tasks. For example, she describes how she and her siblings were taught to use umbrella staves as large needles for stringing apple quarters to dry, and that apple peeling/stringing parties in the drying house her father built were popular gathering occasions for neighboring youngsters. But the narrative then turns to Grandma Samantha, who always "kept a little fire in the grate summer the same as winter . . . to keep the chill out of the room," and had a different way of drying apples and pears. Booth writes: "She had a large rack built from strips like a picture frame, papered on the back. It had two rows of nails. She would hang her strung apples on this and set it in front of the fireplace through the day when she was busy" (48–49). With its depiction of multiple ways to accomplish a singular task—stringing and drying apples—Booth's autobiography emphasizes the ability of rural women to conceptualize a goal and to assess the contextual elements that determine the most efficacious method of achieving that goal, whether one is an elderly woman who keeps a fire going or part of a community of young people seeking social opportunities.

In sum, then, Booth's autobiography richly depicts farmwomen's labor in the West Virginia mountains. Her accounts of women weaving, preparing meals, preserving food, and attending to their families' needs serve as opportunities to trace the mental processes necessary to accomplish work that is often judged to be less than intellectually substantial. Given the deeply varied cognitive capacities that their daily chores demanded, it is not surprising that many rural women, like Booth, valued their identities as workers and expressed this through the textual artifacts they produced. Women's work on family farms in Appalachia was physically demanding, but it could also afford women an array of mental challenges and a sense of agency and accomplishment.[6]

Being Neighborly: Work and Civic Life

The autobiographies, diaries, and other texts in which some rural women have documented their labor often stand as more than records of individual achievement and cognitive sophistication. Through such literacy performances, farm women could suture their work to their civic identities. Rather

than acquiesce to metropolitan models of civic engagement that favor structured enterprises, such as philanthropic organizations, social clubs, and
political parties, rural women like Booth composed texts that positioned
women's labor as a sustaining force in their communities. Tending to aging
relatives, women in childbirth, and neighbors injured in accidents; hosting
parties to prepare and preserve food during harvest; sharing one's home with
kith and kin in need of shelter—such activities are mentioned throughout
Booth's autobiography and exemplify the "neighborliness" described by many
rural women across the United States as well as by historians and sociologists
who have studied rural life in a variety of contexts (Raine; Walker; Neth;
Holt).[7] A significant—though often unrecognized—form of civic participation, such neighborliness allowed farm women to create a sense of mutuality among themselves and establish an informal system of social welfare to
sustain their communities.

Booth's description of the small gristmill operated by her parents reveals
this commitment to an ethic of common cause and shared labor. Frustrated
by the arduous wagon trips to a distant mill in Centerville, Daddy Dan, as
Booth referred to her father, built his own gristmill on Hicks Ridge. After
detailing the inventive design of the mill so that it would be serviceable even
when the river was low, Booth notes that her father was soon "grinding all
the people's grain in the community" and that he was flexible in accepting
remuneration from his neighbors. Seldom offered cash, he was instead content to keep a portion of each bushel of grain he ground as payment. Having
thus a steady supply of grain, Booth's father could loan ground meal to his
neighbors who might arrive when the mill was not operating (32).

Booth's mother also shared in the work of the mill. Recognizing the effort
required of her neighbors to bring their grain even to the mill on Hicks Ridge,
Mother Agnes would not make them wait in her husband's absence: "I have
heard Mother Agnes say, 'If Dan was away and there came a good rain, I'd
close the gate to make the water run through the race and I'd grind people's
grain so they wouldn't need to wait any longer'" (32–33). Booth depicts her
parents' mill not as a for-profit enterprise but as a shared community resource, and in her autobiography she emphasizes that both Daddy Dan and
Mother Agnes ran the mill in ways that respected those who came to have
their grain ground as neighbors, not as customers.

In representing her own labor as an adult, Booth similarly positions her
work within a network of community relationships. In addition to maintaining her household, Booth took on the responsibility of serving as cook at the
one-room schoolhouse her children attended. She writes (again referring to
herself in the third person):

Agnes Conrad had been cooking for the hot lunch program. She quit, so rather than see it close down, Myrtle decided to cook. She walked the half-mile and cooked for six years, for she felt the children needed the lunch. It was during the depression and there were several one-parent children, and they needed the hot lunch. They only paid her $1.00 a day at first, then later they paid her $1.50 a day. It took her three hours out of every day, five days a week, to go fix hot lunch for 39 children; but she felt it was worth it to keep the hot lunch program in the community for the sake of the children.

They had had the hot lunch program for two school terms before Myrtle started cooking. Both years it had closed in the red. The first year she cooked, Myrtle closed it out with $57.00 surplus. Myrtle didn't ask for the money. She did it for the community. (99)

Booth is clearly proud of her skillful financial management, but she wants her readers to know that her true accomplishment lies in how she helped neighboring children. By composing her autobiography, she used her literacy skills to gain a measure of control over how her work as a school cook would be interpreted. Rather than focusing on herself as a wage-earner, Booth works with words to construct herself as a contributor to her community.

The ways in which Booth's autobiography situates women's work within neighborly networks contrasts sharply with how she depicts the activities of the mining, railroad, and timber companies that were beginning to extract natural resources from the West Virginia mountains on an industrial scale in the early twentieth century. In describing how a representative of the B & O Railroad approached her father about laying narrow gauge track through his meadow to facilitate the removal of a lumber company's timber, Booth writes proudly of her father's refusal to accept the company's cash offer. Having seen two neighbor children maimed and another child killed along the tracks, Daddy Dan resisted the overtures of the railroad until he could build a new home on a more remote corner of his land. Booth describes her father explaining to his wife "I want my children away from here before those tracks get this far" (37). In Booth's narrative, those who oversaw the mining and timber enterprises violated the communal ethic that sustained her relatives and neighbors. Just as the students studied by Sara Webb-Sunderhaus engage in communal literacy practices that allow them to coordinate their performances of academic and Appalachian identities (see chapter 12 in this volume), so too does Booth use her autobiography to emphasize that her sense of self cannot be separated from her community.

Booth's representations of the immigrant workers—mostly from Austria and Italy—who arrived to lay track, fell timber, and mine coal demonstrated, though, that a sense of neighborliness may not be particularly inclusive. For Booth, "these foreigners" were a source of anxiety and fear (56). When they make a rare appearance in her narrative, it is as brawling drunkards who cannot be contained in the temporary camps created for the itinerant workforce. According to Booth, their presence in the community consumes the attention of the country doctor who must constantly stitch up their wounds; frightens women who discover strange men sleeping off the effects of binge drinking in their barns; and forces long-standing rural residents into awkward ethical positions as they must decide whether to intercede on behalf of those victimized by their coworkers in the unruly camps. In contrast to the culture of mutual aid that emerges from Booth's autobiography as a defining characteristic of her rural community, the incursion of the extractive industries endangered local residents and altered the social as well as the natural landscape.

In recording her life story then, Booth also documents the impact of industrialization on her rural landscape and challenges the economic and civic relationships that accompany it. To be sure, there is perhaps more than a tinge of nostalgic agrarianism in "The Life Story of Myrtle A. Booth" as its author recalled loved ones long dead and scenes far removed from the small room in her daughter's house where the medical devices that made the final years of her life possible increasingly crowded out treasured mementoes that helped her recall the meaning of that life. Amplifying the voices of farm women like Booth and attending closely to how they described their work— its too easily overlooked cognitive sophistication and its value to a community—can, though, help to diminish the force of unflattering caricatures of rural women from Appalachia that have circulated for far too long. Though often dismissed as a sentimental documentation of family history, the self-published autobiographies and memoirs of rural women merit further study by scholars in rhetoric and literacy studies. Such autobiographies typically have no commercial value, but they stand as potent arguments that critique the forces that have affected rural lives, and they can shape how future generations understand their rural roots. As literacy performances, such texts give voice to an understanding of writing and other labor as activities that circulate outside the marketplace and give rise to a wide range of sustaining human relationships. But there is more work to be done.

Conclusion

With great wisdom, Mike Rose has noted that

> When we think about problem solving, creativity, acts of the mind, we tend to think of the grand moment, the clarifying insight, the breakthrough, the

tough nut cracked. Fair enough. Such moments are worthy of acknowledgment. But I think it also worth dwelling on the commonplace, ordinary expressions of the mind that every day, a thousand times over, enable the work of the world to get done, and that, more than we think, are critical in solving the less common, more dramatic problems that face us. (72)

The sustainability of rural communities both in the United States and around the globe is surely among these "more dramatic problems" in the twenty-first century. Among other factors, industrial farming techniques have altered the physical, economic, and social landscape for rural residents in the United States, and the many rural residents employed in service or manufacturing sectors of the economy must negotiate a precarious job market as companies respond to financial pressures by downsizing or outsourcing. Beyond U.S. borders, women living in rural communities also confront complex challenges in a global economy. While new economic opportunities arise as multinational corporations and international development experts insinuate themselves into local communities, rural women may have new income generating opportunities but find themselves feeling less than empowered by the new roles they must inhabit when they join the industrial workforce.[8]

To undertake a detailed analysis of the impact of industrial agriculture and globalization on rural women in places ranging from West Virginia to Nebraska and from Sri Lanka to Chile and to consider the diverse literacy practices that might enable or constrain their abilities to shape their own lives is far beyond the scope of this chapter. The ways, though, in which rural women from decades past have represented their own labor remind us of the power of the everyday intelligence and force us to look past caricatures of agricultural labor as physically demanding and mentally deadening.

Intellectually astute and keenly attuned to the worth of their work as it sustained their communities, rural women, like Myrtle Booth, call on us to consider alternative ways to understand our relationships to the land and to each other. For example, the neighborliness limned in Booth's autobiography stands as an informal but important alternative form of civic engagement that might productively complicate the efforts of nongovernmental organizations (NGOs) seeking to improve the lives of poor women around the world through microcredit policies and entrepreneurial activities. Closer to home, Booth's stories—a mother teaching a girl-child to weave rag carpet; a husband and wife working as partners to run a gristmill as a community resource; a mother repurposing yet again a suit of clothes to be worn by a child on a special occasion—all point toward mentoring/training strategies, organizational models, and resource management philosophies that, as Rose says, "foster . . . the expression of intelligence" and could serve as touchstones for rethinking practices in contemporary workplaces (208–9). Failing to appreciate the ways in which people—rural and urban, around the corner and around the globe—put their work into words will only "reinforce our social separations and cripple our ability to talk across our current cultural divides" (Rose 216).

New regional and global relationships will necessitate the continual re-conceptualization of labor, literacy, intelligence, and civic life. Such efforts should be undertaken with an awareness of the intellectual sophistication, creativity, and resourcefulness that women workers—in both rural and urban settings—have historically brought to their daily tasks as well as the literacy practices that have been available to them to represent their work and challenge their relegation to the margins of public life.

Notes

1. As one of Booth's fourteen granddaughters, I received an inscribed copy of her autobiography for Christmas in 1985. I am embarrassed to admit that at the time I was largely uninterested in the story my grandmother wanted to share. In my last semester as an English major at a small liberal arts college, I had little patience for a text that seemed so obviously inferior to the "great" works of literature I had been studying for nearly four years. The gifted professors and generous mentors I met during my years as a graduate student at Ohio State University and my own nontraditional students at the University of Missouri–Kansas City have helped me see the lessons that can be learned from the texts produced by seemingly ordinary people, like my grandmother. She died a decade ago, and I can only regret the conversations that she and I never had about the textual legacy she left for her family.

2. See the stories of Will Wallace Harney, Mary Noailles Murfree, John Fox, Jr., and James Lane Allen.

3. For insightful analysis into extension programs and how rural women responded, see Walker; Holt; and Hogg. See also chapter 13 in this volume. Butler describes how New Deal programs designed to aid rural residents, including his grandparents, required that they make themselves available to the ministrations of government experts in agriculture and domestic science. For Butler's grandmother, the visiting "homemaker" was not a bother, but this expert on household management had nothing of particular value to share with an experienced farm woman.

4. See Casey for more on rural women using agricultural journals as a forum for disputing widely circulating images of their lives.

5. My understanding of Booth's work is influenced here by Rose's description of the cognitive and physical accomplishments of waitresses (6–24).

6. See Cowan's landmark study, *More Work for Mother,* for a history of housekeeping in the United States. Cowan posits that rising standards of living and increased access to modern conveniences in the early twentieth century lead women "to believe not just that their place was in their homes but that the work that they did there had enormous value" (191). While I would not dispute Cowan's trenchant analysis, placing the writing of women themselves at the center of study leads me to believe that for some women the intellectual challenges they found in their domestic chores and the ways in which they felt they were sustaining their communities also contributed to their sense of their work's worth.

7. Indeed, neighborliness or "helping out" remains a powerful theme in conceptions of literacy articulated by contemporary rural residents. Sara Webb-Sunderhaus in chapter 12 of this volume describes how college students in Appalachia view a college degree as more than an individual accomplishment. Instead, educational achievements are seen as opportunities for uplifting the entire community.

8. See, for example, Bee's study of women farm workers in northern Chile; and Gune-wardena's analysis of the impact of agribusiness practices on women in Sri Lanka. Among rhetoricians who have begun the important work of analyzing how arguments about women's labor circulate across transnational boundaries in a globalized economy, see Dingo; and Hesford and Kulbaga.

Works Cited

Allen, James Lane. "Through the Cumberland Gap on Horseback." *Harper's New Monthly Magazine* June 1886, 50–66. Print.

Bee, Anna. "Globalization, Grapes and Gender: Women's Work in Traditional and Agro-Export Production in Northern Chile." *Geographical Journal* 166.3 (2000): 255–65. Print.

Billings, Dwight B., and Kathleen M. Blee. *The Road to Poverty: The Making of Wealth and Hardship in Appalachia.* Cambridge: Cambridge UP, 2000. Print.

Booth, Myrtle A. "The Life Story of Myrtle A. Booth." Typescript. 1985. Print.

Brinton, Ada Mae Brown. "Eighty-Six Years in Iowa: The Memoir of Ada Mae Brown Brinton." Ed. Glenda Riley. *Annals of Iowa* 45 (Winter 1981): 551–67. Rpt. in *Writings of Farm Women, 1840–1940.* Ed. Carol Fairbanks and Bergine Haakenson. New York: Garland, 1990. 171–87. Print.

Buffalobird-woman (Maxi'-diwac). "Planting a Garden." *Agriculture of the Hidatsa Indians: An Indian Interpretation.* Minneapolis: U of Minnesota P, 1917. 9–15, 119–20. Rpt. in *Writings of Farm Women, 1840–1940.* Ed. Carol Fairbanks and Bergine Haakenson. New York: Garland, 1990. 3–17. Print.

Butler, Thomas, and Jacqueline Edmondson. "Sustaining a Rural Pennsylvania Community: Negotiating Rural Literacies and Sustainability." *Reclaiming the Rural.* Ed. Kim Done-hower, Charlotte Hogg, and Eileen Schell. Carbondale: Southern Illinois UP, 2011. Print.

Casey, Jane Galligani. "'This is YOUR Magazine': Domesticity, Agrarianism, and *The Farmer's Wife.*" *American Periodicals* 14 (2004): 179–211. Print.

Cowan, Ruth Schwartz. *More Work for Mother: The Ironies of Household Technology from Open Hearth to the Microwave.* New York: Basic Books, 1983. Print.

Dingo, Rebecca. "Linking Transnational Logics: A Feminist Rhetorical Analysis of Public Policy Networks." *College English* 70 (2008): 490–505. Print.

Fox, John, Jr. *The Kentuckians.* New York: Scribner, 1904. Print.

Furman, Lucy. *Sight to the Blind.* 1914. Champaign, IL: Project Gutenberg, 2004. Web. 11 June 2008.

Gunewardena, Nandini. "Gendering Sugar: Women's Disempowerment in Sri Lankan Sugar Production." *Women's Labor in the Global Economy: Speaking in Multiple Voices.* Ed. Sharon Harley. New Brunswick, NJ: Rutgers UP, 2007. 221–45. Print.

Harney, Will Wallace. "A Strange Land and a Peculiar People." *Lippincott's Magazine* Oct. 1873, 429–38. Print.

Hesford, Wendy S., and Theresa A. Kulbaga. "Labored Realisms: Geopolitical Rhetoric and Asian American and Asian (Im)migrant Women's (Auto)biography." *JAC* 23.1 (2003): 77–107. Print.

Hogg, Charlotte. *From the Garden Club: Rural Women Writing Community.* Lincoln: U of Nebraska P, 2006. Print.

Holt, Marilyn Irvin. *Linoleum, Better Babies, and the Modern Farm Woman.* Albuquerque: U of New Mexico P, 1995. Print.

Jones, Bessie. "Making the Best." *We Didn't Have Much, but We Sure Had Plenty: Stories of Rural Women.* Ed. Sherry Thomas. Garden City, NY: Anchor Books, 1981. 33–48. Print.

Murfree, Mary Noailles (Charles Egbert Craddock). *In the "Stranger People's" Country.* New York: Harper and Brothers, 1891. Print.

Neth, Mary. *Preserving the Family Farm: Women, Community and the Foundations of Agribusi-ness in the Midwest, 1900–1940.* Baltimore: Johns Hopkins UP, 1995. Print.

Orpen, Adele. *Memories of the Old Emigrant Days in Kansas, 1862–1865*. Edinburgh & London: William Blackwood, 1926. Rpt. in *Writings of Farm Women, 1840–1940*. Ed. Carol Fairbanks and Bergine Haakenson. New York: Garland, 1990. 79–93. Print.

Powell, Katrina: *The Anguish of Displacement: The Politics of Literacy in the Letters of Mountain Families in Shenandoah National Park*. Charlottesville: U of Virginia P, 2007. Print.

Pudup, Mary Beth, Dwight B. Billings, and Altina L. Waller, eds. *Appalachia in the Making: The Mountain South in the Nineteenth Century*. Chapel Hill: U of North Carolina P, 1995. Print.

Raine, James Watt. *The Land of the Saddle-Bags: A Study of the Mountain People of Appalachia*. New York: Council of Women for Home Missions and Missionary Education Movement of the United States and Canada, 1924. Print.

Rankin, Katharine N. "Governing Development: Neoliberalism, Microcredit, and Rational Economic Woman." *Economy and Society* 30 (2001): 18–37. Print.

Rose, Mike. *The Mind at Work: Valuing the Intelligence of the American Worker*. New York: Viking, 2004. Print.

Salstrom, Paul. *Appalachia's Path to Dependency: Rethinking a Region's Economic History, 1730–1940*. Lexington: UP of Kentucky, 1994. Print.

Shapiro, Henry D. *Appalachia on Our Mind: The Southern Mountains and Mountaineers in the American Consciousness, 1870–1920*. Chapel Hill: U of North Carolina P, 1978. Print.

Smith, Sidonie. *Subjectivity, Identity, and the Body: Women's Autobiographical Practices in the Twentieth Century*. Bloomington: Indiana UP 1993. Print.

Stewart, Cora Wilson. *Country Life Readers: First Book*. Atlanta: B. F. Johnson, 1915. Print.

———. *Country Life Readers: Second Book*. Atlanta: B. F. Johnson, 1916. Print.

———. *Country Life Readers: Third Book*. Atlanta: B. F. Johnson, 1917. Print.

Thomas, Jerry Bruce. *An Appalachian New Deal: West Virginia in the Great Depression*. Lexington: UP of Kentucky, 1998. Print.

Walker, Melissa. *All We Knew Was to Farm: Rural Women in the Upcountry South, 1919–1941*. Baltimore: Johns Hopkins UP, 2000. Print.

Watson, Martha. *Lives of Their Own: Rhetorical Dimensions in the Autobiographies of Women Activists*. Columbia: South Carolina UP, 1999. Print.

Webb-Sunderhaus, Sara. "Living with Literacy's Contradictions: Appalachian Students in a First-Year Writing Course." *Reclaiming the Rural*. Ed. Kim Donehower, Charlotte Hogg, and Eileen Schell. Carbondale: Southern Illinois UP, 2011. Print.

Whisnant, David E. *All That Is Native and Fine: The Politics of Culture in an American Region*. Chapel Hill: U of North Carolina P, 1983. Print.

6

Latent Abilities: The Early Grange as a Mixed-Gender Site of Rhetorical Education

Carolyn Ostrander

> The Grange was the first organization to recognize that
> farming is a partnership business and that the women are
> full partners with men. From the very first, the Grange saw
> that farming cannot succeed without the home and the
> home-makers and that the women have just as much right
> and duty to participate in public affairs as the men do.
>
> —E. R. Eastman

Founded in 1867 as an agrarian secret society (Kelley), the Grange is of-ten depicted as different from other fraternal organizations of the day because it admitted women to full membership from its inception. A second view is that Grange women are supporting members, cooking for "dish to pass" suppers and interesting themselves in domestic topics (Nordin; Marti). In this essay, I argue that Grange rhetoric blended a discourse of "mutuality," or shared responsibility for farm and household productivity (Nancy Grey Osterud cited in Marti), with cultural expectations in Grange rituals, articles, manuals, and the structure of Grange offices. Innovative arguments for women's right to advocate, participate in public meetings, vote, and hold office within a mixed-gender organization enhanced women's efforts to ne-gotiate their own presence in the Grange Hall.

This innovation was possible in part because the Grange was designed as a site for the development of rhetorical skills. The Grange's sponsorship of oratory and literacy practices encouraged but also shaped women's negotia-tions of their roles.[1] The role of lecturer was significant because women as well as men represented the Grange to the public and encouraged others to speak and write in and for the Grange.

Grange Aims and Organization

The Grange was founded as a mutual aid organization modeled after fraternal societies, but its aims were broad: to enhance "the general happiness, wealth, and prosperity of the country . . . by promoting the education and elevation of the largest class of producers in the nation, the fountain-class of its prosperity and greatness." (William Saunders qtd. in Grosh 66–67). Over the course of its history, the Grange advocated or helped to develop many innovations in American life: mutual health, fire, and life insurance, rural electrification, cooperative buying, rural transportation, a cabinet-level Department of Agriculture, rural mail delivery, passage of the 1906 Food and Drugs Act, popular election of senators, and the Hatch Act authorizing Cooperative Extension services (Robinson; Gardner). Even today, Grangers encourage community involvement, promote legislative action benefiting farmers and rural dwellers, and meet to celebrate agriculture and rural life.

From the start, Grange meetings addressed these varied aims within a framework of ritual that celebrated farm life and the importance of rural laborers—both male and female. Initiation rituals and the annual installation of officers emphasized the dignity and importance of agriculture. Short rituals opened and closed each business meeting. Topics under "new business," "old business," and "suggestions for the good of the Order" might include news about the success or trials of local cooperative ventures, market conditions, rural education initiatives, agricultural innovations, legislative initiatives, and a request for news about "members [who are] sick or in distress" (National Grange 1874, 4).[2]

The Grange in the late nineteenth century offered agency and a call to battle political and economic forces that held prices for grain and dairy products low while driving up critical freight prices and taxes (along with similar organizations like the Farmer's Alliance). Through participation in Grange-sponsored cooperatives, individuals benefited directly from collective action. Grangers in the Midwest were particularly active in the development of the Populist Party (Nordin). But financial and political interests were (and are) only part of the reason for joining the Grange.[3]

Rural social structure in the nineteenth century depended on cooperation and was centered on family life (Osterud). While rural American culture incorporated the concept of "separate spheres" for men and women, the realities of isolation, heavy workload, and limited civic infrastructure increased the importance of the labor of all members of the farming family, tied to the land by the demands of cultivation and animal husbandry. The Grange lauded farm families for their intelligence, hard work, and importance to the life of the nation. Granges welcomed all members of the farming household, and their meetings offered opportunities for socialization and a break from daily routine, adding "dish to pass" suppers, and (after 1888) a Youth Grange to keep children busy. Grange programs participated in a tradition of oratory in America and a culture of lifelong learning such as recitations at school, sermons in church, "lyceums," and traveling lecturers.[4] The combination of cooperative, economic, legislative, educational, and social aims made the Grange a strong force in rural life for over a century (Goldberg 39).[5] It also made the Grange an important site for rhetorical skill-building beyond and along with formal education.

Grange leaders wanted to improve the image and economic success of farmers and rural dwellers, encourage young people to enter farming, and find effective ways to advocate for farm-friendly legislation (Kelley; Grosh). Early Grange leaders were interested in ideas like "scientific farming" and "domestic science," which they hoped to disseminate through lectures and publications. Public speaking and writing skills were important to these agendas, and actively practiced in each meeting's centerpiece, the lecturer's program (Buell, *Grange Master*). Typically presented by the lecturer with assistance from other Grangers, the lecturer's program might revolve around a specific theme or presentation or several short items and was designed to fulfill multiple aims. The social nature of the activities and the variety of a good lecturer's program added to social enjoyment at the same time that they encouraged and supported frequent, small contributions by less confident participants.

Gender and Rhetoric in Rural and Urban Settings

As Deborah Brandt reminds us, "literacy abilities are nested in and sustained by larger social and cultural activity" (3). In the nineteenth-century framework of the domestic sphere, much of women's self-expression was directed to other women (what Nan Johnson calls "parlor rhetorics"). Nineteenth-century women in both rural and urban settings were heavily indoctrinated in the "cult of domesticity" (Cott), which outlined women's appropriate role as mothers and wives, absorbed in household affairs. Outside of women-centered spaces, the position of women in public rhetoric was tenuous.[6] Within the Abolitionist movement of the 1830s–50s, for example, the presence of women on speakers' platforms was hotly debated.[7] Most women who publicly advocated for abolition were careful to position themselves within domestic roles as guardians of morality and mothers of future citizens (Warren; Bacon). The very arguments that established the *ethos* of a woman platform speaker validated and reinforced the expectation that "true" women would shrink from public display whenever possible, and public participation in these movements was justified most often as unavoidable because of the urgency of an issue.

Nancy Grey Osterud argues that the separation of men's and women's "spheres of influence" into public and private was far more strict in urban middle- and upper-class society than in rural areas, partly because women provided labor and contributed to the farm's material success. Throughout the nineteenth century, rural women helped settle and build farms and farming communities, promoted education for daughters as well as sons, and built networks both in person and through their writing. The writings of rural women consistently show that though their duties were clustered around child care and housekeeping, they also contributed significantly to the production of agricultural products and the income of the farm family (Osterud; see also chapter 5 in this volume).

In towns more than in the country, men and women established single-gender clubs, which "often viewed each other with suspicion" (Goldberg 42). If women revered domesticity and considered themselves its guardians, men had their own language about the *tyranny* of domesticity (Marti; Romero) and were encouraged to seek the support of masculine peers (Rogers). Men's groups developed as settings for civic or "public sphere" pursuits such as politics or business, though many were formally structured as fraternal organizations. Fraternal orders like the Freemasons maintained gendered spaces at regular meetings.[8] Masons claimed fraternal meetings were central to male roles and masculine values, and separate "auxiliary" organizations were founded for different ages and genders.[9] Male membership needed to be initiated and practiced apart from the constraining influence of women (Rogers).

In carrying out business, promoting organizations, and communicating with members, men practiced invention, argumentation, and oratory along with other elements of rhetoric. Ritual, whether secret Masonic rites or the informal rituals of business meetings, provided a framework that supported public speaking skills (again, more frequently in urban than in rural settings). The tradition of rhetorical training in public education for men was linked with practical participation in civic life, even for those who did not play active leadership roles (as, for example, ministers and politicians did). Even in rural settings, men attended more public meetings, and did most of the public speaking whether the topic was related to business, politics, or religion.

Women in early antebellum society seldom took active part in business meetings or held key posts in civic committees. Even in Sunday schools and missionary societies that seemed to be an extension of women's affairs, men often held the majority of the leadership posts (Ryan). But during the mid-nineteenth century, many women became involved in a wider range of social issues, including the abolition movement, the temperance movement, and women's rights organizations. Women became schoolteachers in increasing numbers (Goldberg 136) and were required to teach recitation, composition, declamation, and debate—all of which were common aspects of the school curriculum (Buchanan). Women also attended popular lectures such as Lyceum events even in small towns (Radner), and their contributions to women's magazines increased as the century progressed.

By the end of the Civil War, women were learning to organize and ready to become leaders. In 1867, the year the first local Grange was founded, the women's clubs often cited as America's first (Sorosis and the New England Woman's Club, both in 1867–68) were also established.[10] Throughout the late nineteenth century, the women's club movement trained urban middle-class women to run meetings, write, edit and publish their opinions, and make presentations within their meetings (Gere). The Women's Christian Temperance Union (WCTU), organized in 1873–74, joined the growing number of organizations encouraging women's efforts to develop their persuasive skills.

In context, the tradition of platform speaking within the early Grange movement was a natural element of organizations at the time. The Grange joined a range of communal activities that sponsored literacies and rhetorical training, providing experience in leadership and public presentation in agricultural districts just as men's societies and women's clubs were doing in towns. The particular opportunities the Grange created for women arose together with forces that opened the way for the Grange to succeed as a rural organization with an egalitarian vision. These opportunities were supported and expanded by the Grange's commitment to continuing education and the rhetorical structure in which women's roles were framed. Perhaps the more unusual features were the mixed-gender audiences in the Grange Hall, inclusion of both men's and women's daily experiences in the recitation of ritual, and the participation of both men and women in program planning and presentation. Women could take part in programs in spite of the divisions created by different expectations based on gender (Marti).

Grange leaders insisted that the organization's success depended on the active involvement of members. Early leaders claimed that women's participation was vital, that their presence would exercise a beneficent influence, and that the Grange was good for women too.[11] Grange meetings added variety and social contact to lives that, they argued, were circumscribed by low population density and long hours of labor.[12] This innovation required the development of new methods for inclusion and a rationale that would fit the circumstances of farm families.

Discourse on Women's Roles in the Grange

Rhetorical performances of women's roles within the Grange were designed to reflect women's supposed interests and daily practices but were negotiated between narrow interpretations of the domestic sphere and wider agricultural, economic, educational, and political issues that affected the entire rural community. Grange rhetoric blended nineteenth-century claims about the role of virtuous women ("ennobling" the private sphere of the home, training up the future as Republican mothers) with subversive claims about rights to formulate independent opinions and to address "mixed" audiences. The Grange initiation explained the goals and expectations of the order through ritual symbolism and instructions by officers. In each of the four subordinate degrees or levels of the Grange, initiates were given a new title: Laborers and Maids, Cultivators and Shepherdesses, Harvesters and Gleaners, and lastly, Patrons and Matrons of Husbandry (National Grange 1874). Though the titles are gendered, they are balanced to indicate that both women and men contribute to the farm, opening a potential space for female participation in the mixed-gender meetings. Movement through the degrees mimics an imaginary apprenticeship, with increasing authority and responsibility bestowed symbolically to match the experience and wisdom attributed to each rank.

For example, the Overseer taught women in their initiation into the first degree (Maid) that "Woman is the educator of youth and our co-student through life, and to be this she must acquire knowledge and wisdom" (National Grange 1874, 21). Though employing the claim of "Republican motherhood," men and women were instructed to share discussion as "co-students." Men and women might have different interests but could participate as equals in continuing self-education that benefits both.

The context in which the ritual was written shows that its authors intended statements like this one to be read literally. Anson Bartlett points out in a letter to founder Oliver H. Kelley that the new organization was asking women (as well as men) for support, and that the promise of equal rank was a reward for their participation.[13] "We ask the co-operation of woman, and advance the idea that she is to be held and considered the equal of man in all respects. This is right. It is just" (qtd. in Kelley 71).

Grange goals and expectations for women were paired with other familiar themes: the importance of family, the central role of agriculture in American culture, and the need for farmers to work together. The language of the Grange ritual was borrowed from the Bible, Greek mythology, and well-known literature.[14] Repetition helped the Grange perspective seem familiar and right. Language that tied women's roles in the family and in agricultural production to a new role as equal partners with men was carefully embedded in that ritual.

Biblical justification for including women in the Grange is a good example of this. The story of Eve was frequently referenced in sermons as proof of women's sin and weakness of will. In Grange ritual, Eve represents a complex set of values to account for the integration of women into society. On the one hand, the lecturer tells women during initiation that "when God created the Garden of Eden . . . His last great work was to adorn it with woman," a comment that might seem dismissive (National Grange 1874, 20). But Eve is also being evoked when Anson Bartlett reminds Kelley that woman is "intended by her Creator to be neither the slave, the tyrant, nor the plaything of man, but to be his help-meet, his companion, and his equal" (qtd. in Kelley 74). Bartlett's argument is incorporated into the initiation ceremony when the chaplain reminds women that "the interests, the social relations, and the destiny of man and woman are identical. She was intended by our Creator to be the help-meet, companion, and equal of man: each shares the glory or the shame of the other" (National Grange 1874, 21).[15] The claim that "the interests, the social relations, and the destiny of man and woman are identical" stresses mutuality and establishes partnership as the base from which Bartlett's "help-meet, his companion and his equal" transcends limiting arguments based on "separate sphere" arguments. Embedded in rites for initiation and officer installations, this representation would be frequently reinforced.

Structured Roles for Women

The Grange vision of society described women and men as equally important within separate spheres, consistent with nineteenth-century American social structure. It also emphasized shared domestic life and agricultural labor. The influence of the founders' visionary language was not the only mechanism for supporting women's participation, however. The organizational structure of Grange offices permitted women to vote on business and serve as elected officers. Four positions were reserved for "ladies only": lady assistant steward and the three graces: Ceres, Pomona, and Flora. The graces represented aspects of agriculture—grains, fruits, and flowers—but also represented the claims that women are integral to agriculture and society and that "woman's counsel" is appropriate, even in mixed company. Though some early office-holders saw the graces' roles as purely symbolic, others took up the challenge offered by their office to support education, home beautification, community service, and health as their particular causes as well as aiding members "sick or in distress" (National Grange 1874) by visiting them or sending letters of encouragement or condolence.[16] The lady assistant steward and the graces all had speaking parts in initiations and the installation of officers, and the lady assistant steward played a substantial role in each Grange meeting.

Because four of the thirteen offices were reserved for women, no Grange could have ignored women members completely. In New York State, South Onondaga Grange No. 880 "was organized March 3, 1897, at the home of Brother and Sister Almeron Fenner. Brother B. F. Hulbert was instrumental in organizing the Grange . . . but not knowing much about the Grange he called only men; therefore, when the County Deputy arrived they found there could be no election until the women were present." At the next meeting, women were elected to the secretary's chair as well as the "ladies' chairs" (Hazard 103–4). On the other hand, the salience of the graces' roles might imply that voters need not consider women for all offices. Certainly many Granges only elected women to the "ladies' chairs." Yet Austerlitz Grange No. 819, founded in 1896, elected Mrs. D. W. Lasher to the office of steward at its organizational meeting. Charlotte Grange No. 669, formed in 1890, elected Mrs. Ola Landers as lecturer at its first meeting and two years later elected Addie Thompson as chaplain, raising the proportion of female officers to 6 of 13 (Grange Collection, Cornell Archives).[17]

The Role of the Grange Lecturer

Especially urge and encourage the young and the
diffident to become writers, readers and speakers in
Grange meetings, and thus develop and direct to greater
usefulness the latent abilities of your fellow-members.
—National Grange 1953

Of all the general offices, the lecturer's office seems to have attracted women most often, and the lecturer's role was held by women with increasing frequency through the first half century of Grange history. Marti cites Kenyon Butterfield's 1901 conjecture that the majority of lecturers were women, in contrast to other major roles such as master, chaplain, or overseer (141). Thomas Summerhill argues that "Subordinate Granges frequently elected [women] to the offices of lecturer, treasurer, secretary, and chaplain, which Kelley had reserved originally for men (along with master, overseer, steward, assistant steward, and gatekeeper)" (200); but neither Kelley nor A. B. Grosh, another founder, confirms this plan. Grosh does specify in his 1875 guide, *Mentor in the Granges and Homes of Patrons of Husbandry,* that "there is no legal prohibition, and there can hardly be any objection, in any Grange, to choosing any devout, intelligent sister as Chaplain" (361); and he describes the lecturer as "he or she" (365) but calls the treasurer "he."[18]

There is no doubt, though, that lecturers played a central role in every Grange meeting and in the Grange as a whole. Education from cradle to grave was a key value, reflected in Grange initiatives, from public school advocacy to lectures and articles on farming, household economy, and conservation techniques (Arthur). Nor was this a mere public service initiative, or "edutainment." Kelley wrote about his intention to raise the agricultural literacy level from simply "able to read" to active participation in a literate program of farmer education: "Where we find one [farmer] who reads agricultural books and papers, there are ten or more who consider 'book farming' as they term it, nonsense. This average is too small . . . yet but very few could not read and write" (17). Kelley's plan for agricultural training and other educational goals fell within the lecturer's purview. Lecturers provided a program for every meeting and were expected to include topics relevant to both household and agricultural concerns in a variety of genres.

The lecturer's program was presented to a mixed audience, exposing both men and women to a broad range of topics: agrarian techniques and policies, child rearing, food preservation and other "domestic sciences," art, literature, music, and awareness of other cultures (Buell, *Grange Master*).[19] Essays, lectures, debates, pantomimes, creative writing, demonstrations, recitations, spelling bees, dramatizations, and contests (all potential elements of the lecturer's program) were familiar in the context of public education (Buchanan). As with the early Lyceum movement (Ray), a member might be asked to share a skill or experience, to recite a set piece, or to present information on a preassigned topic. Such opportunities permitted adults to polish public speaking and composition techniques in a friendly environment.

We might assume that women were primarily interested in "women's concerns" (and men in "men's concerns"). D. Sven Nordin suggests that topics were rigidly gender-divided:

> Male members studied such things as fertilizers, cotton, tobacco cultivation, meat preservation, potato bugs, fruit culture, and a wide range of other items dealing with the maintenance of a productive farm. When ladies conducted the lecture hour, they discussed cooking, baking, canning, gardening, sewing, and embroidering. (86)

However this description is too simple, for the charge to the lecturer in the annual installation of officers asked them to "include the house and the home, as well as the farm and the field" (National Grange 1874, 62); meetings always had mixed-gender audiences, and lecturers prepared and led programs of both types during their tenure in office. Though the charge separated interests by gender, all members of the Grange were expected to take part in the ensuing conversation: "led to contribute their thoughts to the common stock," as A. B. Grosh described it (865).

Participation in Grange meetings actively encouraged women to think of themselves as public citizens, entitled to take active roles. A primary advantage for the Grange in promoting rhetorical skills among its membership was that rhetorical practice increased the effectiveness of Grangers as advocates for rural causes, whether male or female. Increased involvement in meetings was also thought to increase the local Grange's ability to recruit and retain members (Buell, *Grange Master*).

Not all Grange women—or men—became confident public speakers, but the development of oratory skill was an explicit goal, and members were aware of its importance. "Another direct and important result of Grange work is that it has taught farmers to express themselves . . . The Grange was a forum. It taught farm people to speak out in thousands of meetings" (Eastman 15). In a passage in Jennie Buell's *The Grange Master and the Grange Lecturer,* she relates an anecdote about a farmer and longtime Granger who admits that he has failed to become a skilled public speaker. The farmer's assumption that Grangers *should* learn to speak in public is underlined by Buell's response: she lists *other* benefits gained by the farmer, including knowledge of improved farm methods and regular social interaction as a consolation (169–70).

Some lecturers did become popular platform speakers, including Mrs. Mary A. Mayo of Michigan (Buell, *One Woman's Work*) and Mrs. "B. B." (Elizabeth K.) Lord of Sinclairville, New York (Allen). Mayo and her husband joined the Grange after the Chautauqua study movement. Mayo traveled extensively in the Midwest, lecturing on "women's concerns," children's issues, and the potential importance of the Grange in rural women's lives (Buell, *One Woman's Work*). In addition to her skill as a public speaker, Lord was elected to the posts of master and lecturer at the local and county (Pomona) levels, was New York State lecturer from 1902 to 1904, and was a delegate to the New York State Grange from 1886 to 1906 (Allen 111–12).

Women who played strong advocacy roles might have prior experience in public speaking at abolitionist, temperance, or woman's rights meetings but also drew on business procedures and rhetorical skills practiced in Subordinate Granges. At the same time, many rural women gained organizational experience and confidence in public self-expression through Grange work and used it in other kinds of activism and civic engagement.

Conclusion

The early Grange provided rural women a training ground for platform speaking, opportunities to express themselves, and new justifications for their presence at a time when women were entering the public sphere in increasing numbers and seeking more active roles. The Grange provided a rationale for mutuality (Marti) and the sharing of roles across gender lines. Women participated in the Grange as voting members whose activity was valued and whose value was reinforced regularly in ritual language. In Anson Bartlett's words, the Grange "inaugurated the idea of equality between the sexes without doing violence to any person's feelings or prejudices," because the vision of equality it encompassed was consonant with rural culture and because, through education and the example of an egalitarian social order within the Grange Hall, artificial social "disabilities [could] be removed" (Kelley 75). Though that vision was not fully realized in some important ways, it did move women into the public sphere in others.

The "mutuality" of Grange membership served as a bridge from domestic roles to public ones, providing a training ground for important rhetorical skills. For many rural inhabitants, this discourse of productive partnerships between men and women opened a space for literacy and rhetorical practices to be extended. A strong emphasis on knowledge-sharing as a process that developed literacy and rhetorical skills attracted members to the Grange, but, as I have tried to show, did not originate with it. By developing, practicing, and sponsoring rhetorical skills through Grange work, women in the role of lecturer modeled an expanded definition of women's roles and appropriate public performances by rural women.

Notes

Portions of this essay were presented as "Matrons of Husbandry: Literacy Sponsorship in the Nineteenth-Century New York State Granges" at the American Society for the History of Rhetoric forum at the National Communication Association conference, San Antonio, Texas, November 2006. Thanks to Eileen Schell, Virginia Connor, New York State Grange, and the Cornell University Archives.

1. Deborah Brandt's concept of literacy sponsorship is a useful model for the influence of an institution on the rhetorical development of its members: literacy sponsors act as "agents . . . who enable, support, teach, and model, as well as recruit, regulate, suppress, or withhold, literacy—and gain advantage by it in some way" (19). Learners then expand and adapt skills for their own purposes, including economic gain. It could be argued that the Grange acted as a sponsor of literacy and rhetorical development.

2. Examples used here are drawn from the 1874 manual because I am focusing on the Grange's early years.

3. The National Grange urged adoption of the Rochdale principles of cooperative organization as early as 1877 (Gardner).

4. See Clark and Halloran on the use and importance of oratory in American culture. Ray depicts a movement that began as a self-education program in local communities. According to Radner, Lyceum-like local meetings persisted beyond the early Lyceum era in rural areas and shared many characteristics with Grange lecturers' programs.

5. In spite of the egalitarian vision of the Grange's founders, Grange membership was somewhat self-selective and at times openly exclusionary. Race, ethnicity, and religion were more limiting than gender or class, two areas in which the Grange actively promoted inclusion. Some reasons for exclusion can be explained more easily than others (Roman Catholics, for example, were discouraged from joining secret societies in general). Nordin reports that in the

South, some—but not all—Granges may have acted as fronts for Ku Klux Klan activities and specifically barred African Americans (32–33). The reasons for other kinds of self-selection (for example, reluctance of some immigrant groups to join) are less evident.

6. Early Lyceum programs were designed around knowledge-sharing within the community, but later relied on a lecture circuit toured by paid speakers, including some well-known women platform speakers by the late nineteenth century (Ray). Radner's essay focuses on programs in which local inhabitants took turns composing texts, including handwritten newsletters and reading them from a podium.

7. See, for example, letters between Catherine Beecher and the Grimké sisters debating appropriate methods of addressing civic issues in Sklar.

8. Early attempts were made in both Europe and America to establish mixed-gender "Adoptive Rite" orders within the Masonic umbrella. The Order of the Eastern Star, the most successful of these, was established in the 1850s and still exists today, although it took nearly thirty years to formalize its relationship with the Masonic Lodge (Engle).

9. The Order of the Eastern Star is the women's auxiliary to the Masonic Order. Women are not permitted to join the all-male Masons, but a male Masonic officer must head every Eastern Star slate of officers. The Order of DeMoLay and Rainbow Girls are children's organizations for boys and girls, respectively, both sponsored by the Masons. See nymasons.org.

10. Gere reports that a history of the Salt Lake City Ladies' Literary Club listed educational societies formed as early as 1833 (108). It is the rising popularity of such groups that I want to highlight here.

11. Kelley's and Grosh's accounts show that, while the decision to include women was broadly supported, there were some missteps in designing a mixed-gender "fraternity." Oliver H. Kelley suggested that they truncate women's degree work in order to get the organization up and running more quickly, and Anson Bartlett objected, arguing that full membership required full initiation. In the end, negotiations resulted in full degree work for both men and women.

12. Although this might seem overprotective from a modern, urban viewpoint, Grosh rejected the construction of women as "weaker vessels" and made very specific recommendations that underscored how physically labor-intensive women's lives could be. Women should not, he argued, get up earlier than farming men in the household, nor work long into the night, only to rise a few hours later to start another day (Grosh 434–35).

13. Anson Bartlett, an Ohio fruit farmer, was recruited by William Saunders, one of the Grange's founders (Nordin 6). Bartlett, while not considered a founding member, apparently collaborated with Kelley on much of the first draft of Grange ritual. He argued strongly that women needed the social distractions and community support of an organization like the Grange to find relief from constant toil, but also that the Grange could not succeed without women's support—both common themes in early Grange rhetoric (Marti).

14. One letter from Oliver H. Kelley indicates that he thought Cowper's poetry provided "magnificent and appropriate language" for part of the Grange ritual (Kelley 47).

15. The representation of a "universal woman" as a (heterosexual) partner who is "female-but-equal" is consistent in Grange ritual, though it is interpreted differently in different contexts.

16. See Robinson for some twentieth-century examples of "women's projects" in the Grange.

17. A fuller survey of Grange officers in upstate New York is currently in progress.

18. One might argue that the lecturer's role became "feminized" over time. However, there is no indication in the records I have found so far that men rejected the post as "women's work." Most "open" events (to which nonmembers were invited) were extensions of the lecturer's program, and thus the lecturer's role extended into the wider community, with both men and women lecturers performing public functions.

19. These examples are drawn as much from my experience as a child growing up in the Grange in the 1960s as from lists of suggested topics provided by state lecturers and minutes of actual lecturers' programs.

Works Cited and Consulted

Allen, Leonard L. *History of New York State Grange.* Watertown, NY: Hungerford-Holbrook, 1934. Print.

Arthur, Elizabeth L. *The History of New York State Grange, 1934–1960.* New York State Grange, 1961. Print.

Bacon, Jacqueline. *The Humblest May Stand Forth: Rhetoric, Empowerment, and Abolition.* Charleston: U of South Carolina P, 2002. Print.

Brandt, Deborah. *Literacy in American Lives.* New York: Cambridge UP, 2001. Print.

Buchanan, Linda. *Regendering Delivery: The Fifth Canon and Antebellum Women Rhetors.* Studies in Rhetorics and Feminisms. Ed. Cheryl Glenn and Shirley Wilson Logan. Carbondale: Southern Illinois UP, 2005. Print.

Buell, Jennie. *The Grange Master and the Grange Lecturer.* The Farmer's Bookshelf. Ed. Kenyon L. Butterworth. New York: Harcourt, Brace, 1921. Print.

———. *One Woman's Work for Farm Women: The Story of Mary Mayo's Part in Rural Social Movements.* Boston: Whitcomb and Barrows, 1908. Print.

Clark, Gregory, and S. Michael Halloran, eds. *Oratorical Culture in Nineteenth-Century America: Transformations in the Theory and Practice of Rhetoric.* Carbondale: Southern Illinois UP, 1993. Print.

Cott, Nancy F. *The Bonds of Womanhood: "Woman's Sphere" in New England, 1780–1835.* New Haven: Yale UP, 1977. Print.

Eastman, E. R. "Hats Off to the Grange." *The History of New York State Grange, 1934–1960.* Ed. Elizabeth L. Arthur. New York State Grange, 1961. 14–15. Print.

Engle, Willis D. *A General History of the Order of the Eastern Star.* Indianapolis: Self-published, 1901. Print.

Gardner, Charles M. *The Grange: Friend of the Farmer, 1867–1947.* Washington, DC: National Grange, 1949. Print.

Gere, Ann Ruggles. *Intimate Practices: Literacy and Cultural Work in Women's Clubs, 1880–1920.* Urbana: U of Illinois P, 1997. Print.

Goldberg, Michael Lewis. *An Army of Women: Gender and Politics in Gilded Age Kansas.* Baltimore: Johns Hopkins UP, 1997. Print.

Greer, Jane. "Women's Words, Women's Work: Rural Literacy and Labor." *Reclaiming the Rural.* Ed. Kim Donehower, Charlotte Hogg, and Eileen Schell. Carbondale: Southern Illinois UP, 2011. Print.

Grosh, A. B. *Mentor in the Granges and Homes of Patrons of Husbandry.* New York: Clark & Maynard, 1876. Print.

Hazard, Dora M. *Onondaga Pomona Grange, 1883–1915.* Oswego, NY: Lake City Print Shop, 1915. Print.

Hogg, Charlotte. *From the Garden Club: Rural Women Writing Community.* Lincoln: U of Nebraska P, 2006. Print.

Kelley, Oliver H. *Origin and Progress of the Order of the Patrons of Husbandry in the United States: A History from 1866 to 1873.* Philadelphia: J. A. Wagenseller, 1875. Print.

Marti, Donald B. *Women of the Grange: Mutuality and Sisterhood in Rural America, 1866–1920.* Contributions in Women's Studies, no. 124. Westport, CT: Greenwood, 1991. Print.

National Grange. *Manual of Subordinate Granges of the Patrons of Husbandry.* 5th ed. Philadelphia: J. A. Wagenseller, 1874. Print.

———. *Manual of Subordinate Granges of the Patrons of Husbandry.* 29th ed. National Grange, 1953. Print.

New York State Patrons of Husbandry records [ca. 1874–1995]. Unpublished minutes of inactivated Granges. Collection no. 3381. New York State Archives, Division of Rare and Manuscript Collections, Cornell U Lib., Ithaca, NY. Print.

Nordin, D. Sven. *Rich Harvest: A History of the Grange, 1867–1900.* Jackson: UP of Mississippi, 1974. Print.

Osterud, Nancy Grey. *Bonds of Community: The Lives of Farm Women in Nineteenth-Century New York.* Ithaca, NY: Cornell UP, 1991. Print.

Radner, Joan. "Mrs. Editress v. The Village Store Court of Law: Women's Public Discourse in Rural Postbellum Maine." *Of Place and Gender: Women in Maine History.* Ed. Marli F. Weiner. Orono: U of Maine P, 2005. 133–60. Print.

Ray, Angela. *The Lyceum and Public Culture in the Nineteenth-Century United States.* Rhetoric and Public Affairs. Ed. Martin J. Medhurst. East Lansing: Michigan UP, 2005. Print.

Robinson, William L. *The Grange, 1867–1967: First Century of Service and Evolution.* Washington, DC: National Grange, 1966. Print.

Rogers, Barbara. *Men Only: An Investigation into Men's Organizations.* London : Pandora, 1988. Print.

Romero, Lora. *Home Fronts: Domesticity and Its Critics in the Antebellum United States.* Durham, NC: Duke UP, 1997. Print.

Ryan, Mary P. *Cradle of the Middle Class: The Family in Oneida County, New York, 1790–1865.* Interdisciplinary Perspectives on Modern History. Cambridge: Cambridge UP, 1981. Print.

Sklar, Katherine Kish. *Women's Rights Emerges within the Anti-Slavery Movement, 1830–1870: A Brief History with Documents.* The Bedford Series in History and Culture. Ed. Natalie Zemon Davis and Ernest R. May. Boston: Bedford St. Martin's, 2000. Print.

Summerhill, Thomas. *Harvest of Dissent: Agrarianism in Nineteenth-Century New York.* Urbana: U of Illinois P, 2005. Print.

Warren, James Perrin: *Culture of Eloquence: Oratory and Reform in Antebellum America.* University Park: Pennsylvania State UP, 1999. Print.

7

"I Pledge My Head to Clearer Thinking": The Hybrid Literacy of 4-H Record Books

I. Moriah McCracken

I pledge
My head to clearer thinking,
My heart to greater loyalty,
My hands to larger service, and
My health to better living,
For my club, my community, my country, and my world.

—4-H Pledge[1]

At the turn of the twentieth century, the exodus of rural residents from farms to more urban centers was quickly becoming a source of concern for educators, politicians, and even clergy members across the United States.[2] The explanations for this exodus varied, but the consensus was that industrial work was displacing agricultural work as a more lucrative employment opportunity, and these shifts in production were creating trouble for an agricultural way of life. As William Bowers suggests in *The Country Life Movement in America, 1900–1920*, fewer bodies were needed to labor in the fields as traditional farming methods were replaced with new technologies and scientific knowledge. These economic and technological factors, when coupled with "dissatisfaction with poor schools, lack of conveniences and recreational facilities, inadequate roads, isolation, and the alleged general sterility of farm life" (13), led to an outward migration of rural residents, and the farm as a way of life soon fell behind more urban areas in perceived middle-class standards of living. With farm life offering little in the way of entertainment, few conveniences such as indoor plumbing and electricity, and virtually no opportunities for advancement, many Americans from across the country worried about the collapse of the family and sought ways to increase rural residents' satisfaction with life on the farm.

One area identified for change was rural education. Advances in scientific techniques now made new demands on farmers to achieve proficiency in varied areas, including "strength, endurance, mechanical aptitude, knowledge of scientific agriculture, and financial ability" (Bowers 8–9), and educators speculated that "rural education was not performing its proper function and should be changed" (15). Some believed the traditional three R's of education (reading, writing, and arithmetic) were too far removed from the realities of rural and farm life to meet the changing needs of youth, but these educators faced the challenge of convincing local school boards of the value of an in-school, practical education (Keathley and Ham 193).

Building on John Dewey's call for abstract instruction combined with "learning by doing," educators sought an approach that could better connect the daily lives of students to educational opportunities by focusing more on manual arts and skills. One such proponent of learning by doing was Cornell University's Liberty Hyde Bailey, chair of President Theodore Roosevelt's Commission on Country Life in America.[3] Bailey, much like Dewey and other proponents of what became the country life movement, believed education could cure the problems faced by rural youth (Bowers 56), but this kind of curative education would require in-depth study of the physical aspects of natural surroundings (46).[4] Because Bailey believed that a focus on only "books and abstract subjects" would result in a "'pouring-in-and-dipping-out process'" of learning, he argued that "education should always start with the pupils and their environment" (57). Foreshadowing Paulo Freire's opposition to the banking model of education, Bailey outlined a teaching philosophy that prioritized the use of local environments in curriculum development, valued activity over memorization and recitation, and attempted to dismantle the false separation between a liberal education and technical training.

According to Bailey, any intellectual activity could foster "mental growth and power," regardless of application (Bowers 60). But Bailey railed against the use of cities and urban centers as the focus for rural education. When teachers in rural schools talked about life in cities in their classrooms, Bailey contended, they (unknowingly and unintentionally) encouraged students to seek opportunities elsewhere. These urban-focused discussions created a scenario in which, as Bailey suggested, an education "may unfit the child to live in its normal and natural environment. It is often said that the agricultural college trains youth away from the farm. The fact is the mischief is done long before the youth enters college" (Bailey qtd. in Wessel and Wessel 3). For Bailey and others, there had to be a way to educate rural youth without (psychically or physically) removing them from their home environments.

Changing the aims of education and literacy learning at school was not feasible, and Bailey never suggested that schools eliminate the fundamentals of education. Bailey was certain, however, the solution could be found in "extension" work: if agricultural colleges could build on the experiences of successful farmers by demonstrating proven methods and techniques, then learning and training could occur beyond the schools' walls and, more importantly, rural residents could find solutions to their own problems by experimenting with more scientific methods and approaches (Bowers 60). This idea of extension work, of taking the university to the people, became the genesis of youth club work in the United States. Both adult extension work and youth club work were envisioned to be integral components of a larger educational movement, one that began with "educators who grasped the need and had developed plans for practical education" and included "land-grant colleges which had put together the necessary building materials for a newer, stronger agriculture" (Keathley and Ham 193).

Advocates of the country life movement and faculty at land-grant colleges worked to design a more "practical education in agriculture, manual arts, and homemaking" (Reck vii).[5] Together, these reformers believed they could make explicit connections between the work of home and the work of school by combining the theoretical, abstract work of a liberal education with the skills-based, manual work completed on family farms. With a voluntary approach to education and the support of the extension service, club work in the United States began as a means of creating "opportunities for youth to understand their dependence on nature's resources and to value the fullest development of hand, head, and heart" (Kress 133).

Constructing 4-H from Club Work

For more than one hundred years, the 4-H organization has been the face of club work in the United States, supporting millions of youth.[6] In 2007, the 4-H organization had approximately 6 million active members in fifty states, making it the nation's largest nonacademic youth organization. Even though the organization and many institutions of higher education share a common past—both owe their beginnings to the Morrill Act of 1862—4-H remains largely unknown to scholars outside of extension work; moreover, academics outside of land-grant universities often misunderstand the organization to be (almost always) an exclusively *rural* and *agricultural* youth organization—one aimed solely at teaching manual competencies for farm life. Often confused with Future Farmers of America (FFA), 4-H is incorrectly seen as a way for youth to learn how to grow vegetables or raise animals, skills that have little relevance for higher education or contemporary studies of literacy.[7]

Academic misrepresentations and/or mischaracterizations of 4-H are rooted in history; after all, club work was originally designed to fill in perceived deficiencies of rural life by focusing on educational needs; club work aimed to encourage young members to love and value rural life and farming by connecting farm-life skills with secondary-school learning.[8] But *contemporary* perceptions that 4-H prepares *rural* youth solely for agricultural trades are no longer accurate. Today, only 12 percent of 4-H members live on farms. In fact, 52 percent reside in cities and suburbs with more than 10,000 residents ("4-H Youth"), and club work has expanded to include projects in engineering, technology, healthy living, and (as always) citizenship.

More importantly, for (rural) literacy scholars and researchers, the hands-on work integral to 4-H is, and has always been, supported by writing activities and literacy practices. To participate in 4-H club work, young people enroll in projects designed to help them acquire a basic manual skill (or nontraditional literacy), such as raising sheep. This practical, "learning by doing" activity is then supplemented and reinforced with more traditional literacies, specifically the completion of report forms and the structuring of a 4-H story (personal learning narrative). Thus, the organization gives literacy meaning through nonacademic forms of writing by asking youth to self-select a skills-based project and then document and reflect on learning.

After sketching a historical account of how 4-H began in Texas, I examine a single family's writings in 4-H Record Books (a compilation of local and national report forms and narratives) to determine how the skills-based, manual competencies of 4-H projects are reinforced by more conventional (albeit bureaucratic) literacies. Then, by examining the literacy narratives embedded in the documents, I argue that the completion of a 4-H Record Book allows youth to experiment with a hybrid literacy genre, one that implies that the literacies needed to survive in a "normal and natural environment" are of the head *and* the hands. By asking 4-Hers to reflect on their learning in forms and to compose the narrative-driven 4-H Story, the organization not only provides the tropes necessary for structuring the narrative of learning but also (perhaps unknowingly) allows the youth an opportunity to control the presentation of information, creating a scenario where the goals of the 4-Her may trump those of the organization.

4-H Club Work in Texas

Through the Morrill Act of 1862, the U.S. government donated land to the states so that each might establish land-grant institutions to provide an education in practical professions, such as agriculture, home economics, and the mechanical arts. One byproduct of these agricultural universities was the county extension agent, sent out from the university to share institutional knowledge with farmers and ranchers to create a cooperative extension.[9] In Texas, the site for my investigation, the development of 4-H club work illustrates how government officials and universities used this cooperative work to address real-life concerns by bringing the university to the people.

In 1903, the Mexican boll weevil was destroying Texas cotton crops, reducing production by as much as 50 percent in some areas. There was no tested method for eliminating this new pest, but the United States Department of Agriculture's (USDA) Bureau of Entomology discovered damage caused by the boll weevil could be reduced if farmers combined new varieties of cotton with fall plowing (Reck 51). The USDA sent Dr. Seaman A. Knapp, a man originally hired to promote better farming methods in the South, to Terrell, Texas, hoping he could apply these methods to local cotton crops. Knapp managed to convince a single local farmer, Walter Porter, to cooperate in the new tillage technique, but in persuading Porter to participate, Knapp proved a key concept: "theory and technique were best learned by doing the work" (Wessel and Wessel 11). The success of Knapp and Porter demonstrated that the head and hand could work cooperatively in the field; thus, the USDA created an Office of Farmers' Cooperative Demonstration Work to help reinforce this idea of *learning by doing* as an educational principle. But not everyone was convinced.

Adult farmers in Texas were hesitant to agree that the USDA's techniques were superior to their own tried-and-true methods. Intent on sharing the scientific and technological advances being made at land-grant universities, Knapp and his team turned to rural boys and girls, hoping younger generations would be more receptive.[10] To recruit youth volunteers, the government workers would demonstrate a new farming practice, and then, acting as mentors, guide the youth as they applied and tested the techniques themselves (Reck 53). Knapp and his colleagues were soon sponsoring boys' corn growing contests (Wessel and Wessel 12). The success of these first projects drew national recognition, and boys and girls of all races from across the country began participating in club work at the local level: the boys practiced new technologies for growing corn (often out-producing their fathers), and the girls practiced food preservation techniques in tomato-canning competitions. By 1912, there were approximately 73,000 boys and 23,000 girls enrolled in county clubs all across the nation.

The Report Forms: Adding Data and Shaping Participants

Accumulating Bureaucratic Information

With approximately 100,000 youth participants at the beginning of the twentieth century, the newly formed national 4-H organization needed to document what members were learning in their projects. The concept of record keeping was not new for 4-H clubs; the organization had always taught young people how to keep farm records. Asking youth to synthesize and reflect on experiences in a standard form was a new concept, however, and around 1927 at a National 4-H Council meeting, the *National 4-H Report Form* was born. As club work expanded and the number of projects being offered at the local level grew, this new record-keeping method quickly became more than an organizational tool: records were soon touted as a way to track members' experiences and accomplishments.

For forty-five years, the *4-H National Report Form*, completed by all 4-Hers, asked fill-in-the-blank questions that mimicked form data required on everything from job applications to bank notes.[11] In August 1955, when eighteen-year-old John Van Buren completed the *Standard Report Form for 4-H Club Members,* he identified his state and project type and then read a single line of instructions: "Study this form carefully before filling in. It should be written in ink by the participant. DO NOT TYPE." John then listed his demographic data, identified his educational aspirations, and completed the "Statement by Club Member" section, which requires the 4-H member to affirm: "I have personally prepared this report and believe it to be correct," a statement, approved by four adults, that echoes today's academic honesty statements. By August of 1967, when seventeen-year-old Sarah Norris (who married John Van Buren) completed her *National 4-H Report Form*, the report form still directed members to handwrite answers in ink and voluntarily affirm the originality of their work. In 1989, when John and Sarah's daughter, Lisa, completed her 4-H forms, the opening instructions for the *National 4-H Report Form* had changed very little. Like her parents, Lisa provided standard demographic data, including her "place of home residence" and career path, and she, too, signed the "Statement by 4-H Member" to verify the accuracy of her form.[12]

With the exception of naming the project, the 4-Her's first literacy *event* within the organization began with plugging tracking information into a worksheet. But this "paperwork," which categorizes the member's participation and determines progress in the club, also serves as an inextricable literacy *practice* of the 4-H organization. For 4-Hers, like those in my study, the completion of these report forms introduces children as young as nine (the earliest age for club participation) to bureaucratic (and adult) standards for discourse and literacy. As literacy theorists like Kathryn Jones have noted, the nature of institutional forms can best be understood through the work of Max Weber, who argued that a bureaucracy is composed of a hierarchical organization intent on coordinating individuals' work. Moreover, as Weber contended, the coordinating and organizing work of a bureaucracy is not random; rather, it is geared toward fulfilling the goals of the organization and completing its corresponding administrative tasks. Thus, bureaucracies, even nonacademic youth organizations, accumulate information on individuals as a way to track what they are doing (surveillance) *and* as a way to monitor how participants are completing their tasks (control); in other words, as a way to exert "power and control over a population" (Jones 72). The 4-H organization is no exception. Because it seeks information about who is doing what and where, the initial gathering of information required by the national forms fits neatly into Weber's definition of a bureaucracy. The leadership of 4-H designed a national structure, and county extension agents working with the clubs handled its day-to-day operations. As a result of the organization's need to gather information, its forms ask all participants to declare their state and project as a means of routing data to the national level, just as demographic data are reported back to the government for funding purposes.[13]

But the information supplied by 4-H members on report forms does more than compile demographic data. In many ways, the national forms are also geared toward producing a standard kind of youth participant. As my discussion below demonstrates, the 4-H forms used by two generations of the Van Buren family contain embedded instructions and layout designs that highlight the relationship between 4-H projects and the larger goals of the organization. By determining how and what a 4-Her should report on a standard form, the organization exerts control over the experience, outlining the areas to be discussed and the evidence to be provided. All members know what the organization will assess because they are presented with the means of their surveillance even as they accumulate information. The fill-in-the-blank design (complete with tables and boxes) develops the functional literacy practices undergirding more traditional competencies taught by the 4-H Projects. In short, the literacy practices of the forms support the learning of the club work, the ability to follow directions and supply requested information in appropriate locations on the form), and reinforces the inclusion of some information and the exclusion of other details (the composition of a 4-H identity through learning narratives).

Standardizing 4-Hers and the 4-H Experience

In the 1950s when John completed his *National 4-H Report Form,* he was told only to "study the form carefully." There were no other directions (see Figure 7.1). By the time Sarah completed her forms in the mid-1960s, the page-one instructions varied slightly from those given to John, but following the demographic data were two full pages of directions (see Figure 7.2). So after filling in page 1, Sarah finds a directive: "Please study this form before filling it in." The new instructions include an explanation for why 4-Hers are expected to keep records, and the language written into this explanation highlights the complicated nature of 4-H's literacy genre: the report form (bureaucratic surveillance instrument) should stand as a material and written representation (traditional and functional literacy) of the learning that occurred while the 4-Her was working with her hands (skills-based competency). Unlike John, Sarah is told that any accomplishments and successes she reports should represent her growth and progress. The new form also spells out the bureaucratic regulations that govern completion of the form, which call on the 4-Her to demonstrate basic writing skills as well as the acquisition of (or at least the ability to record the learning details of) a life-skill competency. It is not enough for the 4-Her to plug in rote details about the expenses incurred while learning to raise beef cattle; she must also contrast previous skills with gained knowledge.

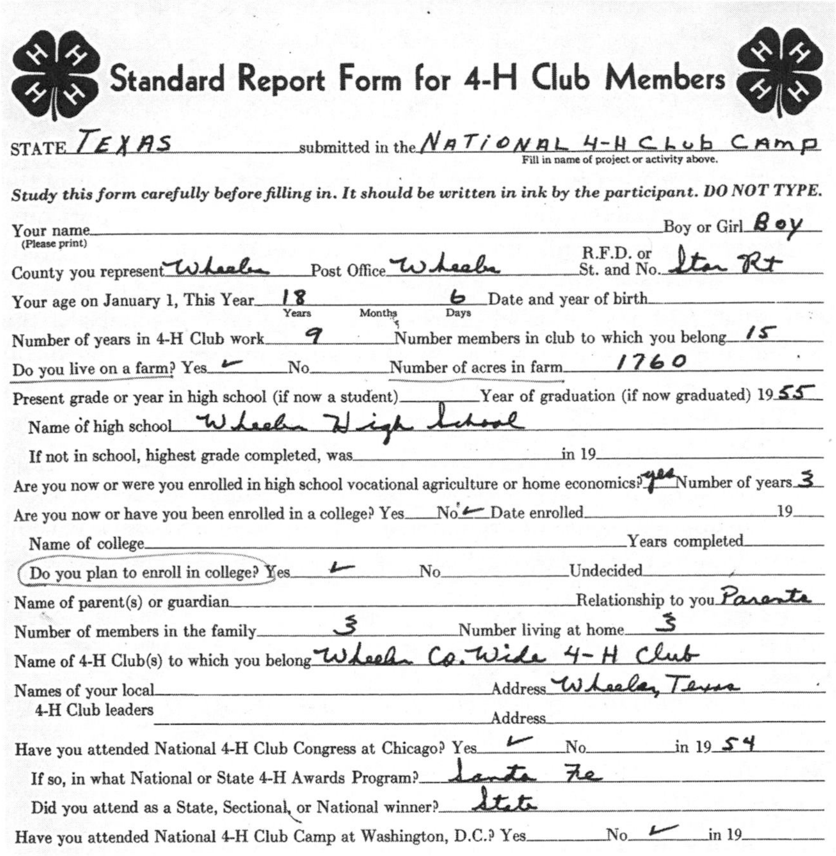

Standard Report Form for 4-H Club Members

STATE TEXAS submitted in the NATIONAL 4-H CLUB CAMP
Fill in name of project or activity above.

Study this form carefully before filling in. It should be written in ink by the participant. DO NOT TYPE.

Your name (Please print) ______ Boy or Girl Boy

County you represent Wheeler Post Office Wheeler R.F.D. or St. and No. Star Rt

Your age on January 1, This Year 18 Years ____ Months 6 Days Date and year of birth ______

Number of years in 4-H Club work 9 Number members in club to which you belong 15

Do you live on a farm? Yes ✓ No ____ Number of acres in farm 1760

Present grade or year in high school (if now a student) ____ Year of graduation (if now graduated) 1955

Name of high school Wheeler High School

If not in school, highest grade completed, was ______ in 19____

Are you now or were you enrolled in high school vocational agriculture or home economics? yes Number of years 3

Are you now or have you been enrolled in a college? Yes ____ No ✓ Date enrolled ______ 19____

Name of college ______ Years completed ______

Do you plan to enroll in college? Yes ✓ No ____ Undecided ____

Name of parent(s) or guardian ______ Relationship to you Parents

Number of members in the family 3 Number living at home 3

Name of 4-H Club(s) to which you belong Wheeler Co. Wide 4-H Club

Names of your local 4-H Club leaders ______ Address Wheeler, Texas
______ Address ______

Have you attended National 4-H Club Congress at Chicago? Yes ✓ No ____ in 1954

If so, in what National or State 4-H Awards Program? Santa Fe

Did you attend as a State, Sectional, or National winner? State

Have you attended National 4-H Club Camp at Washington, D.C.? Yes ____ No ✓ in 19____

Figure 7.1. John's 1955 4-H Report Form. Used with permission of "John Van Buren."

2

Please study this form before filling it in.

WHY 4-H RECORDS?

Your 4-H record is an organized presentation of what you have learned and accomplished in 4-H. When properly kept and carefully assembled, it is a useful tool for determining your own progress and personal growth. For persons who are not personally acquainted with you or who have not witnessed your good work, it is the only information available to them in evaluating your growth and accomplishments in relation to other 4-H members. Your 4-H record is a ready reference, the result of learning experiences which will be helpful to you throughout life.

Your valuable 4-H record is accurate, complete, organized in an appropriate sequence (see page 15 of this report, The Way To Assemble Your Record), neat and contains a minimum of repetition. It is the result of careful planning, conscientious recording of facts and figures and the selection of the most important information.

To the person examining your 4-H record, it is you at your very best.

This Report Form

This, The National 4-H Report Form, has been designed to help you outline completely, your 4-H experiences and accomplishments and is an important part of your 4-H record. Major sections in the report form include—

Section I: EXPERIENCES IN 4-H PROJECTS AND ACTIVITIES
Section II: EXPERIENCES IN 4-H LEADERSHIP DEVELOPMENT
Section III: GROWTH AND DEVELOPMENT IN PERSONAL, COMMUNITY
AND CIVIC RESPONSIBILITIES

You will note these section heads correspond to the principal divisions of the score sheet on page 16 of this report form.

Pages 4 and 5 have been provided for reporting experiences in the 4-H project or activity in which the record is being considered. Additional sheets may be inserted if necessary. See page 3 of this report for examples of information which may be included and the form in which it is to be recorded.

Page 6 is to be used for a summary of your participation and accomplishments in other 4-H projects. Examples are given at the top of the page.

Summarize your participation and accomplishments in other 4-H activities on page 7. Follow examples provided.

Learning situations which you experienced in projects and activities recorded on pages 6 and 7 are to be outlined on page 8. Follow examples provided.

On page 9, using these same projects and activities, list in outline form, important things you have learned, skills you have acquired and attitudes you have developed. Follow examples given.

Page 10 is to be used for summarizing your honors and recognition earned in 4-H projects and activities recorded on pages 6 and 7. See examples given.

Pages 11, 12, 13 and 14 provide space for summarizing your experiences in 4-H leadership development. Examples of information to be included and the form in which it should be reported are given. Additional pages may be inserted if necessary.

Page 15 briefly explains how your growth and development in personal, community and civic responsibilities will be shown throughout your 4-H record. Suggestions are given for writing Your 4-H Story.

Page 15 also outlines The Way To Assemble Your Record and gives specific recommendations for the selection of supporting materials and suggestions for displaying these materials.

When completely assembled your record will include:

Two Photos of Yourself	Project Pictures
A Table of Contents	News Clippings
The National 4-H Report Form	4-H Correspondence
Your 4-H Story	4-H Project or Activity Record Book

Figure 7.2. Sarah's 1960s National Report Form Instruction Page. Used with permission of "Sarah Norris Van Buren."

Because of the surveillance built into the forms of the 1960s, Sarah receives a message John did not: she is expected to construct herself and her actions in writing. The "you" examined for its "very best" must be properly framed and contextualized according to the instructions provided. Sarah also learns that the form's layout has been designed to help her "completely" account for her learning experiences, which is why she must even compose a narrative explaining what and how she learned from completing a manual competency. For example, the three major sections composing the report form (Experiences in 4-H Projects and Activities; Experiences in 4-H Leadership Development; and Growth and Development in Personal, Community and Civic Responsibilities) "correspond to the principal divisions of the score sheet on page 16 of this report form," which is why there are even explicit instructions for how each page should be completed. As Figure 7.2 shows, Sarah must summarize her participation in activities by following the examples provided on page 7. She's even given recommendations for the kind of supporting material she might include (on page 15), which also detail how she will assemble her completed Record Book. The forms and instructions make it clear: any learning Sarah acquired with her hands must be supported by her head and documented in writing.

Unlike her mother, Lisa first encountered the explanations and justifications for record keeping on a more localized state form, her 1989 *4-H Project Record for All Projects except Animal and Poultry*. Like her mother, however, Lisa is given an explanation for why records are part of 4-H projects, and the explanation shows how interwoven surveillance and learning outcomes had become over the past twenty years: "Recordkeeping is an important part of the 4-H program. Records: (1) teach the skill of recordkeeping, (2) encourage good work, (3) show progress, growth, and accomplishment, (4) help direct future plans, and (5) help determine recognition." In the late 1980s and early 1990s, at least at the local level, 4-Hers were no longer told that report forms would serve as representations of themselves; instead, the streamlined presentation reinforces the bureaucratic nature of the reporting method, emphasizing the purpose and use of the form for tracking what exactly was learned.

Like the national form completed by her mother, Lisa's project record form asks for standard demographic data. Now, however, the 4-H member must plan her project in advance. Completed "at the beginning of project," the form asks Lisa to explain what she wants "to learn and/or do in this project this year." In a blank table, Lisa records her project goals (see Figure 7.3), and this preplanning operates as a kind of learning outcome for the project, which cannot be static; after all, "As a member gains knowledge and experience, the size of the project may be increased and additional projects selected."

Thus, 4-Hers are expected to refine manual competencies with more abstract understandings. This is why Lisa's form suggests that by age 12 or 13 (after three or four years of participation), a 4-H member should select a project that she can follow throughout the rest of her 4-H career and identify other projects that might support the primary one. The evolving aims of the bureaucratic forms—at least by the early 1990s—align more with the goals of academic learning: each participant should acquire and build on a particular set of literacies, achieving benchmarks and documenting learning.

Planning Your Project

What do you want to learn and/or do in this project this year?

Project Goals	Date Accomplished
Research the history of textiles, the worldwide economic impact, and the future of the textile industry.	July 31–August 4 & December 1–January 1
Explore careers in textile research and production.	July 31–August 4 & January 18–19
Further investigate community needs and develop leadership skills.	Throughout the year
Discover the different uses of commercial dyes and equipment in the textile industry.	July 31– August 4 & January 18–19
Pursue more tailoring techniques and other construction and detail techniques.	Throughout the year
Investigate southwest fashions, weaving and knitting, and opera house costuming in Santa Fe.	March 23–35

Figure 7.3. Lisa's Project Goals on 1989 Project Record Form. Used with permission of "Lisa Van Buren."

Spanning forty years, the Van Buren family's records show how 4-Hers were never just plugging information into the columns or blank spaces of report forms; instead, relying on the directions provided by the organization, 4-Hers used the materials to demonstrate how they achieved 4-H's learning goals through skills-based projects. The forms track individual progress through the various levels of the organization (allowing the bureaucracy to fulfill its administrative tasks), and these forms also show the work required to participate in 4-H's literacy practices. The literacies practiced while filling in the charts, tables, lines, and white space of the report forms were "part of the substance and process of the work itself" (Defoe et al. 225). The work of a project (including the surveillance of its learning) did not end when the corn was grown and the expenses tracked. The work of the project continued on into the reading, deciphering, and completing of local and national record forms. In this final section, we will see how writing and reflecting on 4-H Club Work became part of an extended narrative of learning.

The Record Book: A Head-and-Hand Literacy of Learning and Doing

In "Reading Literacy Narratives," Janet Carey Eldred and Peter Mortensen examine how literary genres employ the themes of literacy and education, and to begin their work, they tease out (albeit minor) differences in definition. For example, they identify *narratives of socialization* as (coming-of-age) stories in which the character may talk about literacy or even a renewed understanding of how language works, but the main purpose is a chronicle of the "character's attempt to enter a new social (and discursive) arena." *Literacy narratives*, however, are stories that place the character's language acquisition and literacy development in the foreground, discussing details of schooling and/or teaching through "learned, internalized 'literacy tropes'" or "'prefigured' ideas and images" (513). I argue that the instructions accompanying report forms and 4-H Record Books result in literacy narratives and narratives of socialization. After all, the forms provide John, Sarah, and Lisa with the literacy tropes they need to construct themselves as ideal "4-Hers." The forms outline the expectations and parameters for learning within the discourse community, which is why the compositions completed by these 4-Hers—smaller paragraphs and extended stories—detail and reaffirm their membership within the club. Together, the documents' instructions and design outline the performance expectations of the discursive community (resulting in a narrative of socialization), and the compositions of the 4-H self within the forms operate as the representation of an *ideal* 4-Her.

Building on Eldred and Mortensen, Morris Young argues that literacy narratives may also "act to confirm, transform, or even reject a person's participation in [a] culture" or "raise questions about community identity and membership" (35). While Young focuses on how racialized minorities use literacy narratives to demonstrate their legitimacy as (potential) citizens, his assertion that identities constructed through literacy narratives may affect individuals' participation in a culture and/or affirm their community participation has relevance for my study of 4-H's literacy practices. Every 4-Her must bring the manual competencies of the hands into conversation with the reflective learning of the head, and to be *ideal* 4-Hers, they must construct narratives of learning to explain how they embody and represent the values of the 4-H organization. This is why I argue the literacy practices of 4-H clubs must be treated as a hybrid form: members gain manual literacies by participating in projects, but this is only one-half of the learning process. They must also explain *in writing* how these experiences resulted in a more advanced and sophisticated version of their 4-H selves. They must describe accurately what they learned and select appropriate evidence for learning.

I. 4-H PROJECTS AND ACTIVITIES

(a) 4-H PROJECTS COMPLETED.

Indicate size of your project from year to year by stating number of animals, number of quarts, number garments, number of acres, etc., involved each year.

List the first year first, giving projects by columns. If necessary, attach additional columns.

EXAMPLE:

PROJECT	Corn	Canning	Dairy	Garden				
1949	3 acres	25 qts.		1,000 sq. ft.				
1950	10 acres		2 calves 1 cow	¼ acre				
PROJECT	Swine	Beef Club Calves	Beef Breeding Cattle	Commercial Steers	alfalfa	Wheat		
19 47	1 Boar	1						
19 48		1		1				
19 49	2 Fat Pigs	1						
19 50	2 Fat Pigs	3	2		15 acres			
195 1		2	8	1	15 acres	26 acres		

Figure 7.4. John's 1955 National Report Form. Used with permission of John Van Buren.

The composition of the 4-H learning narrative begins when the member confronts the white space of the forms, which each 4-Her had to "fill up" with his or her learning data (see Figures 7.4 and 7.5). As the discussion below illustrates, the space provided on the form dictates the presentation of information, restricting the learning that can be demonstrated. For example, as Figure 7.5 partially illustrates, John had blank lines, tables, and directive instructions guiding the composition of his 4-H self in 1955. For his 4-H Projects and Activities section, John indicates the size and scope of his projects, and within the tables, he may add columns if necessary, but the learning experiences are predetermined by the space he's given. But the work of the forms also required John to consider the arrangement and placement of information. In his 4-H Leadership Record section, John must figure out how to record his public 4-H appearances and how to code the data according to location and number of appearances (see Figure 7.5). When tables give way to blank lines, John takes a cue from his form and uses explanatory paragraphs to detail the financial arrangements that made his project possible: presenting himself as resourceful, John notes that his father fronted the money for his initial projects, but his profits grew, and he was soon able to self-finance projects. He also connects the importance of his work to his home situation: "I live on a stock farm and my family derives most of its income from livestock, alfalfa, and small grains. My projects naturally would be centered around things which I have known all of my life."

(d) Number of talks you have given, TV appearances made or news stories written relating directly to 4-H Club Work. Indicate your participation with appropriate letter. Local (L) County (C) District (D) State (S) Interstate (I) National (N) and number of times as L3 or S1. List first year first.

Year	Talks Before 4-H Groups	4-H Talks Before Other Groups	Radio Appearances	TV Appearances	News Stories Written	Other 4-H Appearances (Explain)
1949	L1	L1				
1950	L1		I1			
1953	L1		I1			
1954	L2	L3	I5		L2	Guest of Whalen Kiwania
1955	L2	L2	I1		L2,I1	

Figure 7.5. John's 1955 Leadership Record information. Used with permission of John Van Buren.

John then uses his 4-H story to explain he has found a career, a nod to his identification with the 4-H community. He opens with a simple statement about the learning opportunities that contributed to his development, echoing the founding principle of club work. John's story then details how "learning by doing" in a 4-H project provided him with necessary life skills, a connection he makes later in his story (see Figure 7.6). John's story demonstrates his ability to craft a narrative, document the skills he acquired, and reflect on what he learned in conjunction with the goals and mission of the 4-H organization. But John's entire 4-H Record Book doesn't bypass the surveillance and control built into these materials. His narrative about a learning activity shows how his hands were linked to his head (see Figure 7.6).

I have always tried to have a well rounded program but my main interest has always been with beef cattle and show calves. I have learned a lot of things about my show calves that I think are necessary to produce champions and then when I get to thinking about these same things I find that you can take them and apply them to everyday life. One of those which you can do that with is gentleness and kindness.

Figure 7.6. Excerpt from John's 1955 4-H Story. Used with permission of John Van Buren.

Because 4-H doesn't value one above the other—he must be able to raise his fat calves and keep accurate records—John doesn't seem to know that what he did with his hands might not be valued by those focusing on the work of the mind; all he knows, it would seem, is that he had better be able to explain the work he completed with his hands in a way that makes sense to readers and justifies his inclusion in 4-H club work. So John focuses on how animal husbandry lessons helped him find his life's vocation, and, as I suggest, his use of paragraphs and personal anecdotes document how academic work is not separated from manual work in the literacy events of 4-H participation.

In 1967, Sarah had written confirmation about the surveillance undergirding her report forms; her instructions state that her progress would be evaluated against other members and not according to her individual growth. She is told that her forms may represent her within the community and beyond—language that mirrors traditional assumptions about the moral imperatives of literacy (see Brandt; Graff; and Soltow and Stevens). By touting the Record Book as the only information available to people unfamiliar with her 4-H work, Sarah's form becomes a material means of surveillance: a stable representation through which the organization can determine how each member meets the expectations for participation within the community, and because "not only the writer but also the reader [make] meaning from the narrative" (Young 35), the 4-H member gains an early lesson in the construction of self for an audience.

Sarah doesn't record her 4-H Projects and Activities in a table; instead, she has two lined pages to outline her yearly participation in projects. She summarizes her activities and what she accomplished, but she starts ignoring directions in the Learning Situations in Other 4-H Projects and Activities section (see Figure 7.7). She shifts from a listing of competencies practiced to a narrative explanation of learning. Rather than outlining skills she mastered, Sarah composes short learning statements. Just as workers might use a distinctive marking system to "express creativity even in situations that demand standardization, and even when such individual expressions may risk getting them into trouble" (Belfiore 39), Sarah explains how her junior leadership role led to new learning opportunities. Her use of sentences in lieu of list-driven record keeping extends into her next project.

Following the provided format, Sarah explains that as a junior Foods Project leader she learned the value of patience and time management: "I learned to manage my time with such a busy schedule and that the girls will be more interested and willing to participate if they are given a type of food group & [*sic*] told to select what they would like to make (which they've never made)." Rather than simply accumulating data in the required format, Sarah ignores the instructions to "list" and writes herself into the action, explaining how she met larger 4-H goals. She pays no attention to the imperatives of her literacy sponsor, choosing instead to dictate the parameters for her literacy development by controlling how she constructs her learning, diverting the sponsor's resources and materials for her own self-development (see Brandt).

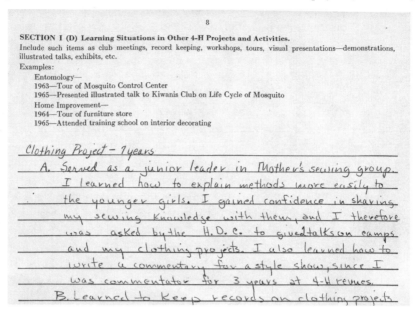

Figure 7.7. Sarah's 1967 Learning Situations information. Used with permission of Sarah Norris Van Buren.

Sarah's 4-H story continues this pattern of self-determination; she explains that she joined the San Perlita Girls' 4-H Club in 1958 and for six years worked on projects that could be directly correlated with her home situation. Though many of her initial projects centered on domestic arts, Sarah wasn't limited to cooking and sewing. Whether she was judging range grasses or raising beef cattle, she learned to use her life-skills experiences (manual competencies) for academic requirements. In fact, her sanctioned narrative explains how the everyday tasks of her 4-H projects gave her the skills she needed to succeed at school, and her 4-H story shows her proficiency with composing a narrative of learning.

In 1989, when Lisa completed her final report forms, composing paragraphs was not an option. The lines and tables her parents worked with had been replaced with white space, and the forms of the 1980s and 1990s require 4-Hers to tightly control documentation. The 4-Her must decipher the best way to record and organize the learning experiences. For example, when Lisa reports on the size and scope of her major project, Clothing, the instructions tell her to use numbers (only) to "show size, growth, profits, losses, or savings" associated with her project. But there are no tables to code data. Instead, Lisa must create her own form to show how long she spent sewing pajamas and costumes over the last eight years (see Figure 7.8). Like her father, she must find a way to explain the "significant" awards she received according to various levels, but the instructions detailing the coding system are on page 14,

---

SECTION I — EXPERIENCES IN THE 4-H _Clothing_ **PROGRAM**

This section of the National 4-H Report Form is devoted to the program in which you are submitting your record.

A. SIZE AND SCOPE

1. List size and scope of your participation in this program; use numbers when appropriate to show size, growth, profits, losses or savings.

Items Constructed	'82	'83	'84	'85	'86	'87	'88	'89	'90	Totals
Dresses/Jumpers	1	1		1	1			1	1	6
Jackets/Vests	1		1		1	1	1			5
Blouses	1		2	3	1	1	1	5	3	17
Pajamas		1								1
Pants/Shorts			1			1	2	2	2	8
Skirts		1	1		1	2	4	4	1	14
Formal Wear							1			1
Costumes					2		2			4
Coats							1	2	1	4
Accessories						4		7	4	15
Items Mended						35	71	83	10	199
Alterations							2			2
	3	3	5	4	6	44	85	104	23	227

Costs Savings & Hours Spent										
$$ saved by sewing	$25	25	100	75	150	237	402	961	985	$2960
$$ saved at sales & resale shops		$300	266	250	398	751	1169	1219	1014	$5367
$$ made by sewing for others							$68	34		$102
Hours spent	15	21	42	19	45	42	161	88	54	487

Activities										
Tours/demos/talks	2	4	1	6	5	5	26	20	12	81
Meetings/workshops	7	8	14	7	8	7	16	29	18	97
People taught				30	102	436	434	35	112	1149
Jr./Teen Leader			x	x	x	x	x	x	x	7 years
Exhibits	1	4	6	8	12	16	7	6	11	71
Times modeled	1	1	4	5	8	5	8	16	4	52
Community service projects	1	1	2	1	3	6	14	6	4	38

2. List significant awards received that indicate quality of your work.

Year	Type of Award	For What Received	Level/Number
1982–1990	Ribbons, Fabric	Clothing Contests, Demonstrations	
1984	Trophies/Patches	Clothing & Wool Contests	L-11
	Best Wool/$$$	Project Show/TOT Clo. Celebration	C-28
1985	Fabric/Trophies/$$$	Clothing & Wool Contests	D-42
1986	Trophies/$$$/Fabric	Clothing & Wool Contests	R-11
	Scissors/Medal	Project Shows/Record Book	S-21
1987	Patches/$$$/Fabric	Record Book/Fairs/Clothing &	N-1
	Trophies	Wool Contests	
1988	Fabric/$$$/Medals	Clothing & Wool Contests	
	Patches/Sewing Machine	High Point Senior at County	
1989	Fabric/$$$/Medals	Clothing & Wool Contests/Proj. Show/Judging Cont.	
	Scholarship/Natl. Congress	State Fashion Show Winner, Record Book	
1990	Fabric/Scissors/$$$	Wool Contest, Fair	

Figure 7.8. Lisa's 1989 National Clothing Report Form. Used with permission of Lisa Van Buren.

not embedded in the section. The organizational system Lisa developed likely aligned with examples provided (she didn't include the instructions in her final Record Book), but regardless of whether she copied the example or designed her own structure, the literacies required to complete the bureaucratic forms had increased. Now 4-Hers design the systems required to present their evidence of learning.

Lisa's 4-H story opens with an anecdote about her legitimacy as a member: "When I was about six years old, I thought I must be a 4-H member because I had been attending 4-H meetings and activities since I was 3. . . . I asked [Mom] if I was a 4-H member. She said, 'No, you have to be nine years old.' I said, 'Well, I sure do go to a heck of a lot of 4-H meetings!'" Lisa's eagerness shows an inherited connection with the organization, and as the daughter of ex-4-Hers, both of whom completed narratives of learning to justify membership, it is no surprise that Lisa used her membership as an entry point: she likely received guidance and coaching from her 4-H leader parents on how to begin telling her story. This may also explain why Lisa's 4-H story is more focused and direct than her parents'. She does not write about her occupation, life skills or even about connecting projects to her home situation; instead, she connects the goals listed on her local report form to her manual competencies. She explains how she learned to talk in front of crowds, to focus on the fit and construction of garments (even on ready-made clothes), and to organize closets and de-clutter her room. Like her mother, Lisa participated in homemaking activities, but she was also able to visit colleges and complete scholarship applications because her institutional sponsor, adapting to the needs of its members, seemed to recognize Lisa needed literacies aimed directly at preparing her for college—an opportunity that was not available to her parents. But the work of her hands and head were never far apart: "As I look back on my 4-H career, I can see how I have grown physically and mentally."

The Literacy Events and Practices of 4-H

Produced approximately fifty years after the creation of 4-H club work in the United States and spanning some forty years, the Van Buren family's 4-H Record Books document the literacy practices embedded in the 4-H organization not at its inception, when the organization was defining itself, and not in its current form, when it is changing and adapting to the educational needs of the twenty-first century. Rather these historical examples reveal the systematic pattern surrounding 4-H's literacy training as it was beginning to take root in the nation's club work landscape. By considering the work of a single family, we see the evolution of 4-H forms. The 4-H record forms were bureaucratic documents meant to assemble composite portraits of the organization's participants, and in the three examples discussed above, each 4-Her had to plan, sequence, and present her or his information according to the contemporary requirements of the forms. Across two generations, the forms recorded demographic data and controlled the information presented by the 4-Her, dictating what could be included (content) and how that information would be recorded (genre/presentation). The composition and reflection required by the forms extended into the 4-H stories, and together these documents offer evidence of an organization using writing to achieve bureaucratic goals, of teaching basic life skills through reflection *and* record keeping. These 4-Hers' narrative reflections on learning demonstrate their acquisition of manual competencies *and* show how they used literacy for self-representation.

As members of their various local 4-H chapters, all three members of the Van Buren family completed the required forms in an "accurate, complete, organized" sequence, and they relied on literacies learned in school to record data and report information about their nonacademic endeavors. To accomplish this, they had to use their traditional, school-based literacy experiences to support their continued participation in skills-based learning projects. David Orr has argued that a truly liberal education develops balanced and whole persons, and 4-H record books show participants and an organization working to create whole 4-Hers by requiring "the integration of the personhood of the student . . . the intellect with manual competence." By asking youth to write about their learning (even in restricted ways), the organization focuses the 4-Her's attention on the "friction between an alert mind and practical experience" (101), thereby creating thinkers who can do, and doers who can think.

If culture is a powerful force in shaping public notions of rural literacy (see Donehower, Hogg, and Schell), then 4-H clubs have been pivotal in shaping the perceptions and applications of literacy for millions of rural, suburban, and urban youth, helping them see the possibilities of a collaboration between functional skills and academic applications. I do not, however, believe that 4-H has served as the sole sponsor of literacy for rural youth; in fact, there are local and community organizations across this country that helped young and old alike find purpose and meaning in literacy practice. But by reconsidering the work required to complete a 4-H record book, I aim to create a space where even bureaucratic uses of writing can be reconsidered and reclaimed as we challenge what counts as literacy.

For some 4-Hers, the contemporary record book has become a "mundane, outdated chore" (see Diem and Devitt), but I believe if literacy researchers can follow the model of 4-H and take the university to the people, then we might begin conversations about how bureaucratic writing events may prepare youth for more complicated writing tasks. Borrowing a cue from research in second-language literacies, we should explore how structured and bureaucratic practices may operate as "funds of knowledge" in our classrooms (see Moll and Gonzalez) or how controlled writing situations fit into the adoption, adaptation, and alienation of familial literacy practices embedded in our students' heritage literacies (see Rumsey). Beth Daniell has suggested that we, as researchers, only study what we value and value what we study. We may not like bureaucratic control of youths' reading and writing habits; we may not even fully accept that our hands and head may operate together in a hybrid literacy practice, but as researchers and scholars, we must recover and reclaim the documents surrounding us or risk losing part of our literacy history.

Notes

1. The 4-H pledge is still recited at the opening of county, district, and state meetings and highlights the organization's educational imperative.

2. As Bowers notes, the rural population of the United States decreased from 63.9 percent to 53.7 percent between 1890 and 1910. The ten-point decline was accompanied by an even greater decline in the number of people employed by agriculture: in 1890, 42.5 percent of the population was employed on farms versus 30.7 percent of the population twenty years later in 1910.

3. The commission outlined four principles for resolving the deficiencies of rural life: knowledge, education, organization, and spirituality. Three of these four principles appear in the educational aims and goals of the 4-H organization and documents produced by 4-H members. One common academic criticism of the Commission on Country Life was that it represented the "Progressive Era's manipulative technocratic social engineering, aimed at benefiting urban elites by remodeling and urbanizing country life and industrializing agriculture in order to make it more scientific, productive, and efficient" (Peters and Morgan 291). In fact, Bowers is often cited as criticizing Bailey for being an "agrarian sentimentalist," and the commission itself is seen as being solely focused on finding ways to make agriculture more efficient and productive. The report frames its work around the deficiencies of rural life, and that is not in dispute, but the recommendations also suggest that the impetus for creating a more sustainable rural life resides in the rural citizenry's ability to organize themselves and serve as the local change makers (which also assumes this was not already taking place). I cite Peters and Morgan to point out the complexity of rereading the report and to note how it cannot be treated simply as an either/or binary for rural life in America.

4. While John Dewey and Liberty Hyde Bailey may seem to share educational philosophies, they were developing these ideas "independently" (Bowers 60).

5. The interests of land-grant colleges, as noted by Keathley and Ham, were much more focused on convincing farmers to "try the new promising methods and practices" they had developed (193).

6. The history of the organization, as I acknowledge, is not clearly delineated by the historians who work on its national presence. Much of its history can be found in state-level histories. It is clear, however, that the name 4-H was adopted once the clubs identified a pledge and the motto "To Make the Best Better."

7. In 2005, I conducted an informal, online survey focusing on academic perceptions of rural places and spaces. I asked respondents to describe their perceptions of the purpose of 4-H. All sixty-six responses connected 4-H to rural lifestyles and indicated that they understood 4-H to be focused on educating youth for lives in an agricultural trade.

8. I use the terms *4-H* and *club work* interchangeably because the 4-H organization began as club work at the local, county, and state levels.

9. The passage of the Smith-Lever Act on 8 May 1914 established Cooperative Extension Work at the government level, "thereby making the government of the United States an actual promoter of boys' and girls' club work" (Hinshaw 17).

10. At a Texas Farmers' Institute meeting, the organization's president, J. H. Connell, suggested that a statewide organization be formed to "encourage rural school teachers to supervise crop growing and domestic science work" (Reck 24), thus creating an environment in which Knapp's intervention and assistance might have been more welcome.

11. When I participated in 4-H, John Van Buren and Sarah (Norris) Van Buren (pseudonyms) were leaders in 4-H Clubs in the Texas Panhandle. They were generous enough to share the artifacts with me for my study.

12. I cannot compare the instructions provided to Lisa in 1989 because she did not keep the instruction pages in her record book; the layout and progression of information remains in sequence: Experiences in 4-H program, 4-H Leadership Experiences, Citizenship and Community Service Experiences, Summary of Other 4-H Project Learning Experiences.

13. Four-H is funded through national, state, and county governments. The national and state funds pay for administering the program, while county funds pay for managing local programs.

Works Cited

"4-H History." National 4-H Headquarters. Web. 6 Sept. 2005.

"4-H Youth Development: Statistics." Web. 23 Jan. 2007.

Belfiore, Mary Ellen. "Literacies, Compliance and Certification." *Reading Work: Literacies in the New Workplace.* Ed. Mary Ellen Belfiore et al. Mahwah, NJ: Lawrence Erlbaum, 2004. 19–62. Print.

Bowers, William L. *The Country Life Movement in America, 1900–1920.* Port Washington, NY: Kennikat, 1974. Print.

Brandt, Deborah. "Sponsors of Literacy." *College Composition and Communication* 49.2 (1998): 165–85. Print.

Daniell, Beth. *A Communion of Friendship: Literacy, Spiritual Practice, and Women in Recovery.* Carbondale: Southern Illinois UP, 2003. Print.

Defoe, Tracy, Sue Folinsbee, and Mary Ellen Belfiore. "Implications for Practice." *Reading Work: Literacies in the New Workplace.* Mahwah, NJ: Lawrence Erlbaum, 2004. 221–40. Print.

Diem, Keith G., and Annette Devitt. "Shifting the Focus of 4-H Record-Keeping from Competition and Subject Matter to Youth Development and Life Skills." *Journal of Extension* 41.6 (2003). Web. 27 Mar. 2009.

Donehower, Kim, Charlotte Hogg, and Eileen Schell. *Rural Literacies.* Carbondale: Southern Illinois UP, 2007. Print.

Eldred, Janet Carey, and Peter Mortensen. "Reading Literacy Narratives." *College English* 54.5 (1992): 512–39. Print.

Graff, Harvey J. *The Legacies of Literacy: Continuities and Contradictions in Western Culture and Society.* Bloomington: Indiana UP, 1986. Print.

Hinshaw, Kenneth. *4-H: A Story Weaving Together Actual 4-H Experiences, Historical Sketches of Boys' and Girls' 4-H Clubwork, and Chronicles of Important 4-H Events.* New York: Orange Judd, 1935. Print.

Jones, Kathryn. "Becoming Just Another Alphanumeric Code: Farmers' Encounters with the Literacy and Discourse Practices of Agricultural Bureaucracy at the Livestock Auction." *Situated Literacies: Reading and Writing in Context.* Ed. David Barton, Mary Hamilton, and Roz Ivanič. London: Routledge, 2000. 70–90. Print.

Keathley, Clarence R., and Donna M. Ham. "4-H Club Work in Missouri." *Missouri Historical Review* 71.2 (1977): 193–203. Print.

Kress, Cathann. "Twenty-First Century Learning after School: The Case of 4-H." *The Case for Twenty-First Century Learning*. Ed. Eric Schwarz and Ken Kay. San Francisco: Jossey-Bass/Wiley, 2006. 133–40. Print.

Moll, Luis C., and Norma Gonzalez. "Lessons from Research with Language-Minority Children." *Literacy: A Critical Sourcebook*. Ed. Ellen Cushman, Eugene Kintgen, Barry Kroll, and Mike Rose. New York: Bedford/St. Martin's, 2001. 156–71. Print.

Moore, Danny. "'To Make the Best Better': The Establishment of Girls' Tomato Clubs in Mississippi, 1911–1915." *Journal of Mississippi History* 63.2 (2001): 101–18. Print.

Orr, David. *Ecological Literacy: Education and the Transition to a Postmodern World*. Albany: State U of New York P, 1992. Print.

Peters, Scott J., and Paul A. Morgan. "The Country Life Commission: Reconsidering a Milestone in American Agricultural History." *Agricultural History* 78.3 (2004): 289–316. Print.

Purcell-Gates, Victoria. *Other People's Words: The Cycle of Low Literacy*. Cambridge, MA: Harvard UP, 1995. Print.

Reck, Franklin M. *The 4-H Story: A History of 4-H Club Work*. Chicago: National Committee on Boys and Girls Club Work, 1951. Print.

Rumsey, Suzanne. "Heritage Literacy: Adoption, Adaptation, and Alienation of Multimodal Literacy Tools." *College Composition and Communication* 60.3 (2009): 573–86. Print.

Soltow, Lee, and Edward W. Stevens. *Rise of Literacy and the Common School in the United States: A Socioeconomic Analysis to 1870*. Chicago: U of Chicago P, 1981. Print.

Wessel, Thomas R., and Marilyn Wessel. *4-H, an American Idea, 1900–1980: A History of 4-H*. Chevy Chase, MD: National 4-H Council, 1982. Print.

Young, Morris. *Minor Re/Visions: Asian American Literacy Narratives as a Rhetoric of Citizenship*. Carbondale: Southern Illinois UP, 2004. Print.

8

"They Make a Lot of Sacrifices": Religious Rhetorics in the Formation of the Mexican Rural Education System

Susan V. Meyers

> I really think people lose something when,
> instead of looking for self-development or
> professionalization, they just look for more stuff.
> —Secondary school director, Villachuato,
> a rural town in central western Mexico

Since the decade following the Mexican Revolution of 1910–20, primary and secondary education have become increasingly accessible in rural areas of Mexico. Despite this apparent increase in opportunity, however, teachers in many outlying areas remain baffled as to why more students aren't choosing to continue their education.[1] For instance, in the small town of Villachuato, drop-out rates remain high, and only a handful of students go on from ninth grade (the last year of mandatory education in Mexico) to high school. In contrast, many young people in Villachuato choose national or international migration as a means of increasing their earning potential. While this phenomenon is part of larger global forces (Grey and Woodrick 370), what particularly interests me in this chapter are local responses to young rural Mexicans' educative decisions.

Primarily, the two perceived areas of concern are (1) individuals' faulty choices about the best means of self-improvement, and (2) the damage that migration causes to the social fabric. As the secondary school director explained, he believes that the community members of Villachuato "just want more stuff: I have this, so I want that and that. So instead of trying to improve themselves, they just try to increase the things that they have. They don't try to build themselves intellectually, or in terms of knowledge. They should try to learn more, try to improve things. But they just look toward having more and more things." Comments like this suggest a partial impasse between communities like Villachuato and the teachers and schools that serve them. Whereas the teachers in Villachuato believe that formal education is the single best means of improving one's self and one's life chances, Villachuato citizens continue, in many cases, to choose other avenues.[2] What is the reason for this discrepancy in values? Why aren't young people in Villachuato choosing to professionalize? One cause, certainly, is the cumulative effect of a global market system (Grey and Woodrick 371). However, as this chapter suggests, another source of current frictions between rural Mexican communities and the schools that serve them are the particular historical circumstances that shaped the development of the Mexican public education system itself. In what follows, I will outline the principal stages of this process, explore commensurate teacher training programs, and suggest ways in which long-standing legacies of institutional power continue to shape the rhetorics and realities of the school experience in rural Mexico. I will also demonstrate the ways in which Mexican public schools emerged out of the nation's need first to create political allegiance and later to support economic development. As a result, I argue that Mexican schools, particularly in rural areas, are often more self-serving than attentive to local needs, and this discrepancy may well account for lowered motivation on the part of local community members, like those of Villachuato. However, through the use of traditional rhetorics that utilize religious themes of self-sacrifice and personal redemption to appeal to the values of rural culture, the *secretaria de educación publica* (secretary of public education), or SEP, does successfully garner a certain amount of support, most importantly through the young professionals who become teachers.

Literacy, Culture, and Identity: A Framework for Critical Response

In order to situate an analysis of the historical formation of the Mexican public education system and its contemporary impact on rural communities, I borrow from several related theories of literacy and education. To begin with, increasing numbers of literacy scholars agree with Brian Street's assertion that literacy is in fact ideological: "Literacy is a social practice, not simply a technical and neutral skill. . . . [I]t is always embedded in socially constructed epistemological principles. It is about knowledge: the ways in which people address reading and writing are themselves rooted in conceptions of knowledge, identity, and being" (78).

One implication of Street's logic is that formal manifestations of literacy, like schools, are always embedded with a specific agenda. That is, they are always working, either implicitly or explicitly, to promote the ideology that they reflect. The social institutions that determine these ideologies are, to borrow Deborah Brandt's terminology, the literacy *sponsors* that, in turn, shape and promote formal literacy. For instance, Brandt's analysis cites religion as the first sponsor that dominated schools in the United States. Later, however, the Church's influence was replaced by state interests, and later still by capitalism (28). Louis Althusser's theories take this analysis further to argue that ideology represents powerful, self-replicating ideas that are expressed in physical settings like schools (113). Similarly, Pierre Bourdieu asserts that formal education replicates cultural knowledge and, therefore, social standing ("New Capital" 19). These composite theories identify education as a vehicle for ideology, one that employs particular rhetorics to achieve the loyalty of its practioners but actually reinforces social inequity—and compliance with that inequity.

According to Bradley Levinson, an education scholar whose work focuses on identity politics in Mexican education, particularly in secondary schools, this loyalty is achieved through a process of identity transformation. While Levinson recognizes the important role that Mexican education plays to create a sense of nationalism, solidarity, and shared identity, he also believes that, particularly at higher levels of education, students are required to release the ties to their original community in order to adapt themselves to the community of educated society—a society that, as Bourdieu would argue, is steeped in cultural capital. In rural areas like those that both Levinson and I have worked in, however, this call to educated life is challenging for students as they find themselves torn between discourses: those of their schools, as opposed to those of their families and community (Levinson 216). Further, it is likewise true that the economic opportunities available in these rural areas are often not commensurate with higher levels of educational training (218). In order to make use of this training, then, the only option often available to these students is to migrate to urban centers, thereby finalizing the break with their home communities. While this phenomenon is, in many ways, congruent with the shift that Deborah Brandt describes as literacy moves from religious to state to commercial sponsorship, it is interesting that, in Mexico, older rhetorics grounded in the missionary origins of the colonization period endure. Further, it is likewise important to note the ways in which teachers, like students, are required to relinquish their home identities in order to support SEP's agenda and to employ the important religious rhetorics of self-sacrifice and personal salvation that carry this agenda forward.

Formal Education in Rural Mexico through the Revolution

While formal education traditions can be traced throughout Mesoamerica beginning with the Olmec civilization from 1500 B.C.E. to 150 C.E. (Reagan 92), the first external literacy sponsor was the Catholic Church. In conjunction with Spanish political colonization, religious schools were founded throughout contemporary Mexico as a means of spreading both the Catholic faith and the Spanish language. Moreover, while missionaries' core intention was religious conversion (Flores 12), general literacy instruction became necessary as they realized that, "era necesario enseñarlos primero a ser hombres y después de ser cristianos" [it was necessary first to teach them how to be men, and then how to be Christians] (Kobayashi 3). To this end, the missionary schools of sixteenth- and seventeen-century Mexico included basic lessons in reading and writing, but they likewise treated European handicrafts, animal husbandry, music, and literature (Flores 12). In this way, the goal was complete colonialization: to convert people not only to a new faith, but a new set of cultural customs and values. Further, the particular blend of religious orders that arrived in New Spain is likewise significant. Among the most important of these were the Dominicans, a highly authoritative order who were among the first to arrive, and the Jesuits, who worked extensively in rural areas and were interested in teaching practical reasoning and life skills (Martínez 13). Both of these influences would be later expressed in the creation of a public education system that, on the one hand, claims a pragmatic focus but that, on the other hand, maintains a highly centralized structure that often overlooks the needs present in individual rural sites.

The second major historical stage in Mexican education took place between the Independence movement (1810–1821) and the Revolution (1910–1920). During this transitional timeframe, the state became the custodian of education and established its goal of realizing universal education within Mexico. The most important figurehead of this era was Benito Juarez: a man of indigenous origin who eventually rose to take the presidency of his newly independent nation in 1858. Well aware of the importance of education to nation-building, Juarez declared education to be both a right and an obligation of all Mexican citizens (Martínez 15). Although schools were expanded under Juarez's leadership and subsequent presidencies, the new nation lacked the economic resources to extend education to its entire population. Part of the source of these economic difficulties was the continued influence of foreign interests. That is, although Mexico had won its political independence, European and American interests were still largely dominant in Mexican economics (Villegas 83). Among these factions, the Catholic Church itself still owned enough land to be able to wield strong political influence (Martínez 27). Even so, Juarez worked to separate church and state in many important social institutions, including education. However, educational growth was slow throughout Juarez's presidency and subsequent leadership during the nineteenth century. By the turn of the twentieth century, only half of the Mexican population had attended some form of schooling, and only 30 percent of Mexicans could read and write (Rockwell 307; Vaughan 138). Further, those who were educated under this system were primarily the elite, urban members of society (Bernardino 7). So, while public education existed between the wars, equal access to it did not.

The period following the Revolution, roughly 1920–30, represents the most important period in the formation of a formal system of public education in Mexico. Following the battle cries for "land and education" (Hughes 10), new leadership after the Revolution recognized, as Juarez had before them, the importance of a national education system. In 1945, SEP officials consulted by research delegates from the United States explained that "Illiteracy is one of the greatest obstacles to our goal of attaining common ideals for the different cultural groups that constitute our nation and to the achievement of economic and social well-being among our workers and farmers" (Federal Security Agency vii). Implicit in this statement is an assumption of the importance not only of cultural unity and economic development but also of political control. If illiteracy (i.e., the lack of reading and writing skills in Spanish, as opposed to indigenous literacy skills of any kind) was perceived as an obstacle to nation-building, the related assumption was that nationalism relies on a degree of both hierarchy and homogenization. According to Althusser's theory of ideological state apparatuses, schools in the capitalist system impart skills and culture, creating a homogenized yet stratified work force (87); and, as Pierre Bourdieu further outlines through his notion of *habitus*, a set of core values and behaviors that are internalized as symbolic social standing ("Social Space and Symbolic Space" 8). Both theorists identify the workings of social reproduction—Althusser via institutions and Bourdieu via social interactions—and they are, therefore, helpful to our understanding of the processes that students encounter in schools. Specifically, as students move through their formal education, they become a part of larger patterns of social reproduction as they learn both state allegiance, as well as acceptance of their social class.

This kind of enculturation began to take place in Mexico in 1921, when José Vasconcelos took charge of the newly reconstituted *secretaria de educación pública* (secretary of public education), or SEP, and began to design a national curriculum for use throughout the new nation (Schell qtd. in Hall 387). This work was not without its challenges, as two-thirds of the population still lived in rural areas, and 65 percent of Mexicans were illiterate (Ramírez 10). Moreover, the education system itself was still grossly underdeveloped, and there was no sustained means of training teachers: "In 1922, approx 100 untrained teachers were struggling to maintain a few federal rural schools" (Federal Security Agency vii). Even so, under the new constitution, primary education was made obligatory, and many new schools began to be constructed in rural areas. It was at this point that communities like Villachuato finally began to have access to at least a primary education, including basic reading, writing, and arithmetic skills. However, it is important to note that Vasconcelos's crusade toward education access, like Althusser's theory described above, was not altruistic. Indeed, the new state had a strong nationalizing agenda that it actualized in large part through the public schools.

In order to appreciate the role of this nationalizing project, it is important to understand the nature of the Mexican Revolution itself. The Revolution did not operate as a single, concentrated force, but rather as a series of localized conflicts and staged resistance efforts at the regional level. As such, the Revolution was a loosely connected collection of guerilla efforts, rather than a carefully staged war with a united front. The result was a liberated but very fragmented nation, and loyalties were most strongly felt at the regional level (Rockwell 303). One of the principal efforts in the aftermath of the war, then, was a movement to nationalize: Finally independent of both foreign political and economic control, Mexico had to pull together its identity and loyalties so as to build a new democracy and a sustainable domestic market. Congruent with Althusser's theory of schools as important political tools (103), the spread of public education in Mexico took on utmost importance: "The educators and anthropologists of the 1920s who articulated the ideal of the *Escuela Rural Mexicana* proposed a 'civilizing mission' to transform rural society" (Rockwell 304).

In the remainder of this chapter, I pay special attention to the period following the Revolution, both because it is historically important as the period during which Mexican education was formalized and because it is ideologically important to the way that this education system was spread. While I agree with Deborah Brandt's analysis of the shift in sponsorship from church to state in the United States, in Mexico the former's influence does not appear to have disappeared entirely. Rather, in order to build a new infrastructure and spread its nationalizing agenda, the Mexican government relied on familiar vehicles and rhetorics, particularly religious ones. Like the Jesuits and Dominicans before them, the new rural educators *were* a kind of missionary force—albeit with a new secular agenda and message. Indeed, as Vaughan suggests, this kind of strategy makes sense, as the influence of religion remained dominant up through the beginning of the twentieth century, such that loyalties, especially in more rural areas, remained tied to the Church and family (138). However, as formal education gradually centralized under the new government, education itself became increasingly migratory, such that young people—like rural youth in many contexts (Brooke)—were obliged to leave their home communities in order to seek the personal advancement that education implicitly offered, That is, because quite often no commercial employment options exist in areas of rural Mexico like Villachuato, becoming educated for a profession means sacrificing geographic proximity to one's family and home community. Therefore, in order to motivate people to pursue formal education, the newly formed SEP had to both normalize and glorify the process, which it did in part by employing religious rhetorics of self-sacrifice and personal salvation. In particular, these rhetorics prize the process of sacrificing one's identity affinity and geographic location within the home community in favor of pursuing formal education, which presumably improves one's personal satisfaction and professional opportunities. As I show later in this chapter, the rhetorics that rural educators still use to describe their careers, challenges, and goals is that of a missionary presence that aims to convert and "save" rural communities—even when the curriculum that these teachers advocate is not congruent with the community's actual needs.

A School without Walls: The Roots of Rural Education in Mexico

Following the Revolution, two of Mexico's principal needs were to develop an economic base and to unify a national consciousness. On both counts, education was an important medium that needed to be expanded—most notably in rural areas, where the majority of Mexicans still lived and few schools existed. However, there were at least two important issues to be dealt with regarding education: "The first problem that educational leaders of the post-Revolution period had to face was to select and train rural teachers; the second, and closely related, one was to decide what to teach" (Hughes 10). At the beginning of the 1920s, there was almost no formal rural schooling, and little to no teacher training in these areas. Further, in order to spread rural education, it was important to secure cooperation from rural communities themselves (Méndez 441). To this end, the new SEP office had to determine not only what things were important to teach people, but also what kind of curriculum and delivery modes these communities would accept.

In order to address these issues of school distribution and acceptance, José Vasconcelos administered a program to send professional teachers and practitioners out into rural communities to determine their needs and the kind of education that would best suit these needs (Ramírez 32). These groups of educators, then, had two principal goals: first to investigate communities' whereabouts, conditions, and needs; and second to begin basic instruction, so as to build an infrastructure of schools and teachers: "Supervising teachers, called *missioners* [italics mine], went out individually to work with those who were serving as teachers, to give support for the new schools, and to do all the things necessary to make the rural schools an institution which would actually teach the rural people new patterns of living" (Federal Security Agency). These teams of educators, called "cultural missions," worked on literacy classes for children and adults, teacher training for community leaders, and the creation of community infrastructures, including school buildings, drainage systems, and health services. These activities, particularly the building of schools and community centers, were completed with the help of the townspeople themselves. These centers were intended to serve all levels and interests of the community and became known as "the house of the people" (Hughes 11).

An important leader of this work, Rafael Ramírez was the product of one of the Porfirian normal schools of the late nineteenth century (Ramírez 22). In contrast to his own conservative training, however, Ramírez was strongly influenced by Marxist thought and particularly by Dewey's and Rousseau's conceptualizations of education. He supported, therefore, a vision of participative education focused on community needs. At the same time, he recognized the difficulty of designing localized programs in Mexico because of the nation's extreme cultural and topographical diversity (35). Even so, under Ramírez, the cultural missions—similar to the place-based model that Robert Brooke advocates—worked tirelessly to attend to local needs, and to take education out of the school building and into the fields and related workplaces, producing the foundation for later models of vocational and agricultural curricula. As such, he advocated "a school without walls": localized education that attends to specific community needs and works with individuals to help them solve their own problems (Hughes 16). In this way, Ramírez's pedagogy reflected his belief that economic and social advancement is intimately tied to education. In order to get ahead in life, Ramírez argued, rural citizens need to learn to think critically. That is, the goal of rural education for Ramírez was "que el hombre piensa en el *por qué* hace tal cosa, *para qué* debe hacerlo, y *a quien* beneficia con el productor de su trabajo" [that a person thinks about the *why* of a given thing, the question of *to what end* of doing it, and *who* benefits from the product of such work] (Bernardino 3).

Ramírez's efforts were successful in the sense that they helped create community interest in education: an important foundation for the broader federal project of delivering national curriculum. In contrast, while Ramírez's work with the cultural missions was likewise innovative and socially aware, these more liberal aspects of the project did not endure as revolutionary zeal waned. According to rural secondary school director Fernando Reyes, the grassroots energy of Ramírez's local efforts could not compete with the development of a larger, more organized, and politically powerful education system (personal communication). Discontinued in 1938, the cultural missions were largely replaced by another educational system that had been developing alongside them: the nation's normal schools. In essence, the cultural missions had functioned as traveling normal schools for a decade and a half. However, under the new, more stabilized government, it became increasingly possible to develop and deliver a uniform curriculum to the variety of urban and rural schools that had been built throughout the country. Indeed, by 1942, the curriculum at rural and urban normal schools had been synthesized into one model: a unified curricular model that more effectively served the nation's own ideology and agenda of civic loyalty and economic productivity. In this way, the attention to local issues in education disappeared from the Mexican consciousness, and becoming educated increasingly meant that young people were obliged to relocate to urban environments, much in the manner that Robert Brooke describes as "migratory education-as-usual." What is interesting to note, however, is the way in which both programs—first the cultural missions and later the normal schools themselves—relied on the same kinds of religious rhetorics, casting teachers time and again not simply as educational agents, but as important missionary representatives of a larger state agenda.

A Civilizing Mission: Teacher Training following the Revolution

The most difficult conquest, reports the SEP's self-authored history of public education in Mexico, "es la intelectual y moral de un pueblo entero. . . . El secreto está en la educación de las masas populares y el factor principal en las escuelas normales" [is that of the intellectual and moral fiber of the people. . . . The secret is in mass education, and the principal factor is the normal schools] (Méndez 430). Written in 1981, the SEP's consideration of its own origin betrays a strong awareness of the power of education to unite a nation and the importance of a work force that is willing to deliver the message. SEP found that workforce in its teachers—and it found the means of forming these teachers in a centralized system of normal schools. In this way, teachers became the evangelists for the "civilizing mission" of public education: they were trained under a specific orientation "to subordinate the three Rs to the betterment of rural life" (Rockwell 304). Moreover, by both internalizing and fostering the nation's new conceptualization of the educated person, these teachers likewise spread a new ideology commensurate with liberated Mexico's goal of unifying the nation through the development of "a cooperative, class-conscious, solitary peasantry" (Alan Knight, qtd. in

Rockwell 304). Normal schools are, therefore, an important component of the Mexican education system to understand—in part because of their particular post-Revolutionary history and in part because they are still the principal method used to train teachers. Rather than attending postsecondary classes in a university setting, aspiring teachers in Mexico attend four years of normal school training focused on the grade level they wish to teach: preschool (kindergarten), primary (1–6), or secondary (7–9). Thereafter, rather than applying for jobs directly, graduating teachers are assigned to a school based on the qualifications and needs of the teachers' union and SEP.

Based in part on foreign influences like John Dewey's progressive education models and in part on the existing Porfirian normal schools, the new generation of normal schools developed slowly, emerging first in urban centers and spreading gradually toward more rural areas until it became broad enough to replace the migratory "missionary" model of educational training. In rural areas in particular, these schools were important because they allowed people without prior access to formal teacher training to become professionalized. Moreover, given the geographic diversity of smaller communities, many of these schools were designed as boarding schools—a feature that had the added effect of removing students from their home communities long enough to reorient them toward a new value system (Rockwell 309). Congruent with Bradley Levinson's explanation of identity development discussed earlier, higher levels of education in Mexico require students to sacrifice the values and assumptions of their home community in exchange for a new identity based in the ideologies of the education system itself, which, in turn, responds to specific economic pressures (220). This is, he argues, the real process of becoming an educated person: adjusting one's identity, rather than acquiring a certain set of skills or knowledge (212). And, in fact, the early literacy goals of rural normal schools in Michoacán and elsewhere were formative, rather than comprehensive: "Más importante a la Escuela Normal el aspecto formativo que el informativo" [More important to a Normal School education is the formative aspect, rather than the informative] (Vela 6). Moreover, this identity shift occurs through exposure to the discourses present in the new environment: discourses concerning the nature and value of education. In the case of rural Mexicans attending post-Revolutionary normal school training, these discourses reflected the importance of education to personal development and social responsibility (Rockwell 304). However, because urban centers provide more varied economic opportunities, schools' values (i.e., the promise that formal education will lead to increased life chances) were more in tune with reality. In rural settings, on the other hand, the identity shift that young teachers made tended to be more jarring both because they were often physically removed from their home communities and because the values they learned as educators were sometimes incongruous with the realities in the communities that they had come from.

Recent data that I drew from teachers working today in rural areas like Villachuato and its neighboring town, Puruandiro, the county seat, demonstrate the enduring nature of this process of identity transformation. Of the teachers I interviewed,[3] all but two were from rural areas of Michoacán, and nearly all were trained at state-operated normal schools in the region. Likewise, nearly all of the teachers I interviewed came from the kind of large families (between five and nine siblings) that were common in this area up through the 1970s, and the majority of these families were led by stay-at-home mothers and fathers who worked either as *campesinos* in the fields, or as craftsmen (e.g., shoe maker). As a result of this reliance on a single wage earner, families often could not financially support their children's education. In many cases, teachers-to-be had to work at the same time as attending school, which meant that the process took longer. In other cases, they had to wait a period of time while another sibling used the family resources to become educated before pursuing their own studies. "There were so many of us, and not very many resources," the secondary school director in Puruandiro told me. "So, some of us got to study, and others of us had to rest. Once some of them had gotten through, they could help the others" (Meyers 25).

Once these young professionals finally obtained their teacher training, they did, as Bradley Levinson predicted, begin to identify more with their new, professional community than with their community of origin. The director in Puruandiro was, like so many educators in the area, among the first in his family to become educated. "My parents basically didn't study," he told me in a hushed voice:

> In those times, it was very difficult to do so. My father has told me that he went to primary school, and didn't quite finish. He just went to learn how to read and write, and that was sufficient. And my mother, the truth is it pains me to tell you this, but she doesn't know how to read or write [laughs, embarrassed]. And we're all professionalized [my siblings and I]. So, as you can see, she really worried about us—preparing us. Because she told us that her life experience was very difficult, and she wanted us to prepare ourselves for something better. To be able to defend ourselves. And the most important thing was to learn something. (qtd. in Meyers 25)

The juxtaposition of embarrassment and appreciation with which he narrates his story suggests an important tension in his loyalties. While he understands his parents' hardships and appreciates his mother's work to make possible a better life for her children, he is, at the same time, ashamed of his illiterate parentage. Having actualized their own hopes for him, he has reached a higher social level: a level which brings with it a new set of values, the most important of which is literacy itself. In this way, this school director's experience is an excellent example of the kind of identity shift that Bradley Levinson argues is part of the process of becoming an educated person. At the same time, it likewise suggests to me an enduring pattern of religious themes embedded in Mexican education. That is, having made the necessary sacrifices, educational professionals like this man believe that they have attained personal salvation through the realization of a professional life.

Indeed, these themes of sacrifice and redemption are the first evidence of a missionary-like rhetoric that endures in rural Mexican education. That is, achieving an education requires young people to sacrifice connections to their home community, but it also promises professional reward. Moreover, this kind of rhetoric was apparent not only in rural educators' stories of their own training, but likewise in their discussions of students. Describing the hardships of students from Villachuato who pursue their education at higher levels, the secondary school director admits that:

> I only know a few people who have their kids at the university in Morelia. Very few. Like four or five. And do you know what these kids do? They work—they work a lot. Waiters, shipping. All that. It's hard for them to study. That have to go and rent—they don't have houses. There are some student houses, and they're full of people. So, they go and they make a lot of sacrifices.

Implicit in this school director's conversation with me was his belief that this kind of hard work and self-sacrifice is *how it should be*: we should make sacrifices for education, he believes, most particularly because it offers us a better life. To this end, he spoke glowingly of the few students who have continued on, admiring their work ethic and the wisdom with which they have made their life choices. In a related vein, another teacher explained to me that there is much more hope for students now: "Well, the world is much more up-to-date now, you know. So it's not likely that kids will only go to primary school anymore. They're going to keep studying. And to get work. We have to study, right? To get work. To do better in life." With statements like these one would assume that formal education leads students to acquire professional jobs; however, there is no paid employment in Villachuato beyond agricultural day labor. Further, because the majority of the students with whom I spoke do not wish to leave their family and their town, the promise of education is incongruent with the values and life chances in Villachuato, and many townspeople remain unmotivated to prioritize formal education. At the same time, the assumption that education honorably involves self-sacrifice and personal reward is evidence of a continued association between education and religion that has characterized Mexican education through the colonial period and the cultural missions following the Revolution, and up through the current structure of SEP and its normal schools.

Conclusion

As stated earlier, one problem with rural Mexican teachers' belief that formal education is the single best means to self-improvement is that this paradigm, which emerged historically through Mexico's progression of literacy sponsors from the Catholic Church to the post-Revolution SEP, both masks the larger agendas at work in and around Mexican public education—national cohesion and capitalist development—and often functions as an empty promise for local communities. As mentioned above, youth from Villachuato who do pursue a professional track are not able to return to their communities, for lack of employment. In an area that prizes familial relationships and geographic closeness (Valdes 203), many young people are hesitant to permanently relocate in order to pursue education and professionalization. Further, the fact that teachers do not sufficiently pay heed to this complexity of values and life choices further alienates students and possibly decreases their scholastic motivation. It seems likely, then, that the reason for school desertion—or young people's decisions to pursue temporary migration over permanent professional relocation—has as much to do with the Mexican rural school system and its connection to an economic model that doesn't support it as it does with students' autonomous motivations.

In our work as literacy scholars and practitioners in the United States, these lessons of conflict between students and their schools, drawn from the historical formation and current conditions of education in rural Mexico, extend into further implications. First, the traces of religious rhetorics that remain in rural Mexican schools suggest that literacy sponsors, rather than competing and replacing each other (Brandt 70), may develop more cumulatively, with each new development stage of sponsorship drawing upon or utilizing former sponsors' values, as through the use of religious rhetorics to promote a form of education that supports capitalist enterprise. Second, the continued use of these same rhetorics suggests the ways in which social institutions like schools downplay the ideological interests that they represent in favor of working persuasively to draw increased support from their members. That is, by employing religious messages of self-sacrifice and redemption to describe formal education, school leaders glorify formal education and deemphasize its potential connection to social reproduction and hierarchies. Third, however, this strategy can backfire when community members recognize that the relative "salvation" that formal education promises asks them to sacrifice geographic proximity to their family and home community—a sacrifice that, in many cases, they are not willing to make. In this sense, if we want to increase school participation and satisfaction in rural areas of Mexico or elsewhere, it is important to be frank and realistic in our discussions of the opportunities and limitations of formal schooling as an ideological institution, and to create, as much as possible, a place-based curriculum that attends authentically to a given community's actual values and needs. Whether through applied curriculum like the cultural missions model that followed the Mexican Revolution, or through liberatory programs that have evolved elsewhere in Latin America, it is important to consider local needs and priorities and to work in conjunction with them in order to develop the educational models that will better serve and motivate local community participation.

Notes

1. A recent 9-month field study in the small town of Villachuato, Mexico, revealed that significant numbers of students continue to drop out of secondary school, or they end their formal education after ninth grade, in order to begin work—often in the United States. Data for this study were gathered from August 2007–May 2008 and included seventy-five hours of classroom observations as well as sixty-five interviews with teachers, administrators, parents, and students. The town of Villachuato was selected for its position in the state of Michoacán, which historically has had one of the highest rates of outbound migration in Mexico.

2. Because the economic base in Villachuato is 100 percent small-scale farming, there is no commercial entity available to employ community members. Therefore, anyone seeking employment beyond local, family-operated farming or small businesses must relocate.

3. Interviews for this study were conducted with school administrators and teachers at the kindergarten, primary, secondary, high school, and college levels.

Works Cited

Althusser, Louis. "Ideology and Ideological State Apparatuses." *Lenin and Philosophy and Other Essays*. Trans. Ben Brewster. New York: Monthly Review, 2001. 85–126. Print.

Bernardino, Marta G. *Educación no formal en el medio rural de Mexico*. Mexico City: Central Nacional de Productividad de México, 1978. Print.

Bourdieu, Pierre. "The New Capital." *Practical Reason: On the Theory of Action*. Oxford: Polity, 1998. 19–34. Print.

———. "Social Space and Symbolic Space." *Practical Reason: On the Theory of Action*. Oxford: Polity, 1998. 1–19. Print.

Brandt, Deborah. *Literacy in American Lives*. Cambridge: Cambridge University Press, 2001. Print.

Brooke, Robert. "Voices of Young Citizens: Rural Citizenship, Schools, and Public Policy." *Reclaiming the Rural*. Ed. Kim Donehower, Charlotte Hogg, and Eileen Schell. Carbondale: Southern Illinois UP, 2011. Print.

Federal Security Agency. *Report on the Cultural Missions of Mexico*. Washington, DC: U.S. Office of Education, 1945. Print.

Flores, Jesús Romero. *Estudios históricos*. 2nd ed. Mexico City: B. Costa-Amic: 1966. Print.

Grey, Mark A., and Anne C. Woodrick. "Unofficial Sister Cities: Meatpacking Labor Migration between Villachuato, Mexico, and Marshalltown, Iowa." *Human Organization* 61.4 (Winter 2002): 364–76. Print.

Hall, Anne-Marie. "Keeping *La Llorona* Alive in the Shadow of Cortés: What an Examination of Literacy in Two Mexican Schools Can Teach U.S. Educators." *Bilingual Research Journal* 30.2 (2006): 385–406. Print.Hughes, Lloyd H. *The Cultural Mission Programme*. Paris: UNESCO, 1950. Print.

Kobayashi, José María Kazuhiro. "La conquista educativa de los hijos de Asís."*La educación en la historia de México*. Ed. Josefina Zoraida Vasquez. Mexico City: El Colegio de México, 1999. 1–28. Print.

Levinson, Bradley. "Social Difference and Schooled Identity at a Mexican *Secundaria*." *The Cultural Production of the Educated Person: Critical Ethnographies of Schooling and Local Practice*. New York: State U of New York P, 1996. 211–38. Print.

Martínez, Raúl Bolaños. "Orígenes de la educación pública en México." *Historia de la educación pública en México*. Ed. Fernando Solana, Raúl Cardiel Reyes, and Raúl Bolaños. Mexico City: Secretaría de Educación Pública Fondo de Cultura Económica, 1981. 11–40. Print.

Méndez, Martha Eugenia Curiel. "La educación normal." *Historia de la educación pública en México*. Ed. Fernando Solana, Raúl Cardiel Reyes, and Raúl Bolaños. Mexico City: Secretaría de Educación Pública Fondo de Cultura Económica, 1981. 426–62. Print.

Meyers, Susan V. "So You Don't Get Tricked: Counter-Narratives of Literacy in a Rural Mexican Community." *Community Literacy Journal* 3.2 (2009): 19–35. Print.

Ramírez, Rafael. *La Escuela rural Mexicana*. Mexico City: SEP, 1982. Print.

Reagan, Timothy. "Training 'Face and Heart': The Mesoamerican Educational Experience." *Non-Western Educational Traditions: Alternative Approaches to Educational Thought and Practice*. Mahwah, NJ: Lawrence Erlbaum, 2000. 91–118. Print.

Reyes, Fernando. Personal communication. 20 May 2008.

Rockwell, Elsie. "Keys to Appropriation: Rural Schooling in Mexico." *The Cultural Production of the Educated Person: Critical Ethnographies of Schooling and Local Practice*. Ed. Bradley A. Levinson and Dorothy Holland. New York: State U New York P, 1996. 301–24. Print.

Street, Brian. "What's 'New' in New Literacy Studies? Critical Approaches to Literacy in Theory and Practice." *Current Issues in Comparative Education* 5.2 (2003): 77–89. Print.

Valdés, Guadalupe. *Con Respeto: Bridging the Distances between Culturally Diverse Families and Schools; An Ethnographic Portrait*. New York: Teachers College, 1996. Print.

Vaughan, Mary K. "Women, Class, and Education in Mexico, 1880–1928." *Latin American Perspectives* 4.1 (Winter/Spring 1977): 135–42. Print.

Vela, Arqueles. *Escuela superior de Michoacán*. Mexico City: Organización y Funcionamiento de las Escuelas Normales Superiores, 1975. Print.

Villegas, Daniel Cosío, et al. *A Compact History of Mexico*. Trans. Marjory Mattingly Urquidi. Mexico City: El Colegio de México, 1995. Print.

Section III
Pedagogies

9

Voices of Young Citizens: Rural Citizenship, Schools, and Public Policy

Robert Brooke

> Education's proper use is to enable citizens to live lives that are economically, politically, socially, and culturally responsible.
> —Wendell Berry, *Citizenship Papers*

> The new idea here is that we're not preparing students for tomorrow, we're preparing them to solve the problems of today. You don't learn about ecology so you can help protect nature in the future. You learn so you can make a difference here and now.
> —David Sobel, *Place-Based Education*

Rural communities need a new kind of citizen, and rural education ought to help shape such citizens. In an era of rural depopulation, rural school consolidation, rural out-migration of able youth, and federal farm policies that privilege distant corporate agribusinesses over sustainable family farms, the need for a new kind of rural citizen has never been more pronounced. Citizenship, for rural people, increasingly needs to mean more than voting, more than serving in the volunteer fire department, more than paying taxes that support the common good, more than signing petitions to protest the allocation of those taxes when they don't support initiatives you individually support. Instead, if rural communities are to survive into the next century as places where vibrant, thriving populaces can live well and grow, then rural citizenship needs to become more active, rhetorically effective, and politically savvy.

Nancy Welch, in her polemical article "Living Room: Teaching Public Writing," suggests the term "rhetorical space" for this new kind of more active citizenship. She writes:

> *Rhetorical space*—that is, public space with the potential to operate as a persuasive public sphere—is created not through well-intentioned civic planning or through the application of a few sound and reasonable rhetorical rules of conduct. Ordinary people *make* rhetorical space through concerted, often protracted struggle for visibility, voice, and impact against powerful interests that seek to deny visibility, voice, and impact. (477)

Welch suggests that "persuasive public" action is a key element to citizenship in our era, and that making "rhetorical space" for such action may well be a critical skill we all need to develop as citizens. For her, this skill is key because we live in a time when "powerful interests" seek to deny that space to average citizens like you, me, or Nancy herself. While Welch's immediate context is a semi-rural college town in Vermont, I suspect most rural people will see their own situation represented in her concepts. Across the nation, many rural citizens see themselves with a chronic need for persuasive public action, for "rhetorical space" for making their lives and experiences and viewpoints visible. And many rural citizens see themselves opposed by "powerful interests" seeking to deny visibility. To cite just two national examples, the issues facing rural communities are denied visibility in both educational policy and food politics. According to the 2007 *Why Rural Matters* report of the Rural School and Community Trust:

> *Rural students in urban states are out of sight, out of mind.* The states where rural education is most notably underperforming (that is, the state's performance ranks worse than its socioeconomic challenges would suggest it should) are predominantly non-rural states on the East or West coast where the rural population is "out of sight, out of mind," including, among others, California and Maryland. (Johnson and Strange ii)

Similarly, Michael Pollan's best-selling *The Omnivore's Dilemma* emerges from the denied visibility of the machinations of the food industry. As he puts it:

> What is perhaps most troubling, and sad, about industrial eating is how thoroughly it obscures all these relationships and connections. To go from the chicken to the Chicken McNugget is to leave this world in a journey of forgetting that could hardly be more costly. But forgetting, or not knowing in the first place, is what the industrial food chain is all about, the principal reason it is so opaque. (10)

As I write this from Lincoln, Nebraska, in winter 2009, my rural state is reeling from a court decision that found our Family Farm Act unconstitutional.

Certain "powerful interests" were able to persuade the regional judicial system that our state's policy of requiring some member of the owner's family to be in residence on agricultural property was discriminatory, opening the door in Nebraska to extended absentee, corporate landownership. Here in Nebraska, we certainly could benefit from more citizens who can *make* persuasive public rhetorical space. I expect and believe other areas of the rural United States could benefit from such citizens as well. (See chapter 13 in this volume, for additional analysis.)

And the additional problem is this: education, as dominantly practiced, isn't set up to help rural youth develop the skills and experience required to make persuasive public rhetorical space. As Paul Gruchow, Lisa Knopp, and others have argued, mainstream education in the United States is predominately set up to encourage talented rural youth to imagine their lives elsewhere (see also chapter 8 in this volume). Gruchow writes:

> These are the lessons we teach our rural children today: that their parents were expendable and that their duty is to abandon their dreams and to become cogs in the industrial machine. Here is another message we give them, in ways both subtle and direct: if they expect to amount to anything, they had better leave home. . . . A friend of mine who teaches at a rural university says that the institution ought frankly to offer a class called "How to Migrate." (98)

Lisa Knopp concurs, describing her own rural education this way:

> I saw Burlington as the end of the world where nothing ever had happened or ever would. Certainly, what I learned in school reinforced, perhaps created, this attitude. American history seldom happened in my part of America; world history never happened in my part of the world. Since local history wasn't valued and thus wasn't taught (or vice versa), I learned little about where I was from and what it meant to be shaped by such a place. . . . Neither did I understand that stories about home were stories about me. My lack of imagination banished me from my place of origin. . . . If I had internalized the stories before my decision-making time, I would have been more ingenious and receptive: I would have found a way to stay where I belong. (8–9)

As these two essayists make clear, mainstream education is partly responsible for the decline of rural communities. As predominately practiced, education points elsewhere: to history happening in other parts of the world, to migration as the means of personal advancement in the corporate industrial complex, to an ineffective form of citizenship.

These essayists' claims about education teaching migration are made concrete by the U.S. Census figures on "net migration change" in rural areas. (Net migration is calculated by subtracting the number of people who migrated out of an area from the number of people who migrated into that same area.) For instance, while the current estimates for 2000–2007 show the United States as a whole growing by almost 8 million net migration, in the same time period the largely rural Midwest is estimated to have shrunk by over 380,000 people. For my state of Nebraska, the loss in net migration is tied directly to young adult migration in the 14–29 age range—over half of the people who left our state in the period covered by the last fully reported census (1995–2000) fell in this range. The clear implication is that, at the end of their school careers whether secondary or collegiate, many more young adults leave the area than stay. (Carlson, Hartmann, and Thompson 2).

Place-Based Education: Toward Effective Citizenship

An alternative to migratory education-as-usual is place-based education, an approach to education that centers learning in local issues, both cultural and geographical. David Sobel offers a succinct definition:

> Place-based education is the process of using the local community and environment as a starting point to teach concepts in language arts, mathematics, social studies, science, and other subject areas across the curriculum. Emphasizing hands-on, real-world learning experiences, this approach to education increases academic achievement, helps students develop stronger ties to their community, enhances students' appreciation for the natural world, and creates a heightened commitment to serving as active, contributing citizens. Community vitality and environmental quality are improved through the active engagement of local citizens, community organizations, and environmental resources in the life of the school. (7)

As Sobel describes it, place-based education strives to locate learning in the immediate environments (cultural and natural) that surround the school and community. Such education is "hands-on" and "real-world" because the learners' actual homes and communities are integrated into learning.

From the immediate relevancy of the local community, place-based education then "spirals out" to regional, national, even international issues and ideas (as Paul Theobald describes in *Teaching the Commons*). In fact, once a classroom starts attending to local issues, it's almost impossible not to "spiral out" to wider issues and ideas, because local reality is almost always shaped by much more widespread cultural, natural, and economic forces. As Sarah Robbins, director of the Keeping and Conserving American Communities program in Georgia, explains, local community issues are always embedded in the widespread cultural history that produced them:

> In all these cases, students and their teachers have positioned their study of local communities within a larger cultural context. For instance, they critiqued the competing visions of "America" embedded in a suburban city council's conflict with shop owners setting up Spanish-language signs. Similarly, they researched competing issues of ownership in Atlanta newspaper accounts of a Cherokee tribesman's moving "back" to reclaim land marked off long ago as a state park. These students made connections between shifting American cultural formations and daily community life. (Robbins and Dyer 16)

In making connections between large-scale "shifting cultural formations" and the local realities of "daily community life," place-based education thus helps learners begin to understand the persuasive public "rhetorical spaces" that surround them. In addition, for most place-based educators, a significant part of classroom work involves finding public opportunities outside the school for disseminating student thinking. Foxfire, the Appalachian-region program that has been enacting place-based education since the late 1960s, has made this stretch to audiences for student work outside of the classroom a component of two of their eleven Core Principles:

> Principle 6. Connections between the classroom work, the surrounding communities, and the world beyond the communities are clear. Course content is connected to the community in which the learners live. Learners' work will "bring home" larger issues by identifying attitudes about and illustrations and implications of those issues in their home communities.

> Principle 7. There is an audience beyond the teacher for learner work. It may be another individual, or a small group, or the community, but it is an audience the learners want to serve or engage. The audience, in turn, affirms the work is important, needed and worth doing. (Starnes et al. iv)

Foxfire, in its post-2000 form, is no longer simply a compendium of quaint rural practices compiled by high school students. Instead, the current Foxfire program, available to teachers across the United States, aims at the development of active citizens by connecting the curriculum to the community and by insuring that community members are actively involved in responding to learners' work. (See chapter 6 in this volume for another example.)

Here in Nebraska, in our place-conscious programs of the Nebraska Writing Project, we have similarly made the development of active citizens one of our core guiding principles. As I explained in the introduction to *Rural Voices*:

Place-conscious education is aimed at a certain kind of citizenry. . . . Place-conscious citizens are locally active, engaged in community decision making for their region through their work, schools, local government, and civic organizations. Place-conscious education thus provides an alternative to the focus of mainstream education on the creation of migratory, displaced citizens, equipped with marketable abstract skills and knowledge but lacking a sense of living well in local community. (Brooke 13)

In short, place-based educators relate their work directly to the citizenship issues facing rural communities. If curricular projects can be centered in local community issues, and if learners' work on these projects can actually contribute to public discussion of those issues, then education will become a place where learners can develop the abilities necessary to become a new kind of citizen. School can be a place where learners practice, develop, and engage in the creation of "rhetorical space" on the real work facing their communities and themselves.

One Place-Based Project for Developing Rhetorical Space: Voices of Young Citizens

If Nancy Welch is right about "rhetorical space" as a new need for citizens, then what might education look like if classes sought to create "public space with the potential to operate as a persuasive public sphere"? How might young, future citizens in rural classrooms learn to engage in the creation of "rhetorical space"? These, and related questions about the problems besetting rural Nebraska communities, guided a team of five rural public school teachers in a year-long partnership with Nebraska Educational Telecommunications-Television during 2005–6. The "Voices of Young Citizens" project set out to discover how school-age youth in rural communities might address the same issues faced by their community's adults when offered a "rhetorical space" on Nebraska Educational Television.

In a nutshell, "Voices of Young Citizens" allowed five classes of rural youth to work with NET-Television videographers to produce video segments that addressed rural issues crucial to them. These video segments were collectively broadcast on NET Television's Statewide program June 2, 2006, and DVDs of the program were shown at open houses in the host communities later that month. The video segments remained available through NET Television's website at www.net.nebraska.org/extras/statewide/. The partnership provided rural youth in these five classrooms with:

- Access to the same "persuasive public space" that their community elders had used during the 2005 four-part "Saving Small Towns" Statewide program;

- The opportunity to address the same set of issues facing rural communities that their community elders had addressed; and
- Guidance from professionals in crafting their video segments for the "rhetorical space" of public television.

Working from place-conscious educational principles, these five classes each (1) identified an issue crucial to their rural community, (2) conducted local research (interviews, archival study, writing, and photography) to understand that issue and craft a response to it, and (3) created, with the help of NET-Television, a 5–8 minute video segment for a statewide audience. The five classes and their issues were:

- Albion High School senior class (Ellen Kohtz, teacher) profiled dwindling economic opportunities for their families in north central Nebraska;
- Aurora Elementary School fifth grade class (Amy Wilson, teacher) explored the nature of community in their central Nebraska town;
- Cedar Bluffs High School junior class (Robyn Dalton, teacher) profiled their eastern Nebraska community's reliance on the overused Platte River;
- Heartland Community Schools: Henderson/Bradshaw's senior class (Sharon Bishop, teacher) explored rural depopulation and what elements of rural life are currently vanishing in their central Nebraska community;
- Ogallala Middle School's eighth grade class (Dixie DeTuerk, teacher) explored the drought affecting Nebraska's Lake McConaughy reservoir in relation to water usage and economic controversies across the Great Plains.

Building the "Voices of Young Citizens" Partnership: A Brief Narrative

The "Voices of Young Citizens" project came about through a three-way collaboration between NET-TV, the Nebraska Writing Project (NeWP), and the Nebraska Humanities Council (NHC). All three organizations have a long history of place-based work in video and radio journalism (NET-TV), school programs (NeWP), and civic humanities outreach (NHC). All three have worked together on other programs over the past thirty years.

In spring 2005, NET-TV producer William Kelly approached the Nebraska Humanities Council with an idea. NET-TV had just completed filming a series with adult statewide leaders exploring the question of the survival of rural communities in Nebraska. This series would be broadcast in October 2005 as four half-hour segments of NET-TV's Statewide program under the collective title "Saving Small Towns." The series emphasized the challenges facing rural Nebraskan communities to maintain their population in an era of economic downturn and outmigration of rural youth. William Kelly hoped to follow up this series with some profiles of Nebraska rural youth, as a set of human interest stories on the people most affected by the survival or demise of small towns. Since NET-TV had collaborated with Nebraska Humanities Council on video projects in the past, Kelly hoped to collaborate again.

Over the past decade, the Nebraska Humanities Council had helped fund several Nebraska Writing Project Rural Institutes on place-based education for kindergarten-through-twelfth-grade teachers across the state. Consequently, NHC put William Kelly in touch with me, as director of the Nebraska Writing Project. NHC believed teachers from the Nebraska Writing Project could provide more than Kelly expected: school-age learners who were already active addressing adult issues in their communities. The NeWP helped Kelly select five teachers from across the state, all with several years' experience developing place-conscious curricula in their schools. During the spring, the three agencies worked out a plan for the program, with NET-TV providing telecommunications expertise, NeWP providing place-based classes and teachers, and NHC providing much of the funding for the partnership. Over summer 2005 and the following academic year 2005–6, the participants developed the program.

The "Rhetorical Space" of Voices of Young Citizens

When given a chance to create their own "rhetorical space" for public television, what kind of persuasive, public action do young people create? To provide an extended example for this chapter, I will focus on the video segment produced by the seniors at Albion Public Schools, a community of nearly 2,000 in north central Nebraska. Six years earlier, when teacher Ellen Kohtz had the same group of students as sixth graders, the children had explored the economic opportunities in Albion. In the year 2000, their class projects had focused on their fathers' employment and the roles of those jobs in the community. This earlier project created a pastiche of all the children's family job descriptions. Collectively, the class and community needed to do the mental work to build connections among and between the individual stories in order to see the wider fabric of their rural place. But in 2005–6 during the "Voices of Young Citizens" project, these same students were now seniors and could make the connections themselves. In fact, the issue of economic opportunity was personal for most of the class. Individually, they were facing the choice of what to do after high school (and the issues of outmigration that choice brings). Collectively, they were aware that several of their sixth-grade classmates were no longer in Albion schools because their fathers' jobs had ended and the families had moved away.

The students' issue of net migration loss and economic opportunity is the same issue profiled by the University of Nebraska–Lincoln's Bureau of Business Research in their 2007 article "Brain Drain in Nebraska." This study compared net migration in the students' home town of Albion to eight similarly sized small rural cities in Colorado, Minnesota, Oklahoma, Kansas, Kentucky, Missouri, Indiana and New Mexico. Seven of the studied cities had experienced significant net migration loss (five with 10 percent or greater), while the two cities with net migration gains showed gains of less than 1 percent. Of the studied cities, Albion had experienced the largest net migration loss: 16.36 percent (Carlson, Hartmann, and Thompson 6). In short, the issue selected by the Albion seniors (1) was also identified as crucial by the state's business community, and (2) fits into the national pattern of rural net migration loss.

The Albion seniors worked with NET-TV videographers to address this issue of net migration loss by focusing on their own relationship to their family's work. Their video segment was structured around essays by three students, each with generations-deep local roots ("Voices of Young Citizens," Albion segment). One senior was the son of established area ranchers; one the daughter of a long line of farmers; and one the son of the grain elevator operator. Their essays emphasize their generational pride in family place, the historically changing needs of rural businesses, and their own coming choices after high school graduation.

Alex Wolf's essay on his family's cattle ranch is the most upbeat segment of the three. Framed by opening and closing shots of Alex in the field with family cattle, his essay celebrates the family's business success since the 1890s and his plan to return to run the business after college. Using a sequence of historical photos, Alex's essay describes the founding of the ranch by two brothers (one Alex's great-grandfather) who emigrated from Germany in the 1890s; the expansion of the business by his grandfather and granduncle who combined their talents as rancher and Harvard-educated lawyer; and his own commitment to continuing the business after his turn at college. The essay emphasizes continuity through historical change.

By contrast, Laura Maricle's essay on her family's farm emphasizes the emotional and familial complexity of changes in agriculture during the same century. The Maricle family farm, like the Wolf ranch, has a generations-deep history in Boone County, and the family expects it to continue. But, unlike Alex, whose family position as inheriting son secures his future place in that business, Laura's essay is tinged with the knowledge of loss. Her segment, for instance, ends with a complicated image of her lifting one of her elder brother's two toddlers. Her voice-over describes, in almost the same breath, that the farm is changing as the young folks move away, while, at the same time, through her brother and his offspring "there will always be Maricle men on this land." Her gentle awareness of both the continuity and limited opportunity of the family farm adds poignancy to her essay. As her voice-over reads her words, the camera shows her interacting with the buildings, livestock, equipment, landscape, and people, documenting a sequence of choices to divest the family farm of certain operations as the cost of continuing them became more and more prohibitive. One shot shows Laura and her grandfather inside the now-empty dairy barn on her family farm, examining the now-unused equipment, while her voice-over recounts her grandfather's complex decisions to sell the last dairy cows. (Laura's segment was aired a few months earlier and separately from the rest of the video segments, as a human interest story and advance trailer for the whole program.)

Patrick Koch's segment, like Laura's, emphasizes the complex emotional terrain of rural employment possibilities. In his segment, the camera focuses on his father at work inside the Cargill grain elevator, while Patrick's voice-over describes his changing understanding of the nature of that work. Patrick connects his childhood memory of his father's changing work hours to his current knowledge of corn pricing and harvests. He ponders what Cargill's decision to close the grain elevator and instead open an ethanol plant will mean for his father. With typical midwestern understatement, he emphasizes that there are two sides to everything, and that some folks are hopeful that the new plant will mean new jobs while others decry the increased truck traffic and smell that will affect the city. (And Patrick, writing in 2005–6, couldn't know that Cargill would be considering closing the ethanol plant itself in 2009, as I write this article.) Patrick's segment is noticeably silent on the question of his own future employment choices, emphasizing instead simply the value of hard work that he has learned from his father.

Taken together, while all three seniors are upbeat about their personal future and committed to their family's continued presence in this part of Nebraska, they are also very clear that current economic and agricultural polices work against those commitments. The Albion segment, thus, claims some rhetorical space as a call to action, as a deeply-felt appeal to alter the economic and agricultural paths that rural Nebraskans now must tread.

Central to all three Albion seniors' episodes is the rhetorical strategy of identification, in the Burkean sense of creating a shared common interest through which an audience might "identify with" a rhetor, even across differences, and thereby be moved to action (*Rhetoric of Motives*). The Albion seniors craft their stories so that their families' experiences can represent wider patterns in history and community. Alex Wolf's homage of his entrepreneurial, immigrant ancestors allows rural viewers to celebrate the practical intelligence of rural citizens who have confronted and overcome challenges. Laura Maricle's and Patrick Koch's sections dramatize, through their fathers' lives, the consequences of making certain choices in response to agricultural and economic policy. All three segments place before their viewers certain public controversies (for which, in Patrick's words, "there are two sides"), using their families' stories as representative of the effects of choosing one set of actions rather than another. The family stories thus have what we might call representative force: the seniors speak for others like them in calling for particular resolution of policy debates, and craft their segments so that many viewers can imagine themselves in that group of "others like them" who are being affected.

There is some evidence that the Albion seniors' segment did in fact help create a wider conversation about these issues. About a month after the first broadcast of her segment ("Albion"), Laura Maricle was invited to read her essay as part of the groundbreaking ceremony for a new Heritage Center at the Homestead National Monument outside of Beatrice, Nebraska. As captured by the NET-TV videographers ("Homestead Groundbreaking"), this ceremony placed Laura at the podium next to Senator Chuck Hagel (R-NE), historians, and National Parks Service dignitaries in a public forum devoted to rethinking the historical Homestead Act. While the original Homestead Act has, of course, long been inactive (and is a source of controversy for social and environmental historians of the region), the questions of how government policy promotes or inhibits rural livelihood endure. Senator Hagel's presence at the groundbreaking ceremony, for instance, was linked to his cosponsoring of the 2003 New Homestead Act, a proposal to address rural depopulation by providing federal incentives for jobs, housing, education, and health care in specific rural areas. (The 2003 New Homestead Act was an entirely different proposal than the 2008 New Homestead Act, which addressed the national mortgage and loan crisis.) Laura Maricle's presence at this ceremony suggests that the work of the Albion seniors has increased their abilities to craft rhetorical space.

Citizenship Now, Citizenship in the Future

The "Voices of Young Citizens" project is, of course, just one year-long project from five rural schools in Nebraska. Yet I suggest that this type of project is important for developing the kinds of citizenship we most need. David Sobel, in the epigraph from *Place-Based Education* that starts this essay, points out that the issues that face our youth face them now: "we're not preparing students for tomorrow, we're preparing them to solve the problems of today" (12). Our experience working with Nebraska youth in "Voices of Young Citizens" indicates that our young people are well aware of the "problems of today" that beset them. What they are less aware of is how to engage the citizenship work that might allow them to address these problems. If Nancy Welch is right that the crucial task facing citizens in the coming decade will be the creation of persuasive, public rhetorical spaces for open debate and action, then schools need to provide ever more opportunities for the creation of rhetorical space.

Programs like "Voices of Young Citizens" allow youth the hands-on, real-world experience of crafting public rhetorical spaces. Our experience developing this program in Nebraska suggests that schools, communities, and public service agencies are eager to engage in such work and eager to form partnerships to promote it.

Works Cited

Berry, Wendell. *Citizenship Papers*. Washington, DC: Shoemaker and Heard, 2003. Print.

Brooke, Robert, ed. *Rural Voices: Place-Conscious Education and the Teaching of Writing*. New York: Teachers College, 2003. Print.

Burke, Kenneth. *A Rhetoric of Motives*. Berkeley: U of California P, 1969. Print.

Carlson, Steve, Hannah Hartmann, and Eric Thompson, "Brain Drain in Nebraska: What Do the Data Show?" *Business in Nebraska* Nov. 2008, 1–7. Print.

Gruchow, Paul. *Grassroots: The Universe of Home*. Minneapolis: Milkweed, 1995. Print.

Knopp, Lisa. *Field of Vision*. Iowa City: U of Iowa P, 1996. Print.

Johnson, Jerry, and Marty Strange. *Why Rural Matters, 2007: The Realities of Rural Education Growth*. Arlington, VA: Rural School and Community Trust, October 2007. Print.

"Homestead Groundbreaking." Prod. William Kelly. NET-TV. 28 Apr. 2006. Television.

"Saving Small Towns." Prod. Perry Stoner. 4 parts. Statewide. NET-TV. 7–28 Oct. 2005. Television.

"Voices of Young Citizens." Prod. William Kelly. 5 parts. Statewide. 2 June 2006 . NET-TV, NeWP, NHC. 2 June 2006. Television.

Pollan, Michael. *The Omnivore's Dilemma*. New York: Penguin, 2007. Print.

Robbins, Sarah, and Mimi Dyer, eds. *Writing America: Classroom Literacy and Public Engagement*. New York: Teachers College, 2005. Print.

Sobel, David. *Place-Based Education: Connecting Communities and Classrooms*. Great Barrington, MA: Orion Society, 2004. Print.

Starnes, Bobby Ann, Angela Carone, and Cynthia Paris. *From Thinking to Doing: Constructing a Framework to Teach Mandates through Experience-Based Learning*. Mountain City, GA: Foxfire Fund, 1999. Print.

Theobald, Paul. *Teaching the Commons: Place, Pride, and the Renewal of Community*. Boulder, CO: Westview, 1997. Print.

Welch, Nancy. "Living Room: Teaching Public Writing in a Post-Publicity Era." *College Composition and Communication* 56.3 (Feb. 2005): 470–92. Print.

10

The Arkansas Delta Oral History Project:
Understanding Poverty through Literacy Outreach

Christian Z. Goering, David A. Jolliffe, Laine Gates,
Kelly Riley, and Hillary Swanton

In Arkansas, as in many places, *rural* and *poor* are de facto synonyms. In Arkansas, the dual forces of mechanization and globalization have combined to convert an agricultural economy once based on family farms— an economy where it was possible to establish a comfortable, middle-class existence—to an agribusiness economy where large corporations serve as absentee landlords and where relatively few landowners prosper by sharing in the agribusiness profits while the formerly subsisting middle class largely disappears.

When an economic shift like this happens, schools suffer. Businesses and industries shut down and leave; populations decrease; tax revenues decline; teachers' salaries lag behind those in more prosperous districts; schools are hard-pressed to offer a full range of courses, let alone such co-curricular activities as plays, student newspapers, literary magazines, and speech and debate teams that enrich students' "literacy lives."

In such circumstances, many students with aspirations for a better life look for the first opportunity to "get the hell out of Dodge"—to get whatever credential they need to establish themselves in a locale with better socioeconomic prospects. (See chapter 9 in this volume.) Others come to see school as unavoidable seat time, a burden to be borne until they can drop out or graduate into the local economy, where good jobs for high school graduates are scarce, or move into the one employment category where "jobs" are always plentiful, the military. For most students, school becomes a synecdoche for the local culture as a whole; one that has seen better times in the past; one that is struggling to earn and retain viability in the present; one that is trying valiantly, against all odds, to shape a better future.

These conditions were part of the motivation for a literacy-outreach project developed by the University of Arkansas at Fayetteville in an effort to help the Delta honor its past, thereby providing its citizens, particularly high school students, with an intellectual platform to support initiatives designed to reclaim and revitalize its communities, economies, and prospects. The scheme, called the Arkansas Delta Oral History Project, involves high school students from the Delta working in writing groups led by University of Arkansas student mentors. Both the high school students and their university mentors spend an entire semester producing oral history projects that culminate in a range of final products—essays, stories, plays, videos, brochures, and so on—that are performed publicly and then archived in both the University of Arkansas library and in the local high school libraries.

A central element in the curriculum of the project has been an emphasis on how issues related to poverty and socioeconomic class affect the Delta high school students whom the university students mentor. Put simply, the University of Arkansas students generally come from privileged, middle-class or upper-middle-class backgrounds, and the Delta high school students are, in large measure, working class or poor students, many of whom live in the midst of intergenerational poverty. About a quarter of the university participants have been African American. The African American populations at the participating high schools have ranged from 70 to 90 percent. Because this mentor-mentee mismatch caused some unexpected, yet palpable, tensions in the first year of the project, the instructional staff, in the second year, made Ruby Payne's popular but controversial book, *A Framework for Understanding Poverty,* required reading for the university students. We asked them to reflect regularly on any connections they saw between Payne's claims about how poverty affects students and their own perceptions about the ways these influences shape their mentees' lives.

We operate the Arkansas Delta Oral History Project as an intentional reclamation task, similar to the "place-based education" Brooke describes in chapter 9 of this volume, and we acknowledge that if the University of Arkansas hopes to contribute to efforts to revitalize the Delta, then our students must have a well-grounded understanding of the dynamics and forces of poverty they will encounter in such efforts. In this chapter, after offering a thumbnail sketch of the Delta and an overview of the project, we draw on the reflections of three of our University of Arkansas students as a basis to interrogate whether Payne or her principal critics ultimately offer a conceptual basis sufficient for understanding the interaction of poverty and rural life in eastern Arkansas.

The Arkansas Delta—Rich Past, Uncertain Future

What is the Arkansas Delta? From a geographical standpoint, that's apparently not an easy question to answer. The United States Department of Transportation says the Delta comprises 42 counties; Arkansas historian Willard Gatewood, by contrast, refers to the Delta as "one-third of the state's counties," or 25 of the 75. Many would maintain, however, that the best definition of the Delta is the one promoted by the Delta Byways Commission: the 15 counties that either have a Mississippi River shoreline or sit between the river and an odd geological feature, Crowley's Ridge. This crescent-moon-shaped bump stretches from just south of Cape Girardeau, Missouri, to Helena, Arkansas, and is the only high ground in the otherwise flat alluvial plane of the region.

The most influential geological feature of the Delta, however, is not so much the flat plane as it is the rivers: the Arkansas, the White, the Cache, the St. Francis, and, of course, the Mississippi. These rivers flood regularly, and with receding floodwaters comes a superabundance of rich soil, so the Delta economy has always been agricultural. Cotton has consistently been a strong crop in the Delta along with rice, soybean, and sorghum grain (or milo) crops. An old saying seems true about the Delta: The soil is so rich that you could toss out a pound of nails and harvest a bucket of crowbars.

There is nothing resembling a big city in the Delta. One might claim that Jonesboro, with a population of 53,515, represents something like a population center in the north end of the region, while Helena, with a current population of 6,333 (having recently combined with West Helena), anchors the southern end. Most of the rest of the burghs are small farming, river, or railroad towns. There was a time, according to Gatewood, when many of these towns were bustling: They had main streets—often two of them, one for whites and one for blacks. They had shops and businesses. They had restaurants, movie theatres, even opera houses.

But a triple whammy hit the Delta. First, like many other sites in small-town America, the interstate came in the 1960s and 1970s and whizzed past the small towns, moving commerce either to larger cities or to malls on the "bypass" outside of the downtown. Second, the agricultural economy that dominated the region was victimized by the twin forces of mechanization and globalization. The cotton plantation that used to take a hundred people to operate now employed three or four people. The Delta cotton that once upon a time was sold directly to the textile mills in the Carolinas now had to compete with cotton grown in South America and Asia. Third, the economy essentially converted from family agriculture to big agribusiness. As a result, despite some rare bright spots in the Delta economy, the region is clearly in decline: businesses go under, industries shut down, populations dwindle, schools suffer. As Gatewood puts it, one clearly notices "the deterioration of the human condition in the Delta. Virtually all the usual indices, from per capita income, unemployment, and housing to health, teenage pregnancies, and school dropouts, provide a statistical portrait of a people in distress" (23). And yet the Delta keeps on trying. Communities institute civic improvement projects; school systems bring in new curricular programs; economic development commissions try to entice new businesses and industries to locate there. In short, a great many people in Arkansas believe that the Delta is worth reclaiming—worth the effort it will take to revitalize the economy, improve the schools, and better the quality of life in the region.

What Is the Arkansas Delta Oral History Project?

The Arkansas Delta Oral History Project emerged from two simple questions that we posed in the autumn of 2006: If students in the Delta could become interested in learning to read and write more effectively, what might they be interested in reading and writing *about*? If these students could recapture, via oral history, some of the rich, pithy lore of their home region, might the project motivate them to consider staying in the Delta, reclaiming its present, and shaping its future?

The project works this way: When it signs on, a high school in the Delta agrees that in *one class*, the teacher will not alter *what* he or she was planning to teach for a semester, but instead will agree to use oral history as a *teaching method*. That is, no matter what the content of the course, each student will identify a topic that in some way involves local history or legend; do some background research on the topic; identify someone with a unique perspective on the topic whom he or she can interview; plan, practice, conduct, and transcribe the interview verbatim; and then write a final project of his or her own design—an essay, a story, a series of poems, a play or video script, a brochure, and so on—that grows out of the interview.

At the same time that the high school students embark on their oral history projects, the University of Arkansas offers an undergraduate colloquium in which students do three things: (a) they read, write, and learn about the history of the Arkansas Delta, including its emerging culture of poverty; (b) they plan and complete oral history projects of their own on some aspect of Delta life; and (c) they act as mentors and role models to the high school students participating in the project.

The semester begins with a day-long meeting in Helena, involving all the university students, all the high school students participating in the project, and instructors from both sets of institutions. At this meeting, four workshops introduce participants to the defining characteristics of an oral history project, to best practices of planning and conducting an oral history interview, to options for converting an interview transcript into a final project, and to the logistics of participating in online discussions. At this meeting, all the participating students are organized into four- or five-person working groups. Chairing each group is a University of Arkansas student; the other members are students from the different participating high schools. The groups are given the agenda for the project, detailing the dates when members should have selected a topic, finished their background research, selected an interviewee, drafted interview questions, practiced the interview, conducted it, transcribed it, and started working on their final projects. At the end of the initial meeting, the students go back to their respective institutions with the agreement that each student will, at least once a week, log on to the University of Arkansas's electronic discussion platform and share drafts, ask questions, participate in discussions—in general, work together on the project.

After about six weeks of this group activity, all participants come to Fayetteville for a weekend of face-to-face work, campus activities, and fun. The visiting students from the high schools tour campus facilities and meet with university admissions and academic officers. The writing groups convene to work on the emerging project. A local playwright, Bob Ford, runs an workshop called "From Page to Stage," which helps students find dramatic moments in their interview transcripts.

After the weekend, all participants return to their home schools and wrap up their work, all the while checking in with their online writing groups. At the end of the semester, the Arkansas Delta Oral History Project concludes with a day of public performances of final projects—stories, plays, videos, poetry sequences, and so on—at the University of Arkansas Community College of Phillips County in Helena.

Everyone involved with the project during its first four years has agreed on two things. First, the students' projects are, in general, unqualified successes. They are well-researched; they are vivid and entertaining; they are compelling—indeed, often harrowing—in ways that typical student projects in traditional schooling seldom are. Second, the experiences of both the high school students and the University of Arkansas mentors—and the relationships that grow between members of these two groups—are poignant. Here are students for the first time in their lives bringing projects of their own design to completion and performing them publicly. Here are students from, generally, two sides of an economic divide, one group learning that perhaps going to college might be possible after all and another doing their best to show their younger counterparts that, yes, they *can* succeed in college. We are, in other words, aiming to achieve two of the pedagogical goals called for by Thomas Butler and Jacqueline Edmondson in chapter 13 of this volume: To counter the strong public discourse that maintains rural schools suffer under an impoverished intellectual climate that can only be countered by subjecting students to standardized tests that tacitly promote a suburban or urban lifestyle; and to try, consciously, to show University of Arkansas students the importance of seeing rural eastern Arkansas as place where important, purposeful teaching can change lives and communities.

Moreover, one of our goals as instructors has been to provide our students with some intellectual "handholds" for understanding how the high school students' socioeconomic class backgrounds affected their success and enriched the sense of urgency we all felt about the project. Particularly with the advent of the No Child Left Behind legislation in 2002, the education community is turning its attention to the characteristics and needs of poor students in a way it has not done for nearly three decades. Since Payne has become such a prominent figure in the discussion of students and poverty, and since many of the university mentors in the first year of the project commented on interactions with students that we suspected were connected to the issues Payne addresses, we assigned her book to our students in the second year. Doing so brought to the forefront of our class discussions some of the tensions and controversies engendered by Payne's approach.

Payne, Poverty, and Her Critics

In her best-selling book, *A Framework for Understanding Poverty* (originally published in 2001, now in its fourth edition), Ruby Payne, a former public school teacher and administrator, takes a taxonomic view of her subject, enumerating and unpacking the characteristics of poverty in a way made popular by Stephen Covey's (1989) explication of "the seven habits of highly effective people." (Payne herself quotes Covey twice in *A Framework for Understanding Poverty*.)

Payne begins by defining poverty as "the extent to which an individual does without resources" and then proceeds immediately to subdivide "resources" into eight categories: "financial, emotional, mental, spiritual, physical, support systems, relationships/role models," and "knowledge of hidden rules" (8). She returns regularly to this list of resources later in the book.

Payne's next move is to explain "the role of language and story" in understanding poverty (27). Citing the linguistic theory popularized by Martin Joos in his 1961 book, *The Five Clocks*, Payne notes that "every language in the world has five registers"—"frozen," or "language that is always the same," such as "the Lord's Prayer" or "wedding vows"; "formal," or "the standard syntax and word choice of work and school," characterized by "complete sentences and specific word choice"; "consultative," a "formal register . . . used in conversation," with a "discourse pattern not quite as direct as formal register"; "casual," or "language between friends . . . characterized by a 400- to 800-word vocabulary," in which the "word choice [is] general and not specific" and the "sentence syntax is often incomplete"; and "intimate," or the "language between lovers or twins" and the "language of sexual harassment" (27). Payne argues, citing the contrastive rhetoric research involving Hispanic students by Montano-Harmon (1991), that "the majority of minority students and poor students do not have access to formal register at home" and indeed that "these students cannot use formal register" (28). These students, Payne suggests, default to casual register not only in word choice and syntax but also in "discourse patterns"—Payne defines a "casual-register discourse pattern" as one in which the "writer or speaker goes around the issue before finally coming to the point" (30)—and in "story structure"—Payne characterizes a "casual-register story structure" as one that "begins with the end of the story first or the part with the greatest emotional intensity," is interrupted by "audience participation," and "ends with a comment about the character and his or her value" (31).

Payne also offers an extended definition of "generational poverty," the state of "having been in poverty for more than two generations" (47). Many of the defining features of generational poverty are the same as those explained under "poverty" in the "hidden rules" taxonomy. For example, in both the hidden rules of poverty and the generational poverty definition, "personality" is seen as "the ability to entertain, tell stories, and have a sense of humor" (51), rather than the propensity to value achievement, as it is in the middle-class hidden rules, or to value "financial, political, and social connections" as in the hidden rules of wealth (43).

Payne proceeds with her excursus on resources by arguing that "emotional resources" come from "role models" that lead a child from "dependence" to "independence" and eventually to "interdependence" (64–65); by explaining that "support systems" fall into "seven general categories," ranging from "coping strategies" and "options during problem-solving" to "positive self-talk" and "procedural self-talk" (70–71); and by focusing on the "cognitive strategy" of "mediation," in which the person tapping into this resource learns three steps: "identification of the stimulus," "assignment of meaning" to the stimulus, and "identification of a strategy" to deal with the stimulus (90).

Several critics of Payne's work have surfaced over the past few years (Gorski; Ng and Rury; Osei-Kofi), the most vocal of whom is a group led by Randy

Bomer, professor of education at the University of Texas, Austin. In a 2008 *Teachers College Record* article, "Miseducating Teachers about the Poor: A Critical Analysis of Ruby Payne's Claims about Poverty," Bomer, Joel Dworin, Laura May, and Peggy Seingson criticize Payne both for the ideas presented in *A Framework for Understanding Poverty* and for the impact she has allegedly had on teachers and the broader educational community. Chief among Bomer et al.'s criticisms of Payne is that she purveys an unsubstantiated deficit-thinking model in dealing with the poor. Bomer et al. further hold that, given the huge popularity of her book (over 800,000 copies sold) and professional development seminars and lectures for teachers (she has appeared before teachers in 38 states), Payne is misinforming teachers about the nature of poverty and poor students. Bomer and his colleagues analyzed the discourse of Payne's text, seeking to determine "what patterns are detectable in Ruby Payne's truth claims about children's lives in poverty" and "to what extent are those truth claims supported by existing research" (2). Examining each sentence for truth claims—those which made specific claims about reality—Bomer et al. created four superordinate headings under which to categorize Payne's tenets: social structures, daily life, language, and characteristics of individuals.

In each category, the central problem they found with Payne's formulations was the same: deficit thinking. Bomer et. al. explain: Deficit thinking "holds that students that struggle or fail in school do so because of their own internal deficits or deficiencies." In deficit thinking, when a pedestrian is hit on campus, it is her fault for not looking before walking in front of traffic. A deficit thinker does not consider that the pedestrian might be deaf, at a cross walk, or that the driver could have been impaired by text messaging and speeding when the accident happened. Rather, a deficit thinker moves toward "blaming the victim" (Ryan) instead of investigating the conditions of the accident. In *Rural Literacies*, Kim Donehower, Charlotte Hogg, and Eileen Schell explain the deficit model too frequently held out as a means of understanding people in rural situations is a stereotype: "Life in rural America is seen as 'lacking': lacking education, lacking economic opportunities, lacking cultural opportunities" (14).

Bomer et al. find in Payne's deficit thinking a parallel situation to public education in the aftermath of the No Child Left Behind Act. Schools around America are "failing" and "on improvement" for not moving their students classified as poor to the levels of proficiency on reading and math assessments. Payne's grouping of students into categories, Bomer et al. maintain, provides the scapegoat the American public needs to feel good about closing already failing public schools.

Bomer et al. suggest some of the most damaging potential effects of Payne's work are in the perceptions that poor people need to be "fixed." "She pathologizes the 'culture' or 'rules' of the poor and valorizes the 'culture' or 'rules' of the middle class" (6); they argue that at a school level, "teachers are called upon, then, to narrativize and envision the lives of poor children in the way that Payne suggests, so that they can have certain kinds of ideas about those children and use particular language in speaking to them and their parents" (6). Leveling a summative claim, Bomer et al. assert, "Teachers may be misinformed by Payne's claims. Poverty in Payne's work is marked only as negative, only as a divergence from a middle-class norm, and students who are 'of poverty' need to be fixed" (13).

The Payne-Bomer tension represents the backdrop against which we asked the University of Arkansas student mentors to write about their perceptions of how poverty and class influenced the lives of the Arkansas Delta high school students whom they were mentoring. We hoped our students featured here, who had read Payne's work but not her critics,' would begin to interrogate the complex relationships involving social, political, and economic forces that influence high school students' educational practices and goals in rural Arkansas. We remained interested in whether Payne, whom the university students read as part of the course, or Bomer were helpful in their work. Since collecting these data, we have added Bomer to the required reading.

The Mentors' Perspectives on Class and Poverty

As the Arkansas Delta Oral History Project completed its fourth year in 2009–10, we brought the tenth, eleventh, and twelfth high schools into the fold, and our combined total of student participants had reached about 350. We look back on the project with pride and circumspection. The university students in year one consistently made note of what they perceived as unwarranted silence, resistance, and even hostility from their high school charges. While these strains eased a bit as the semester progressed and were not evident in the final celebration and performance of the projects, we thought it might be wise to be proactive about these issues. Beginning in year two, we asked our students to write reflectively about whether and how they perceived issues of poverty, race, and class affecting their work as mentors. Reading these reflections, we were particularly interested to see whether our students were displaying the kind of deficit thinking about poverty that Bomer et al. found in Payne's work and whether our students would level the same kinds of criticisms at Payne that Bomer and his colleagues did. What follows are reflections from three of the university mentors, followed by our own observations about how the mentors perceived the influences of poverty in working with the high school students. We use names of the mentors, but the names of their high school charges have been replaced with pseudonyms.

From Hillary Swanton

In working with the ADOHP in the spring of 2008, I was able to see a small part of the intersection between class divisions and how poverty plays a role in high school life. Something that struck me the first day we met them was that during our lunchtime, class lines seemed completely erased in some ways. Groups of guys and girls sat together and associated with each other based on personality more than background. They seemed altogether absorbed in high school life, making jokes to each other and talking about their rival high school. The one distinction I saw was that some of the students who seemed as though they were from more fortunate families already knew more about college life than the ones who seemed as though they came from families that were not as well-off. The latter were more curious about the college experience, asking "Are there parties?," "Are all the parties really crazy?," "What is the basketball team like?," "Do you have a lot of homework?"

The four high school girls, one senior and three juniors, seemed able to relate socially, but I did observe some differences when trying to interact with them on an academic level. It seemed obvious by looking at our online interactions that different students had different experiences just working with the Internet. Some students were more comfortable using the Internet, frequently using "online language," like abbreviations or emoticons. Another student was more formal in her approach, and less frequent in her postings, which made me think that the Internet was associated more with schoolwork and academics than recreation and communication. Also, I would try to include some "fun" questions in my prompts, asking them what their weekend plans were, or what their school day was like, etc. Two students were very quick to respond talking about their extracurricular activities, while one was less responsive in that area. This left me wondering if she had the time or resources to participate in those extracurricular endeavors, or if it was just a personal preference. That student, however, was very enthusiastic working with her group as their project got off the ground. All three of my students were actually very proud of their accomplishments at the end of the semester.

I think the multifaceted issues of poverty and class definitely influence the lives of these high school students on a cultural level. They are able to move easily in the social sphere with students of different backgrounds, but the differences come in the kind of day-to-day interactions that many in the university world take for granted. Students growing up in poverty do not have a familiar connection with college or the lifestyle that comes with it. It is something that can seem very exciting to them, but that I'm afraid can also seem almost exotic and unreachable.

From Laine Gates

The second of the ADOHP meetings includes an all-day playwriting workshop, during which each high school student is asked to create a narrative using his or her oral history interviewee as the protagonist. One of the students in my group, a fifteen-year-old tenth-grader, ran into some trouble with creating a protagonist to provide the conflict for her narrative. Her interviewee was her grandfather, and she was planning to interview him about a tornado that hit their hometown. For her, there was no clear good and bad around which she could create her story. After some discussion about the idea of conflict in narrative, my student thought for a little while, then began to write intently. She wrote a monologue for her grandfather, in which he weighed the potential costs of going to work, despite the danger of a tornado, against the potential costs of missing that day of work. This might seem like a dilemma with an obvious answer, but for many, the danger of losing a job or even a day's wages can seem just as perilous as a random, disastrous act of nature.

Families face this dilemma in many different guises, whether it's weighing the costs of braving icy roads that lie between home and work, staying home to care for an ailing child or parent, or deciding which household necessities to forego in order to afford the gas to get to work. In many financially insecure families, college attendance is not seen as a viable option. Because children learn the tension of living from paycheck to paycheck early in life, they often decide to forego college in order to contribute to the family's immediate financial stability. When labor seems more tangible than academics, college becomes exorbitant and superfluous.

Poverty in America is, of course, not a monolithic concept. The complete profile of a child in poverty is not possible. One of the teachers involved in the Arkansas Delta Oral History Project had this simple advice for the college student mentors: be honest and listen. Students can tell when you're using a formula for dealing with them, and they can tell when you're being honest. As with the student in my group and the narrative written about her grandfather, all that I had to do as her mentor was listen to her questions and affirm that she did, indeed, have compelling and relevant ideas. When students are encouraged to take on subject matter which is relevant to their own lives, that's when mentors have the chance to take that subject matter and help students understand how to guide their own narratives.

From Kelly Riley

Over the 2008 spring semester, I served as a mentor to five female high school students—Vanessa, Lauren, Monique, Tanisha, and Katelyn—all of whom attended various high schools throughout the Delta. Through my interaction with these students, I learned that issues of poverty (both in its traits and its effects) in the Arkansas Delta are extremely complicated. Because of our limited encounters, it is difficult to discern the unique economic background of each of my students. We rarely discussed economic status or class directly. However, I did observe some subtle indicators of poverty and hardship from each member; and collectively, their experiences seem to create a narrative that demonstrates how a region's poverty can deeply affect the individual.

At our first face-to-face encounter in Helena, we attended a meeting that served as a brief introduction to WebCT—the online software and discussion board we were required to use as a means of communication. After the meeting, I gave each student a little slip of paper on which was written their username and password. Both Vanessa and Katelyn accepted their paper with a quick nod and a knowing smile. However, I noticed that Lauren, Monique, and Tanisha took the paper from my hand reluctantly. Because the meeting was over, we immediately broke for lunch and joined the buffet line. When I came back to our table, I found Tanisha waiting for me. She held a plate of catfish in one hand and her username and password in the other. As I sat down, I asked her if she had ever used a discussion board before. "Kind of," she said. I asked if she wanted me to explain WebCT to her again. She nodded enthusiastically. As I started to explain, Lauren sat down next to Tanisha and asked me to start over. Instead, I waited for everyone to return to the table before explaining WebCT again. Both Vanessa and Katelyn added their computer experiences to our conversation. We explored the idea of using Facebook as an alternative means of communication, but the students stated that their high schools had filters to block the use of the social networking site. Once everyone felt better about WebCT, Tanisha told me that she was worried about being able to get online regularly. She explained that she had limited computer access at school. Monique and Vanessa expressed the same concern. I helped to relieve their fears by telling them that they just needed to do the best that they could in keeping up with their online correspondence. By the time we had finished our catfish, everyone seemed to feel more at ease.

It was obvious to me from this exchange that several of my students had very little computer experience, and it also seemed apparent that their schools had a very limited number of computers and that access to them was not guaranteed. These students' experience with computers contrasted sharply with those of the students I had worked with at schools near the university.

Although a part of Arkansas, the Delta is nothing like northwest Arkansas. Being in the Delta often gives me the feeling that I have gone back in time. Crumbling buildings and old store signs from the 1950s and 1970s are ubiquitous; however, computers are not. Around the university, I am constantly surrounded by computers. I find them everywhere I turn. Computers are much fewer and farther between in the Delta. While attempting to conduct a Google search on the region, I have also concluded, based on the pitiful collections of loosely related websites I found, that the Delta's people are not online. It is evident that the Delta has yet to enter the digital age, and I find myself wondering how this will affect the education and the opportunities of the people who live there.

The Mentors as Analysts of Poverty

Hillary, Laine, and Kelly offer glimpses into the lives of students living in rural situations in a very poor region of America. The high school students' lack of resources and exposure to information technology could certainly have lasting effects on their collective futures. When asked, most students were not willing to consider leaving the region for college; familial and friendship ties are too strong to consider abandoning. As Kelly explained, her Delta students' "experience with computers contrasted sharply" with those in the economically booming area around the University of Arkansas, a theme echoed in Hillary's narrative. In much the same way, going to the Delta region for Kelly was like going back in time. Even searching the Internet for information on the Delta nets few results, an indication the region is behind other sections of the country in terms of information access and computer savvy—another theme raised by Hillary's story. Kelly's perspectives following her first experience with the Delta region focus on what these students are lacking and how that will affect their futures. Clearly, while these students' location in the Delta puts them at a deficit in these terms, none of the university students is wont to group the Delta students into a monolithic population. Rather, the university students relate their experiences by comparing their students in the Delta to students at the University of Arkansas and in high schools near the university. Laine's advice from her mentor, "be honest and listen," because "students can tell when you're using a formula for dealing with them, and they can tell when you're being honest," along with her perspectives that, "Poverty in America is, of course, not a monolithic concept" and "the complete profile of a child in poverty is not possible," seem to reflect an understanding of the students in these situations that complicates what Payne could bring to the table. These three mentors reject the deficit thinking that would see the Delta high school students as being responsible for their material conditions. These mentors at least seem to recognize that, in efforts to support the current and future educational goals of students affected by poverty, the initial move ought not to essentialize and reduce, but instead embrace the complexity of the situation and learn from it.

Rethinking Poverty in Rural Literacy Outreach Projects

A fascinating scene transpired at the Fayetteville Town Center, a conference venue near the University of Arkansas, on June 4, 2008. Ruby Payne was the keynote speaker at the second annual University of Arkansas Literacy Symposium. Nearly a thousand teachers—elementary, secondary, and postsecondary—spent three hours listening to Payne and working through scenarios she presented. Clearly, her work is popular, widespread, and, until recently, unchallenged among educators, particularly those who teach reading and writing, literate activities that most often offer a window into the socioeconomic lives of students.

Surely it's a good thing that the discourse about poverty and class has been raised to a new level of consciousness in American education. To be fair, both Ruby Payne and Randy Bomer bring valuable insights to this discourse. Payne's book and in-service series have clearly brought more attention on poverty-in-education issues than any other unilateral effort. Bomer's analysis of Payne's work was approached with stringent research methodology and has been published in major research journals in the field (*Teachers College Record, English Education*) and presented at the American Educational Research Association, considered the premiere educational research conference.

Our original question of whether Payne and/or Bomer really help students, like those at the University of Arkansas, deal with the issues of poverty and class that potentially impinge on rural outreach projects like the Arkansas Delta Oral History Project remains our focus. Despite their distinguished work, neither Payne nor Bomer et al. meet the basic standards, for example, of in-service literacy programs or practices as set forth in the No Child Left Behind legislation. For example, a reading program such as Scholastic's Read 180, a computer-based reading intervention program, must be supported by research standards set forth in NCLB and noted below from the International Reading Association to qualify as "evidence-based." Research supporting Read 180 (or any other programs) must meet the following criteria. It is

> Objective—it uses data that any evaluator would identify and interpret similarly;
> Valid—it uses data that adequately represent the tasks that children need to accomplish to be successful;

Reliable—it uses data that will remain essentially unchanged if collected on a different day or by a different person;

Systematic—it uses data that were collected according to a rigorous design of either experimentation or observation;

Refereed—it uses data that have been approved for publication by a panel of independent reviewers.

Neither Payne nor Bomer offers research-based practical solutions for dealing with people living in poverty. Does Payne's focus on categorizing poor students in order to understand their problems serve as precisely the paradigm shift in thinking elementary, secondary, and postsecondary literacy instruction needs? What are the dangers of approaching kids in poverty with deficit thinking model, as Bomer et. al. criticize Payne for doing? These questions are complicated, of course, but what we know about poverty and its effects on education are simply not sufficient to offer a substantial answer to them.

It should be noted that neither Payne nor Bomer set out to meet the standards of evidence-based practice presented here. But if theirs are the two central voices in the discussion of poverty in education in recent years, shouldn't they? We find ourselves looking for more helpful guidance in these discussions, and while Payne and Bomer might have garnered a great deal of attention, their work falls short of providing guidance for the preparation of university students enacting literacy work with high school students from the Delta.

We must be quick to admit the practices of the Delta Oral History Project are not evidence-based either. These practices for now are simply examples of dedicated university faculty members and student mentors working with real children in a systematic, repeatable fashion, again, very similar to the work featured in Robert Brooke's chapter in this volume. Our work is the product of what Brandt terms "literacy sponsorship," in this case an approach designed to help students not by focusing on what they lack or lag but by examining, and therefore sustaining their ways of life. This pursuit, shared by Kim Donehower, Charlotte Hogg, and Eileen Schell in *Rural Literacies* as public pedagogy modeled after the work of Henry Giroux, seeks to create a sense of shared responsibility in the university students while allowing the high school students to find their literacies in the projects they create.

The practices of the Arkansas Delta Oral History Project could become evidence-based as the project continues to grow. For example, we could move to the point of developing recommendations for literacy-outreach programs that are based on objective, valid, reliable, systematic, and refereed data. This should be a goal not only for the Arkansas Delta Oral History Project but also for other similar projects emerging from other universities and not-for-profit organizations. The work of our colleagues combines to create widespread attention to this work and practical, repeatable, implications for it. As students in years three and four of the Arkansas Delta Oral History Projects grapple with these readings and diverse perspectives, we anticipate their work being even more critically informed, practical, and relevant.

The opportunity for high school students from a rural region with high poverty rates to work in small group settings with other high school students and college mentors could have a profound impact on not only their abilities in literacy but also on their belief that college and further academic pursuits are genuine possibilities on the way to a better life. The University of Arkansas students are spending time away from the flagship university to travel across the state and work with children in the Delta; they are making a commitment to understand and help students in these situations. It stands to reason that high school students creating significant projects based on the histories of the people and places around them develop increased aptitude for reading and writing, which could help them succeed both in high school and, ideally, in college. Beginning to consider the issues affecting both the college and high school students helps move the project from a sort of phenomenon of practice to a repeatable, valid manner of approaching students in similar situations across the country, toward a public pedagogy.

The work of the Arkansas Delta Oral History Project has just begun—we are committed to operating the scheme for at least five years. As it moves forward from a promising beginning, it certainly stands to benefit from the discourse created first by Ruby Payne and more recently by the feud between her and Bomer et al. Though the attention on poverty and education in America has never been so great, it remains a small blip on the radar of national consciousness and one that needs the focused attention of the entire country. We view models such as this and those prescribed in *Rural Literacies* as methods worth repeating and researching to contribute to the conversations about rural and poverty situations. We ultimately would like to be able to tease out how the connections between the projects created and interactions among the university and high school students provide understanding among all stakeholders.

Education is a key to social justice, and literacy is the crux on which all education rests. Education in these regions of America is not equal, as Kelly Riley points out, in terms of computer access. It isn't fair either. When a project can help students see themselves as literate, viable members of an academic community and begin to participate in the discourse inherent to such situations, change can occur. Just as critical to the equation of help-ing people in the Arkansas Delta region is that work there contributes to knowledge and practice in other parts of the state, country, and world. While Payne and Bomer et al. have sparked the dialogue about these issues, it is up to programs like the Arkansas Delta Oral History Project to continue it and to create productive, informed action in response to it.

Works Cited

Brandt, Deborah. "Sponsors of Literacy." *College Composition and Communication* 49.2 (1998): 165–85. Print.

Bomer, Randy, Joel E. Dworin, Laura May, and Peggy Semingson. "Miseducating Teachers about the Poor: A Critical Analysis of Ruby Payne's Claims about Poverty." *Teachers College Record* 1 Dec. 2008, 2497–531. Print. Web. 3 August 2008.

Donehower, Kim, Charlotte Hogg, and Eileen E. Schell. *Rural Literacies.* Carbondale: Southern Illinois UP, 2007. Print.

Gatewood, Willard B. "The Arkansas Delta: The Deepest of the Deep South." *The Arkansas Delta: Land of Paradox.* Ed. Jeannie Whayne and Willard B. Gatewood. Fayetteville: U of Arkansas P, 1993. 3-29. Print.

Gorski, Paul. "The Classist Underpinnings of Ruby Payne's Framework." *Teachers College Record* 1 Feb. 2006. Web. 31 July 2008.

Montano-Harmon, Maria Rosario. "Discourse Feature of Written Mexican Spanish: Current Research in Contrastive Rhetoric and Its Implications." *Hispania* 74.2 (1991): 417–25. Print.

Ng, Jennifer C., and John L. Rury. "Poverty and Education: A Critical Analysis of the Ruby Payne Phenomenon." *Teachers College Record* 1 July 2006. Web. 1 August 2008.

Osei-Kofi, Nana. "Pathologizing the Poor: A Framework for Understanding Ruby Payne's Work." *Equity and Excellence* 38.4 (2005): 367–75. Print.

Payne, Ruby. *A Framework for Understanding Poverty,* 4th ed. Highlands, Tex.: aha! Process, 2005. Print.

Ryan, William. *Blaming the Victim.* New York: Vintage, 1971. Print.

"What Is Evidence-Based Reading Instruction? A Position Statement of the International Reading Association." Web.

11

For All Students in This Place

Valerie Mulholland

Rural Literacies came into my possession during a book-buying frenzy at a national English conference in New York City. (The irony of discovering a book that is ostensibly about my home and my experience in a rural setting while visiting the largest city in North America does not elude me.) In this essay, I draw upon the authors' definition of rural literacies: "the particular kinds of literate skills needed to achieve the goals of sustaining life in rural areas . . . to pursue the opportunities and create the public policies and economic opportunities needed to sustain rural communities" (4). The term "sustaining life" is subject to multiple interpretations. I live and teach in a Canadian province where tensions between rural and urban communities mask a deep underlying current of tension between white settlers and the indigenous peoples, who in Canada include the First Nations, Métis, and Inuit peoples. Until the economic, social and cultural tensions are resolved, sustainable life is not possible. The "particular kind of literate skill" I advocate in this essay requires white settlers like myself to reread our pioneer history and recognize the extent of white privilege in our institutions, in this case public education, in order to sustain an equitable future for all people.

In this essay I advocate for the examination of white privilege in preservice teacher training. Through several years of systematic reflective practice, I have arrived at a method of drawing the attention of my predominantly white-settler students to the privileges they accrue "by virtue of being white" (Schick). My pedagogy is informed by postcolonial theory and supported by self-study research methods (Mulholland and Longman). This chapter is a personal story of learning to teach differently, which I understand now as a rejection of the seduction of the "rhetorics of lack, lag and the rosy past" (Donehower, Hogg, and Schell 1).

The Historical Context of This Place

The university where I teach is located in the northern Great Plains of North America, in the province of Saskatchewan, Canada, covering a vast territory extending from the United States border to the Arctic. The total population hovers around the one-million mark, and has been static since 1930. In the entire province there are only two cities with populations nearing 200,000, which in global terms qualifies both as relatively small third-tier cities. Over half the population live in "146 towns, most of which have populations of no more than 1,000, 376 villages with populations of less than 500, and 297 rural municipalities which, apart from one or two notable exceptions with populations of 2,000 to 5,000, generally have populations of just a few hundred" (Garcea 135). Originally, the territories that now comprise the province of Saskatchewan were inhabited by primarily Cree, Dene, Dakota, and Saulteaux peoples (Ward). In Canada, the term *First Nations* is in common use to identify people who in other jurisdictions are named Amerindian, Indigenous, or Aboriginal people. There are seventy-five First Nations reservations, by definition rural, and only a few with recently purchased urban-land holdings.

The first significant European contact occurred in the late 1700s, when a trickle of French and British fur trade workers arrived by canoe to engage in commerce. A second massive wave of white European settlers arrived between 1880 and 1920, a period that coincided with the decline of the fur trade and the destruction of the Plains bison as well as the traditional way of life the bison sustained. In this region of Canada, there were no extended conventional wars waged with the First Nations; however, there were massacres, armed occupations, and significant acts of violent resistance, notably the Riel Resistance of 1885 (or Riel Rebellion, depending on your perspective). Canadians sometimes suggest that our national motto, "Peace, Order and Good Government," explains how the settlement of the Canadian West was achieved with less violence than that of the American West. Such a suggestion ignores that many chiefs signed treaties because their people were starving (McLeod 34). By the time Saskatchewan joined the Canadian confederation in 1905, by Treaties Four (1874) and Six (1876), First Nations people were restricted to living on reservations, their children were sent to church-run residential schools, and white settlers were buying land for homesteads at rock-bottom bargain prices. Surely definitions of state-sanctioned violence vary according to context and perspective.

Situating Myself in This Place

Like me, the great majority of my secondary English education students are descended from white settlers, raised and educated in small, rural communities. In her essay "When Place Becomes Race," critical race theorist Sherene Razack defines the term *white settler:*

> A white-settler society is one established by Europeans on non-European soil. Its origins lie in the dispossession and near extermination of Indigenous populations by conquering Europeans. As it evolves, a white-settler society continues to be structured by a racial hierarchy. In such societies, it is believed that white people came first and it is they who principally developed the land; Aboriginal people are presumed to be mostly dead or assimilated. European settlers thus become the original inhabitants and the group most entitled to the fruits of citizenship. (1–2)

To be a white settler is to be part of the dominant class of a white-settler society. The pioneer version of our selves is codified through provincial curriculum, language policies, and teaching practices that marginalize people with different stories of origin. Despite the continued presence of First Nations people in the province, and a recent influx of non-European immigrants, most descendants of white settlers persist in accepting the fantasy of "originality and origination" (Bhabha 110) that allows colonizers to believe that they were the first to build civilization in the land they occupy. Many extend this pattern of thinking by insisting that new immigrants should be required to learn English immediately upon arrival, saying, "We lost our language when we came here, so should they" (Trainor 165).

My career as an English teacher began in high schools. Annually, I participated in a variety of large-scale assessments of reading and writing, at the local board, provincial, and national levels, where I observed that what the tests did best was identify social class and racial difference. I was not alone in this observation, by any means, but those in charge clung to the discourse of objectivity. At the time, I was aware of the political implications of curriculum, hidden or official, and knew that as a subject, English was a relatively recent addition to the Western curriculum (Russell; Willinsky, "History," *Learning*).

Later, as a doctoral student reading postcolonial theory, I began to understand my role as a white-settler teacher differently. Meredith Cherland and Helen Harper write: "Postcolonial research demonstrates that education has been a tool for social and political control. Curriculum has been (and remains) a discourse through which the colonizer's knowledge has been distributed and validated" (90). My understanding of the role of English teachers was altered substantially by learning that the original, legislated purpose of subject English was to produce a bureaucracy to govern the Empire, a bureaucracy that was fluent in the language and conversant in the constructed values and morals of the English colonizer (Viswanathan, "Milton," *Masks*). Postcolonial theory is concerned with the workings of colonial discourses to produce the subject positions of the self and the other. Alistair Pennycook writes that the colonizer's insistence on the uncivilized "other," viewed in terms of absence— as lacking language, culture, intellect—exists in tension with the civilized "self" and produces a racialized hierarchy; "such is the politics of everyday life in colonized societies" (24). The self and other are characters in the colonial drama, performing the *ongoing* process of colonization.

In Saskatchewan, the teaching of English remains a site of colonization. For example, Andrea Sterzuk writes that First Nations children who speak indigenous English (in the United States referred to as "American Indian English") are regarded by their teachers as "having a less developed or deviant command of [the] English language" ("Whose English" 12), a judgment that contributes to poor results in school and a very low rate of graduation. Such practices negatively impact not only these students, but the entire school community. Dawn Wallin and Laura Reimer, in their study of Canadian rural education priorities, "suggest that rural school improvements that are genu- inely rural . . . invite contributions from those who are usually marginalized in community development and reform efforts" (611). Since the majority of Saskatchewan's seventy-five reservations are adjacent to white-settler com- munities, how English is understood and taught is a salient feature of sus- tainability. However, this is not only a pedagogical issue. Rural white-settler communities depend on the tax dollars each First Nations child represents to sustain their local schools. When a rural community loses its school, the death knell has sounded. Unless First Nations children succeed in school, rural communities will not survive.

Situating Students in This Place

The issues of race and racism are major tropes in educational research in North America, and I am aware that an extensive body of research exists to support the contention that schools are complicit in the reproduction of racist practices and beliefs (Delpit; Edelsky; Earick; Grande). For the pur- poses of this essay, I rely on theory and research of the Canadian context in which I live and work (Alfred; Battiste and Henderson; Emberley; McKenzie; Razack; St. Denis). Jo-Ann Episkenew writes, "Although the modern Can- adian settler-state purports to be multicultural and inclusive, there is, in effect, an invisible boundary between settler and indigenous society, which creates what John Stackhouse has dubbed a 'quiet apartheid'" (190). The Eng- lish education students whom I encounter in teacher training classes are accustomed to thinking of the United States as a racialized country but are less open to the idea that they live in one, too. The more specific the research cited in my courses is to our shared context, the more difficult becomes their resistance to the idea that we postcolonial Canadians are implicated in the reproduction of racist ideologies.

For example, I avoid assigning readings about Ebonics in language courses, initially, and focus instead on research related to how indigenous and immigrant children fare in mainstream Canadian classrooms. My white-settler students are routinely shocked to learn in Heit and Blair's 1993 study that, "A great deal of damage has been done to Indian and Métis students who have been misdiagnosed as having language and learning problems due to differences in their spoken English that have been misunderstood by educators, who, through no fault of their own, have not been trained in these areas" (115–16). Sterzuk's study of literacy practices in a public school in "urban Saskatchewan" describes "some of the ways that educator beliefs and institutional practices regarding language variation and literacy development help to perpetuate and maintain the race divide in Saskatchewan schools" ("Language" 2). Her research illustrates the racialized differences in teacher expectations and practices and their effects on children. Schick's 2000 study of preservice teachers' replication of racist ideologies in classes and practice teaching in Saskatchewan completes the circle of colonial attitudes and beliefs that infuse our context. Learning that *we* are also *them* catches the attention of my students.

A series of critical incidents early in my career as a teacher-educator caused me to become more intentional in my effort to fulfill the provincial mandate to include First Nations and Métis, as well as multicultural, content in my preservice courses. Partly, I was driven by the naïve hope that if my students were exposed to a greater variety of texts in their undergraduate education, they would replicate this practice in their own classrooms. During the first year, the experiences of the very few students in education who were recent immigrants or First Nations people caused me to reconsider my assumptions and practices. Every nonwhite preservice teacher encountered discrimination in their school placements, often at the hands of their cooperating teachers. Undoubtedly, they encountered discrimination in university classrooms, too.

The first example involved a First Nations intern who was asked by her cooperating teacher to teach the novel *April Raintree* by Beatrice Culleton so that she could "draw on her experiences as a foster child." The intern had read the book, a harrowing tale of two sisters taken into custody by the state because their neglectful parents were alcoholic, only to be further abused by a series of foster parents. Taken aback, the intern told the white settler teacher that she had never been a foster child, nor had she ever lived with anyone who was an alcoholic. The intern was assured that, "If you aren't comfortable talking about your past, I understand completely." Later, when the intern called me to report on her progress, she said, "I knew you'd be mad, but I didn't know what to say to her." It was not that the young woman was without intellectual and personal resources. At another time, I observed the same intern conduct a large group discussion with a group of white-settler students and was impressed with her ability to respond to the students' questions about myths informing their understanding of First Nations cultures.

In another incident, a First Nations intern attempted to correct a white-settler teacher's misuse of an anglicized Cree word, *neechee*. The teacher told the class *neechee* was a derogatory term meaning "dirty Indian." The intern, a Cree speaker, said, "In Cree it means *friend*." Perhaps the teacher genuinely believed she was right, or felt her authority was threatened; in any event, she assured the class that her definition was correct and attributed the conflict to language variation. Another intern revealed that she never spoke of her Métis heritage because of the racist discourse common in the staffroom. A Muslim intern was told that her quiet speaking voice would prevent her from becoming an effective teacher. Her cooperating teacher said, "You'll have to speak up if you want the boys to respect you." All of the interns I have worked with who are culturally and racially different than the dominant white-settler class have been subjected to similar treatment in schools. I am unsure how these interns, who have no power at school, might have countered the discrimination they experienced. In each case, they remained composed and attempted to rebut the challenges with information. They simply were not in a viable position to dismantle racist and sexist systems of privilege while they were being socialized as teachers.

White-settler students in my preservice classroom come from both rural and urban backgrounds, but with the exception of recent immigrants, most people in Saskatchewan are one or two generations removed from the farm. The majority of my students come from rural communities, typically established within the previous 125 years by European white settlers, and seemingly culturally and racially homogenous. The prosperity of these towns and villages is closely tied to the fluctuating fortunes of agricultural or other resource-based economies. Often the brightest in their small graduating classes, these students share a common history of being successful in school. In their communities, teachers are generally recognized as well-paid professionals, so these students do not see becoming a teacher as a step down the social ladder.

While the use of the term *urban* may seem odd to someone living outside of Saskatchewan, students who were raised in either of the two large provincial cities see themselves as distinctly different from their rural counterparts. Many self-identified urban students are from working-class families; often they are the first in their family to complete a university degree. They perceive teaching to be a worthwhile job, offering security, good hours, and decent pay. Students who enter the program holding bachelor degrees may be from very small towns originally, but usually identify as urban once they have graduated. They are eager to find a place in the working world, even if that means becoming a teacher.

There are, of course, additional categories: students who have dreamed of teaching since childhood; students who have been encouraged to become teachers by others; some express a desire to change the world. What they share is a history of being successful in school and of having a white-settler heritage. Being members of the dominant culture is a powerful uniting force. That collective history often excludes knowledge of treaties and the Indian Act as well as a failure to recognize institutionalized racism in daily life. Most important, it results in a desire to be innocent in the ongoing process of colonization (Schick 83). As a group, these students are not positioned to disrupt the systems that produced them as successful people. But as Verna St. Denis writes, "Colonization and racialization are also what tie Aboriginal students to non-Aboriginal. We have long since ceased to be islands onto ourselves. . . . By acknowledging a common experience of colonization and racism educators can enact solidarity and join together to challenge racism and racialization" (1087). What I failed to realize when I began this process was that until I incorporated antiracist theory and practices, my classes would be susceptible to a romantic view of the past that reified entrenched white-settler identities.

My First Attempts to Disrupt White-Settler Discourses

When I began teaching preservice English teachers in 1999, I attempted to prepare students to fulfill the provincial mandate to integrate First Nations, Métis, and multicultural content in their teaching. Many definitions of *multicultural* exist. For the purposes of this discussion, I rely on a definition in common use: texts from marginalized, non-European cultures. In Canadian schools, the canon is comprised largely of British, U.S., and a few internationally recognized Canadian writers. Initially, I included texts written by First Nations and multicultural writers. I was operating in the naïve hope that by kindling awareness, I could encourage preservice teachers to "naturally" introduce new texts in their own classrooms. Often, this happened, but overall, we stalled in the "celebrating diversity" or awareness mode, without tackling the more difficult process of interrogating power and privilege. For example, the projects that resulted from this teaching focused on aspects of culture associated with the "tourist approach" to multicultural teaching, an approach that celebrates food, costumes, and dance of non-dominant cultures. Critics of this approach write: "Children 'visit' non-White cultures and then 'go home' to the daily classroom, which reflects only the dominant classroom" (Sleeter and Grant 105). St. Denis writes that offering cultural awareness has become mainstream practice in teacher education programs but has not resulted in equity: "The historical legacy of the Indian Act and residential schools continues to impact Aboriginal students' sense of community and belonging. Through these historical processes, so many were and, some would argue, continue to be relegated to the margins of the margins" (1073). I contend that the same is true of multicultural perspectives. Although it was not uncommon for some students to assume missionary zeal in their efforts to include marginalized voices in their teaching, many others remained silent, *neutral,* claiming that there were no First Nations and multicultural texts to teach in the schools to which they were assigned.

Imagine my dismay when I read the following suggestions from three different students in my 2004 teaching evaluations: "I wish we had read more real literature, not just First Nations authors"; "I want to study what is actually taught in school"; "We spent too much time on the Other. We need to know how to bring all students up to standard." McCann, Johannessen, and Ricca found in their study of beginning English teachers that they wanted to do what "real" teachers do. By not creating a sufficiently coherent rationale for taking up the challenge of fully integrating other voices in their teaching, I made it easy for students to dismiss my efforts as an unnecessary distraction from learning to teach English. My approach was not working; in fact, as the comments show, in some cases it was making the situation worse.

What I Try to Do Now

Since 2004, I have become more purposeful in my inclusion of First Nations, Métis, and multicultural content in my courses. I use postcolonial theory and self-study methods (Pithouse; Loughran and Russell) with students to show how we are all affected by colonization. Students begin class by writing a literacy autobiography (Agee; Frank, Carpenter, and Smith); self-study as a research method makes the impulse to deny involvement in oppressive practices difficult (LeCourt). A typical introductory lesson I use to support the larger assignment, which also draws students' attention to the legacy of our colonial history, is the "What's in a Name?" assignment. Students must identify how their ethnic, social, racial, and gender identities, among others, are revealed in their first and last names. Many students bear anglicized versions of Eastern European surnames; an alarming number of students have never considered how their Ukrainian names became English.

Almost without exception, white settlers and nonwhite settlers alike find profound similarities in their personal stories of learning to read and write. The majority of students share a social-class privilege that transcends racial difference. As an example, most remember fondly placing a Scholastic Book order every month. The discovery provides fertile ground for uncovering the systems of privilege that have benefited them, and me. (The work of Clare Bradford has been useful in these conversations.) Notably, we recognize and name privileges that have accrued, not because of merit or the valorized virtues of hard work and perseverance that are features of our shared pioneer narrative, but because we are white.

While students are writing their literacy autobiographies, we begin reading excerpts from residential school literature, such as Connie Dieter's *From Our Mother's Arms,* a compilation of first-person narratives of experiences in Canadian residential schools. In *Taking Back Our Spirits: Indigenous Literature, Public Policy, and Healing,* Jo-Ann Episkenew writes, "Indigenous autobiography goes beyond catharsis. It is an act of imagination that inspires social regeneration by providing eyewitness testimony to historical injustices. As such, it is intensely political" (75). My intention is to politicize our shared history through pedagogy. Concurrently, we view the Australian film about their residential schools, *Rabbit-Proof Fence.* It is not uncommon for students to react with shock and horror, claiming either to have never heard that First Nations children were forced to attend state-sponsored, church-operated residential schools or to have never contemplated the effects of the national policy. The stories do not adhere to the Canadian motto of "Peace, Order and Good Government." Each year a few students have related stories of their family members who taught or worked at residential schools, offering a counternarrative to the readings and the film. They claim that the schools "accomplished a lot of good. Those kids had such hard lives on the reserves." Rarely are those family stories interrogated to understand why life is difficult on reserves or for evidence of the tyranny of the Indian Act (as well as Indian agents, Métis scrip, the reservation pass system, not being granted the vote in Canadian elections until 1960, and so on). Many students appear genuinely traumatized by these images and stories, and they write responses filled with compassion and empathy. The discussions emanating from these assignments are vigorous and emotional.

After this introduction, we take up the reading of First Nations and Métis authors differently than students had previously. Previously, I depended solely on the students to create connections between the cultural and literary theories we studied. Now, I provide explicit teaching about our shared history and about postcolonial theory. Neil Besner advocates the use of postcolonial theory as a methodology but also "as an approach to a condition: the colonial condition" (43). With this new approach, many students now indicate that the emphasis on First Nations issues, history, and literature is a strength of the course. In my current practice, novels such as Joy Kogawa's *Obasan* about the Japanese internship in Canada or Lawrence Hill's *The Book of Negroes* about the black Loyalists' flight to Nova Scotia after the American Revolution (published in the United States as *Someone Knows My Name*) are not dismissed by students as historical aberrations, but rather as reflections of a shared colonial past. As we discuss such texts, our conversations and their writing in response are less judgmental. Nor is the impulse to deny racist happenings in Canada's history as prevalent.

These practices are intended to achieve what St. Denis advocates: "Anti-racist education explores the practices, processes, and ideologies of racialization, which includes a study of not only how racism disadvantages some but also how racism advantages others and how whiteness gets produced and constructed as superior" (1087). In her chapter "Moving Beyond the Personal Myth," Episkenew argues that the presence of indigenous literature in the academy "functions as counter-stories to heal the community, as implements of social justice, and as tools of anti-racist education" (146). Although I embrace all three purposes, in preservice teacher education I emphasize the latter two. However, given the history of our part of the Great Plains of North America, to accept understanding as *enough* is a form of violence (Bockarie).

Marx and Trepagnier studied white teachers' attitudes to antiracist pedagogies, and among their findings was white teachers' abhorrence of racism. The teachers in the studies did not want to be labelled racist. They were united in their condemnation of racial slurs and racially based acts of violence but were less willing to recognize, much less condemn, less extreme acts as being racist. Consequently, they had developed narrow definitions of what constitutes racist attitudes and behavior. Not surprisingly, when their own attitudes or behaviors were challenged, they became defensive. Marx explains that "the very ambiguity of White culture is evidence of its colonial past. Groups that are named, bound, and encouraged by the dominant culture to remain 'pure' and 'preserved' (Frankenberg 193) like Native Americans, Inuit, and other native groups, are most likely to be groups that have been marginalized by colonialism. In its dominance, white culture remains unmarked. Indeed, many whites profess to feel resentment and even envy regarding the imagined cohesiveness of these 'other' cultures" (49).

Similarly, Jennifer Trainor provides a useful analysis of white talk about race, revealing that defensiveness, claims of being color-blind, and charges of reverse-racism are common among white educators uncertain of their own positionality as white people and as antiracist teachers. The effort of white teachers to appear innocent of racism, which is perceived as being repugnant and evil, prevents them from seeing the less-heinous, garden variety discrimination. Such acts may be considered unconscious or insensitive, but not racist. Trepagnier writes: "Ignoring racism that is not hateful and intentional effectively hides the fact that white students daily perform acts of everyday racism" (3). Marx, Trepagnier, and Trainor all found that by reducing racism to a binary, that is, racist or not racist, not as part of continuum of complex beliefs, attitudes, and behaviors, denies the existence of unintentional or institutional acts of everyday racism. The combination of self-study methods and explicit teaching of postcolonial theory prevents the preservice classroom from falling into this problematic binary.

Resistances of White-Settler Students

In any course with antiracist goals, a significant number of students openly resist the alternate story of the white-settler past, particularly in their written responses to the texts we write, read, and view. The resistance is welcomed; it is preferable to openly discuss, rather than to take the resistance underground (Marx; Trepagnier; Trainor). Some of the most vocal resistance to antiracist pedagogy comes from rural students who have never attended school with First Nations students, have never before lived in one of the cities where 15 percent of the population self-identifies as Aboriginal, or have never had any direct knowledge of recent immigrants. Recently, a student described his frustration with being a white settler by writing a poem entitled "A Cracker's Lament." *Cracker* is not a term in common use in this part of the world but is an indicator of the struggle some students have with challenges to preexisting ideas. Furthermore, the resistance is understandable given the dominance of white-settler constructed realities. What follows is a simplified version of these students' resistance.

First is the claim of *mystification.* They write, "Why do we need to study this *stuff* when we are not responsible for the wrongs of the past? Our communities are homogenous. We are not implicated in the oppressive practices of the present because our communities do not have anyone to oppress." I read these sentiments every semester: "I don't think there were any Indians in my school. I think those who grew up near reserves are more prejudiced because of what they have seen. I can be neutral in all this stuff." There are a number of assumptions at play in these opinions. By embracing the twin mantles of ignorance and amnesia, this stance allows students to downplay the systems of privilege that benefit white settlers. If proximity to the oppressed was the sole variable in racist systems, then people living in gated communities, however extensive their power and privilege, would be fully exonerated from responsibility for the restrictions the social and political systems impose on others.

A second common claim is that *rural culture is marginalized, too.* Many of these students' grandparents or great-grandparents lost a first language because they were forced to learn English in colonial schools that were compulsory. I understand this story. My own mother did not speak English until she began school at age seven; by the age of eighteen she was teaching Hungarian immigrant children English in a one-room country school. The process of assimilation for most European white settlers was rapid and comprehensive. My Swedish immigrant family were "English" for all intents and purposes in one generation because they were literate, Christian, and white. They moved seamlessly into the dominant British colonial society that ruled Saskatchewan. Giving up their first language was a small price for attaining such privilege.

Many rural students have written wrenching stories of the struggles their parents faced to finance their university educations, citing commodity prices, natural disasters due to weather, and international trade as hardships they endured that are at least commensurate with being "a visible minority." Similarly, in a study of rural educational priorities and capacity, Wallin and Reimer acknowledge that the poverty of farm families threatens the sustainability of rural communities and their schools. For example, "I come from a Century farm [originally a homestead, in the hands of one family for 100 years or more] and my dad says he doesn't know from one year to the next how long he can afford to keep farming." Sentimentality often emerges on the page. The lack of privacy that comes from living in a rural community that students normally complain about morphs into a sunny story of unconditional community support when marshalling their reasons for resistance to accepting the existence of white-settler privilege. Coupled with succumbing to the rhetoric of the rosy past is a more pernicious form of denial that takes of the form of "my life is hard, too, therefore I'm not of the oppressor class." A possible response to this common reaction is to question the assumptions we hold about the place where we live. I say "we" deliberately since I am of this place: I grew up here and returned to make my living here. Perhaps one reason that we cling to the pioneer provenance is the space that story allows for white settlers to identify with struggle and hardship and to deny that the power we have is unjust.

The third claim of resistance is *idyllic simplicity.* Often it takes this form: "I intend to return to my home town where these problems do not exist. There are no reserves near my community. We do not have cultural differences or social problems that create tensions in my home town." In other words, rural communities are somehow immune: "I'm not going to have to worry about this. . . . I'm going home." While it is true that most new immigrants to Saskatchewan settle in the two major cities, where possibilities of employment, contact with their language and cultural groups, and limited government support exists, there are some recent non-European, non-English-speaking immigrants in rural Saskatchewan. Also, some international students attend small rural schools as exchange students. Their tuition is an important revenue source, and their presence a way to boost enrollment in schools in danger of closing because of declining rural populations. Very few supports for immigrants exist in small communities. In more than one rural school, I have witnessed non-English-speaking foreign students sitting together, staring at books they cannot read, in a cone of silence. The Canadian students and the teachers, many of whom are fewer than two generations from not speaking English themselves, are free to remain oblivious to the painful isolation these students experience daily. When students assuming this stance are reminded of pressing problems in rural communities, such as school closures, lack of child care for farm families, limited access to health care, particularly for mental health, economic insecurity, incidents of violence and suicide, and so on, most concede that life in rural Saskatchewan may not be perfect.

James McNinch conflates the social, racial, and class tensions raised in this essay in his study of a sensational 2001 Saskatchewan trial of three white-settler men for the sexual assault of a 12-year-old Saulteaux girl from the Yellow Quill First Nations in the town of Tisdale. After a lengthy trial and subsequent appeals, two of the three accused were acquitted. The judgments exacerbated racial tensions in the town and in the province. McNinch concludes: "To the First Peoples of the Yellow Quill Reserve, the Tisdale town folk [like my university students] carry with them the burden of white privilege. This privilege allows white-settler elites to ignore or be blind to their racism, failing to see how their whiteness has been defined by those they have othered" (91). The resistance to a counternarrative to the white-settler version of history that pervades the school, indeed all institutions in the province, is banal in its predictability. Ours is a postcolonial story. Although I can understand the origin and appeal of the resistance to learning a different story, one that challenges the dominance of one group over another, the failure to respond by teaching differently would constitute a serious failure.

Conclusion: Ways to Work with Student Resistance

Kevin Kumashiro writes: "The reason we fail to do more to challenge oppression is not merely that we do not know enough about oppression, but also that we do not *want* to know more about oppression" (25). Social and political issues are not the sole responsibility of teacher-educators or English teachers, but neither are we exempt from engaging meaningfully in their exposition. The failure of cultural education alone (St. Denis) parallels my own experience of implementing first a multicultural awareness, then a postcolonial approach in my classes. Until I included a critical literacy stance in my teaching, the colonial version of our rural pioneer past persisted.

In response to the stance of *mystification*, I insist that students learn about and acknowledge the implication of our recent colonial history. Since my preservice methods classes are devoted to language and literacy education, we read through a postcolonial lens narratives of the Indian residential schools in our province and in other analogous postcolonial settings such as Australia or New Zealand, places whose histories and language are similar to Canada's. Jo-Ann Episkenew's refrain, "When you are sick you need a cure, and when you have been damaged you need to be healed," a phrase she uses in her scholarly talks about indigenous literature, informs my teaching. I attempt to make her advice concrete in my classes. My approach to First Nations and Métis literary memoir is "to offer a cure."

Second, to counter the claim that *rural culture is marginalized, too*, I offer students contemporary research and my own family's history for them to interrogate. In my literacy autobiography, I include a picture of my first day of school with the caption: "With my English name and ability to read, I could not have failed at school." Most important, I invoke the treaties and their assertion that all the people in our province have an inherited legal responsibility to live in harmony. In the essay "We Are All Treaty People: History, Reconciliation, and the 'Settler Problem,'" Roger Epp argues:

> In such places, mostly rural, interdependence is a difficult but almost inescapable challenge. The casual racism of everyday speech is shocking to outsiders. . . . But it is in such places, places where not one but two working human cultures—aboriginal and settler—have been dispatched to the dustbin of history by the proponents of the new economy, that words of reconciliation must ring true and people must be enlisted in relationships. (127)

Rather than dismiss the very real experience of a struggling agricultural economy, we read nonfiction that addresses the practical and historical realities of our communities. Part of understanding our autobiographies is gaining understanding of our contemporary context. While it is possible to make a strictly moral argument for reconciliation, our collective economic future depends on finding ways to live together.

The third form of resistance, *idyllic simplicity,* is the most difficult to disrupt because it is at once so appealing and so prevalent. Poetry that exhorts the natural virtues of the rural landscape and people is as common in Canadian school literature anthologies as are representations of the Noble Savage that reify destructive images of First Nations and Métis peoples. Earlier I cited one of many court cases involving racialized violence in our recent history as a counternarrative. I have also used popular media to dislodge the myth of idyllic simplicity. A critical reading of the Canadian sitcom *Corner Gas,* which is set in a fictional rural Saskatchewan town, has generated discussion and acknowledgement of the complexity of contemporary rural life.

In summary, I am deliberate about teaching postcolonial theory to preservice teachers to assist us in understanding our setting and the literature written about and produced in this place. I advocate explicit teaching of the reasons for engaging in antioppressive practices, reasons that include moral and pragmatic dimensions. Most important, the self-study methods that I have employed do not apply to the students alone. As a white settler, I am subject to the same process. The discourses that produced most of my students also produced me.

To avoid complicity in colonizing discourses and to engage in resistance and advocacy for social justice, a postcolonial approach in teacher education, particularly in my community, is necessary to disrupt the version of our collective past that continues to interfere with our living equitably in the present. Incorporating First Nations cultural perspectives and practices in English education is a moral and political imperative, more likely to develop when the restrictions created by white-settler discourses are exposed, recognized, and addressed. White settlers have easy access to an idyllic rural mythology that interferes with social justice initiatives. A counternarrative to the heroic pioneer story that is suffused in many Saskatchewan schools may contribute to a more equitable education for all students in this place.

Works Cited and Consulted

Agee, Jane. "What Kind of Teacher Will I Be? Creating Spaces for Beginning Teachers' Imagined Roles." *English Education* 38.3 (2006): 194–219. Print.

Alfred, Taiaiake. *Wasase: Indigenous Pathways of Action and Freedom.* Toronto: Broadview, 2005. Print.

Anderson, Alan. "Population Trends." *Encyclopaedia of Saskatchewan.* Regina, SK: Canadian Plains Research Centre, 2006. Web.

Battiste, Marie, and James Sakej Youngblood Henderson. *Protecting Indigenous Knowledge and Heritage.* Saskatoon, SK: Purich , 2000. Print.

Besner, Neil. "What Resides in the Question, 'Is Canada Postcolonial?'" *Is Canada Postcolonial? Unsettling Canadian Literature.* Ed. L. Moss. Waterloo, ON: Wilfrid Laurier UP, 2003. 40–48. Print.

Bhabha, Homi. *The Location of Culture.* London: Routledge, 2004. Print.

Bockarie, Abu. "Peace Education in a Post-Conflict Third World Country: The Good, the Bad, and the Ugly." SIDRU (Saskatchewan Instructional Development and Research Unit, U of Regina). 7 Mar. 2007. Address.

Bradford, Clare. *Unsettling Narratives: Postcolonial Readings of Children's Literature.* Montreal: Sir Wilfred Laurier, 2007. Print.

Cherland, Meredith Rogers, and Helen Harper. *Advocacy Research in Literacy Education: Seeking Higher Ground.* Mahwah, NJ: Lawrence Erlbaum, 2007. Print.

Culleton, Beatrice. *April Raintree.* Toronto: Peguis, 1984. Print.

Delpit, Lisa. *Other People's Children: Cultural Conflict in the Classroom.* New York: New Press, 2006. Print.

Dieter, Connie. *From Our Mother's Arms: The Intergenerational Impact of Residential Schools in Saskatchewan.* Toronto: United Church, 1999. Print.

Donehower, Kim, Charlotte Hogg, and Eileen E. Schell. *Rural Literacies.* Carbondale: Southern Illinois UP, 2007. Print.

Earick, Mary E. *Racially Equitable Teaching: Beyond the Whiteness of Professional Development for Early Childhood Educators.* New York: Peter Lang, 2009. Print.

Edelsky, Carole, ed. *Making Justice Our Project: Teachers Working toward Critical Whole Language Practice.* Urbana, IL: NCTE, 1999. Print.

Emberley, Julia V. *Defamiliarizing the Aboriginal: Cultural Practices and Decolonization in Canada.* Toronto, ON: University of Toronto Press, 2007. Print.

Episkenew, Jo-Ann. *Taking Back Our Spirits: Indigenous Literature, Public Policy, and Healing.* Winnipeg: U of Manitoba P, 2009. Print.

Epp, Roger. *We Are All Treaty People: Prairie Essays.* Edmonton: U of Alberta P, 2008. Print.

Frank, Carolyn R., Marilyn Carpenter, and Karen Smith. "Mapping Our Stories: Teachers' Reflections on Themselves as Writers." *Language Arts* 80.1 (2003): 185–95. Print.

Garcea, J. "Immigration to Smaller Communities in Saskatchewan." Ed. B. Reimer. *Our Diverse Cities: Rural Communities* 3 (Summer 2007): 134–39. Print.

Grande, Sandy. *Red Pedagogy: Native American Social and Political Thought.* Lanham, MD: Rowman and Littlefield, 2004. Print.

Heit, Mary, and Heather Blair. "Language Needs and Characteristics of Saskatchewan Indian and Métis Students: Implications for Educators." *Aboriginal Languages and Education: The Canadian Experience.* Ed. S. Morris, K. McLeod and M. Danesi. Oakville, ON: Mosaic, 1993. 103–28. Print.

Hill, Lawrence. *The Book of Negroes.* Toronto: Harper Collins, 2007. Print.

Kogawa, Joy. *Obasan.* Harmondsworth, UK: Penguin Books, 1983. Print.

Kumashiro, Kevin. *Against Common Sense: Teaching and Learning toward Social Justice.* New York: Routledge Falmer, 2004. Print.

LeCourt, Donna. *Identity Matters: Schooling the Student Body in Academic Discourse.* Albany: State U of New York P, 2004. Print.

Loughran, J., and T. Russell, eds. *Improving Teacher Education Practices through Self-Study.* London and New York: Routledge Falmer, 2002. Print.

Marx, Sherri. *Revealing the Invisible: Confronting Passive Racism in Teacher Education.* New York: Routledge, 2006. Print.

McCann, Thomas M., Larry R. Johannessen, and Bernard P. Ricca. *Supporting Beginning English Teachers: Research and Implications for Teacher Induction.* Urbana, IL: NCTE, 2005. Print.

McKenzie, Stephanie. *Before the Country: Native Renaissance, Canadian Mythology.* Toronto: U of Toronto P, 2007. Print.

McLeod, Neal. *Cree Narrative Memory: From Treaties to Contemporary Times.* Saskatoon, SK: Purich Publishing, 2007. Print.

McNinch, James. "Queer Eye on Straight Youth: Homoerotic and Racial Violence in the Narrative Discourse of White Settler Masculinity." *Journal of LGBT Youth* 5.2 (2008): 87–107. Print.

Mulholland, Valerie, and Sarah Longman. "Reframing Autobiography in Teacher Education from a First Nations Perspective. *Making Connections: Self-Study and Social Action.*" Ed. Kathleen Pithouse, Claudia Mitchell, and Relebohile Moletsane. New York: Peter Lang, 2009. Print.

Pennycook, Alistair. *English and the Discourses of Colonialism.* New York: Routledge, 1998. Print.

Pithouse, Kathleen. "Self-Study through Narrative Interpretation: Probing the Lived Experiences of Educational Privilege." *Just Who Do We Think We Are? Methodologies for Autobiography and Self-Study in Teaching.* Ed. C. Mitchell, S. Weber, and K. O'Reilly-Scanlon. New York: Routledge Falmer, 2005. 206–17. Print.

Rabbit-Proof Fence. Dir. Peter Noyce. Alliance Atlantis/Miramax/Australian Film Finance Corp., 2003. Film.

Razack, Sherene H. *Looking White People in the Eye: Gender, Race, and Culture in Courtrooms and Classrooms.* Toronto: U of Toronto P, 1998. Print.

———. "When Place Becomes Race." *Race, Space, and the Law: Unmapping a White Settler Society.* Ed. S. Razack. Toronto: Between the Lines, 2002. Print.

Russell, David. "Institutionalizing English: Rhetoric on the Boundaries." *Disciplining English: Alternative Histories, Critical Perspectives.* Ed. D. R. Shumway and C. Dionne. New York: State U of New York P, 2002. 39–58. Print.

Schick, Carol. "'By Virtue of Being White': Resistance in Anti-Racist Pedagogy." *Race, Ethnicity and Education* 3.1 (2000): 83–102. Print.

Sleeter, Christine E., and Carl A. Grant. *Making Choices for Multicultural Education: Five Approaches to Race, Class, and Gender.* 6th ed. Hoboken, NJ: Wiley & Sons, 2009. Print.

St. Denis, Verna. "Uniting Aboriginal Education with Anti-Racist Education: Building Alliances across Cultural and Racial Identity Politics." *Canadian Journal of Education* 30.4 (2007): 1068–92. Print.

Sterzuk, Andrea. "Whose English Counts? Indigenous English in Saskatchewan Schools." *McGill Journal of Education* 43.1 (2008): 9–19. Print.

Sterzuk, Andrea. "Language as an Agent of Division in Saskatchewan Schools." *"I Thought Pocahontas Was a Movie": Perspectives on Race/Culture Binaries in Education and Service Professions.* Ed. Carol Schick and James McNinch. Regina, SK: Canadian Plains Research Centre, 2009. 1-14. Print.

Thobani, Sunera. *Exalted Subjects: Studies in the Making of Race and Nation in Canada.* Toronto: U of Toronto P, 2007. Print.

Trainor, Jennifer Seibel. "'My Ancestors Didn't Own Any Slaves': Understanding White Talk about Race." *Research in the Teaching of English* 40.2 (2005): 140–68. Print.

Trepagnier, B. *Silent Racism: How Well-Meaning White People Perpetuate the Racial Divide.* Boulder, CO: Paradigm, 2006. Print.

Viswanathan, Gauri. "Milton, Imperialism, and Education." *Modern Language Quarterly* 59.3 (1998): 345–59. Print.

———. *Masks of Conquest: Literary Study and British Rule in India.* New York: Columbia UP, 1989. Print.

Wallin, Dawn C., and Laura Reimer. "Educational Priorities and Capacity: A Rural Perspective." *Canadian Journal of Education* 31.3 (2008): 591–613. Print.

Ward, Donald. *The People: A Historical Guide to the First Nations of Alberta, Saskatchewan, and Manitoba.* Saskatoon, SK: Fifth House, 1995. Print.

Willinsky, John. "A History Not Yet Past: Where Then Is Here?" *Advocating Change: Contemporary Issues in Subject English.* Ed. B. R. C. Barrell, and R. F. Hammett. Toronto: Irwin, 2000. 2–13. Print.

———. *Learning to Divide the World: Education at Empire's End.* Minneapolis: U of Minnesota P, 1998. Print.

12

Living with Literacy's Contradictions: Appalachian Students in a First-Year Writing Course

Sara Webb-Sunderhaus

During the summer of 2004, I conducted an ethnographic case study of students in a first-year composition course at State University–Sciotoville,[1] an open-admission, state university in rural, central Appalachia. Literacy micro-sponsorship and identity performance proved to be useful concepts in thinking through ideas of rural Appalachianness and how students grapple with this identity. My other work ("Family Affair") discusses the role of family members as sponsors of college students' literacies and positions the composition classroom as a stage for the performance of student identity. This essay further explores these issues, focusing on the role literacy beliefs and practices play in student identity performances. Drawing on Sylvia Scribner's "Literacy in Three Metaphors," I illustrate how metaphors of literacy emerged from these students' literacy beliefs and practices—metaphors that overlapped with and extended Scribner's framework. I argue that for these students, literacy became, to use Mary Louise Pratt's term, a *contact zone* "where cultures meet, clash, and grapple with each other" (34). These students were living with literacy's contradictions, illustrating how the boundaries of Scribner's metaphors break down and how new metaphors are created as literacy practices and beliefs circulate.

Scribner documents three influential metaphors of literacy: literacy as adaptation, literacy as power, and literacy as a state of grace. Literacy as adaptation is rooted in a functional view of literacy, one "conceived broadly as the level of proficiency necessary for effective performance in a range of settings and customary activities" (73). It recognizes literacy's assimilative value, portraying literacy as a set of skills needed to survive and flourish in any given society. Scribner's second metaphor, literacy as power, "emphasizes a relationship between literacy and group or community advancement" (75).

This metaphor is evident in the work of educators such as Paulo Freire and Myles Horton, who sought to empower and liberate their students. In this view, literacy education can and should be used as a means of social change and transformation, though the power of literacy is one of very different kinds, including social mobility (à la the "American Dream") and transformation. Scribner's final metaphor of literacy, literacy as a state of grace, derives historically from religion and endows the literate person with special privilege and worth. In this metaphor, literacy comes to define and refine the self: "the literate individual's life derives its meaning and significance from intellectual, aesthetic, and spiritual participation in the accumulated creations and knowledge of humankind, made available through the written word" (77).

At State University–Sciotoville, the boundaries between Scribner's metaphors became blurred, mixing together as they circulated throughout the university. Literacy as adaptation, power, and a state of grace were not the only metaphors in play, however. A new metaphor emerged, one that mixed literacy as adaptation and literacy as power into a consuming metaphor of literacy that often, though not always, figured literacy's functional power in terms of increased economic capital. The institutional contact zone of literacy forced students to wrestle with this metaphor's meanings and implications, and students, in turn, developed a more complex model of literacy. While the university's emphasis on the consumption metaphor was often on individual advancement, this was not always the case for the students, who illustrated a concern for community advancement—acts that played an important role in their performance of Appalachian identity.

Literacy as Consumption: State University–Sciotoville

As a participant-observer in the first-year composition course, I sat alongside the students, participated in their conversations, and took breaks with them. Of the fourteen students in the course, twelve consented to participate in my research. Two students (Julie and Katie May) emerged as case study participants, primarily because they were available to be interviewed for thirty to sixty minutes after class once a week for the duration of the course. However, I informally interviewed all twelve consenting students at various and multiple times during the term. These spontaneous interviews happened in the classroom and library, by the vending machines, and during smoke breaks: anywhere and anytime the students were willing and able to talk.

Before my field work began, I was able to learn much about the university and its surrounding community. The university is a two-year campus of a large, state university; approximately 1,800 students were enrolled at the regional campus during the study. Over 60 percent of the students at this campus were women, and their average age was 33. The town of Sciotoville, with a population of nearly 22,000 according to the 2000 census, is the seat of St. Clair County, whose 2000 population was just over 73,000. The county was predominantly white (92 percent), and 11.3 percent of county residents 25 and older held bachelor's degrees or greater, compared with a state average of 21.1 percent. The most common educational attainment levels were high school graduate (42.2 percent) and no high school diploma (23.9 percent). The Appalachian Regional Commission classifies St. Clair County as having a "transitional" economic status, meaning that the county's three-year unemployment average, per-capita market income, and poverty rate are worse than national averages, but better than those of "at-risk" counties ("County Economic").[2] Some 9.1 percent of county families live in poverty, and of those families, 41.2 percent are headed by a single mother. The county's general poverty rate is 12 percent, compared with the state average of 10.6 percent. This part of the central Appalachian region was also familiar to me since my parents were born and raised in the general area before migrating out of the region, and I have many relatives still living there.

Thus, I had some knowledge of the regional and institutional contexts I was entering. However, I was unable to get a sense of the institution's literacy beliefs, since this regional campus did not have a website, catalogues, or brochures distinct from the four-year campus. Posters in the university bookstore were my first indicator of the metaphors of literacy in circulation on campus. While the posters were not produced by the university, they contributed to the implicit and explicit messages about literacy on campus.

The first poster depicts a woman reading a textbook, a man holding a diploma, and a man holding a paycheck under the heading, "Read This. Get This. Earn This!" The implication is clear: by reading a textbook, one will acquire a college diploma and subsequently earn a paycheck. The subtext of the poster—a metaphor of literacy as power—is also evident. This particular type of literacy offers economic power, as the poster uses the language of the stock market ("Invest in your future") to impart the importance of reading one's textbooks.

The second poster notes, "If you don't read your textbooks now, you'll have plenty of time to read them later," with the word "textbooks" highlighted in yellow. Underneath the text is an illustration. At the top of the illustration is a banner that states, "UNEMPLOYMENT. Please wait for your number to be called." Beneath the banner, professionally dressed men and women (the men wearing shirts and ties, the women wearing dresses or skirts and blouses) are sitting, presumably waiting for their numbers to be called. Several are reading a newspaper or brochures of some sort. The man in the center of the illustration has a large textbook resting on his lap—a visual emphasis of the poster's message that the unemployment line offers plenty of time to read.

Finally, the last poster reads, "Textbooks: the difference between the boardroom and the waiting room," and contains a pair of juxtaposed images: one of people sitting on benches; the other of a group of people dressed professionally and gathered around a conference table, as if in a business meeting. This table rests on a large stack of textbooks, making this image literally tower over the image of people in the waiting room. The poster drives home its point—that reading textbooks will enable students to rise above others, both economically and socially—quite literally.

Consuming Literacies: Institutional Contexts

Together, these posters argue that students must develop a particular academic literacy practice—reading their textbooks—in order to function successfully in today's society. It is not *any* type of reading, but the reading of college textbooks, that ensures students' ability to gain employment. Critically reflecting on and writing about these texts apparently play no part in the students' success. The message of these posters is that, if students simply read their textbooks, their transformation into denizens of the boardroom will happen automatically. Engaging in other reading and writing acts is not part of the equation for economic security.

In other words, this type of reading *is* power, though in this conceptualization of literacy, its power is utilized not on behalf of a group, as Scribner suggests, but on behalf of individuals. The transformative power of literacy that Scribner describes is nowhere to be seen. Instead, literacy becomes a neatly packaged object that one can possess, and in turn, use as capital to gain even more capital—namely, employment and wealth (Gee 122–23). This conceptualization of literacy focuses not on group advancement, as does Scribner's metaphor of literacy as power, but on individual adaptation and advancement as a value-neutral way to thrive in a modern economy. At Sciotoville, literacy's power is reduced to adapting to the status quo and its consumerist mentality. Furthermore, the power that literacy could offer for regional change and uplift is not apparent in these posters—even though the county in which the university is located needs to be empowered in these ways. By representing literacy-as-adaptation *as* the power that literacy offers, the university erases the different kinds of power that Scribner describes. The posters' message is that these presumably "upwardly mobile" college students should "go along to get along" and become full members of a consumption-based economy in which literacy will presumably allow them to participate.

The mindset behind these posters overlooks other factors that impact literacy. It assumes equal access to the education and funds needed to enroll in college (and purchase textbooks). It also equates academic literacy with corporate success, as seen in the reference to the boardroom. This assumption is rooted in Harvey Graff's concept of the literacy myth: the idea that literacy independently improves one's social and material conditions. Graff argues factors other than literacy—such as race, gender, and social class—are far more influential in determining, and reinforcing, said conditions. Rather than theorizing literacy as only a means of empowerment, Graff identifies literacy as an instrument of domination and cultural eradication (59). Thus, rather than only seeing poverty and unemployment as resulting from low literacy and education, we should also recognize that low literacy and education levels result from poverty and unemployment, since these factors limit one's chances for pursuing and receiving a meaningful education.

This is not the view of literacy and education evidenced in the posters, however. State University–Sciotoville uses "the vehicle of literacy for the promotion of the values, attitudes, and habits" (24), to use Graff's phrase; the posters in the university bookstore may not explicitly say so, but the implicit meaning is clear: if you are unemployed and/or poor, it's your fault. You should have gone to college and developed specific academic literacy practices—namely, reading textbooks—not so much for the purposes of learning, but for purposes of earning. These posters encourage students to "pull themselves up by their bootstraps" by acquiring a college degree, but as Victor Villanueva writes of himself, "he knows that for most like him, the bootstraps break before the boots are on, that too many have no boots" (xiv).

What these posters, and, by extension, the university at which they were displayed, fail to recognize is that there may not be jobs for these students. Being in the unemployment line may not hinge at all on their status as a college graduate or nongraduate: unemployment and poverty rates in the Appalachian region are higher than national averages. Across the region, there is a lack of jobs, particularly high-paying ones; labor participation is lower than national averages; many jobs that had been available locally have been outsourced; job opportunities for women are particularly limited; and the feminization of poverty is quite real, particularly in St. Clair County. These factors play a role in determining—to paraphrase Villanueva—who has boots, who doesn't, and whose bootstraps will break under the pressure of poverty, unemployment, and gender roles. This disconnect between the message of the posters and the regional and local context of this university makes the placement of these posters in the university bookstore disturbingly ironic, and the metaphor of literacy as consumption in this context so troubling.

Consuming Literacies: Individual Contexts

To some extent, the Sciotoville students share a conceptualization of literacy as consumption, repeating over and over again in interviews that their composition course was important due to the literacy practices they learned that would earn them a college degree and a ticket to a "better life." For example, Katie May remarked in an interview, "We all *have* to take this class, because it's a freshman English class. These skills that we're learning are essential for our other courses that we're taking." Here Katie May connects academic literacy practices ("the skills that we're learning") and success in other courses to success in this class. She must acquire a functional literacy (note her emphasis on skills) in order to succeed in other courses she takes.

I asked Julie, a returning adult student and mother of a kindergartener, why she enrolled in college; her response illustrates the idea that functional literacy *is* power, and its power comes from adapting to the economic status quo:

> Well, you had to, especially for girls. . . . The boys, there were good-paying jobs for them right out of high school. They could go work in the steel mill, the factories. Hardly any of them went to college, because they would be missing out on good money and would be living at home and paying a lot of money to go to college. It was almost like a waste of money to go to college. But for the girls, it was working at McDonald's. That was it. That's why I went back to school: I have to provide for my son, and there just aren't good paying jobs around here for women, unless you have a college degree. Then you can be a schoolteacher, a nurse, that sort of thing.

Julie's goal was to become a lawyer, and her decision was influenced in part by a desire to "make a lot of money." Julie had been poor all her life and did not want the same for her son. Similarly, Katie May hoped to become a pediatrician, and one of the reasons why she wanted to be a doctor was because "doctors make a good living." For these students, academic literacy practices and a college degree are forms of economic power and capital that will assist them in gaining even more economic power and capital—valuable commodities in a region as disenfranchised as Appalachia.

But within Julie's response is a recognition of social forces that the bookstore's posters lacked. As Jane Greer notes, "the place of rural women within the economy remains an ongoing concern in the twenty-first century," and this concern is certainly evident in Appalachia. Julie repeatedly discussed how her employment opportunities were limited due to her gender, an assertion reinforced by the county's high rate of poverty for families headed by single mothers. A college degree was more necessary for women than for men, according to Julie, because a college degree opened the door to traditionally female occupations, such as teaching and nursing.

Julie was not the only Sciotoville student with an awareness of how gender may impact educational and career opportunities. Schueler used the fact he was only one of two males in the class, and one of few boys from his high school class to go to college, as evidence that there are more job opportunities in the area for men without college degrees—a fact that also illustrates the area's gender norms. However, Schueler also commented that things were changing:

> I have a lot of friends, in high school they always went to those tech prep programs, career centers, instead of college. . . . Most of them end up at [a local factory], the steel mill, the sawmills. Where I work, I have a friend who just graduated [from high school], and he quit his job at the pizza place to go work at the sawmill. . . . He was talking about how he was starting out at $13 an hour. And yeah, that's good money for an eighteen-, nineteen-year-old. But he's going to be making that his entire life, trying to support a family on that.

Schueler later added that while many of the factories and mills are closing, the mindset that young men don't "need" college isn't changing. He observed that this mindset could eventually leave his friends "between a rock and a hard place," as he put it, since they would not have the college educations that would enable them to look for work outside of the local area at the very same time that jobs that do not require a college education are leaving the area.

In their own way, these gender roles are just as damaging for young men as they are for young women. The local and regional culture encourages these young men to go to work after high school, since going to college was, in Julie's words, "almost like a waste of money." Yet as these jobs are outsourced from the region and men start to enroll in college, the men will be hit with a one-two punch: they will have lost their jobs, and the blame for that loss will be placed solely at their feet in institutional discourse such as Sciotoville's. In this context, men are in a catch-22: they are encouraged to forsake college for the sake of employment so as not to "waste money," but if they lose that employment, it's their fault because they didn't go to college. What this discourse fails to recognize is the cultural context and the region's lack of jobs for all.

Students such as Julie and Schueler did recognize this cultural context, however. Although they echoed the university's metaphor of literacy as consumption, they complicated it by their attention to place—a subject ignored by the university. They also emphasized the social, rather than individual, nature of literacy via sponsorship of their peers: teaching each other how to use their textbooks, offering revision ideas, providing help to a student struggling to answer a professor's questions. Their literacy sponsorship illustrated another contact zone of metaphors, a space where differing beliefs systems about literacy came into play and blended both institutional and regional contexts.

"We're All in This Together": Students as Literacy Micro-Sponsors

My use of the term "literacy sponsor" is influenced by the work of Deborah Brandt, who defines sponsors as "any agents, local or distant, concrete or abstract, who enable, support, teach, and model, as well as recruit, regulate, suppress, or withhold, literacy—and gain advantage by it in some way" (19). Brandt conceptualizes literacy sponsorship with macro (or top-down) analysis, noting that literacy sponsors—which in her work are large institutions such as the African American church, unions, and the educational system— are the actors through which social and economic forces make themselves known in individuals' lives.

While Brandt's analytical framework is extraordinarily helpful in understanding the circulation of literacy beliefs and practices, literacy lives must be examined from a micro (or bottom-up) perspective as well. In other words, we must also account for how individuals use literacy beliefs and practices as they act within, upon, and without these institutions and negotiate social and economic forces. My conceptualization of "micro-sponsors" departs from Brandt's notion of sponsorship in that I contend that individuals *can* act as sponsors of literacy, rather than conduits of institutionally sponsored literacy. However, my use of micro-sponsorship also complements Brandt's macro view, as the Sciotoville students became micro-sponsors thanks to their exposure to the university as an institutional sponsor of literacy. Given their education, these students could perform some version of that institutional role and "give back" to their communities, as many of them wanted to do; furthermore, thanks to the rural context, it is possible for a few individuals to have an almost institutional level of impact on a community. This type of micro-analysis is particularly important for rural areas—including parts of Appalachia—where many institutional sponsors do not penetrate deeply into the community.

The students of Sciotoville sponsored each other's literacies via communal, cooperative behavior that was evidenced in almost every class session. Time and again, the students worked in groups, assisting each other in acquiring the literacy practices needed for effective college writing. These peer groups functioned as *literacy events*, which Shirley Brice Heath defines as "any occasion in which the production and/or comprehension of print plays a role" (445). This definition of literacy events would certainly extend to the groups I observed at Sciotoville, given the prominent role print texts played in those groups. Most of the time, students in these groups were focused on their own or their classmates' written texts. Moss, Highberg, and Nicolas write that "writing groups sit primarily (but not exclusively) on the productive side of literacy events, and thinking about writing in this context highlights the centrality of oral speech in the development of texts" (3). The authors explain that literacy events can be productive or interpretative in nature, depending on whether the talk in these events focuses on texts that are currently being drafted (productive) or texts that have already been written (interpretative). I observed both types of literacy events in the Sciotoville groups; often, however, groups simultaneously performed productive and interpretative literacy events.

One example of a simultaneous literacy event occurred on the day when the professor returned drafts of the first formal writing assignment at the beginning of the class. When she announced a ten-minute break during class, several students left the room, but six—Katie May, Dixie, Twana, Anna, Beth, and Schueler—remained at their desks and immediately, as well as voluntarily, sought each other out, asking, "Do you want to trade papers?" With this question, peer groups were born.[3]

The students worked in pairs, turning to the person who was sitting closest to them. The groups quickly exchanged papers, trading ideas for revision and helping each other interpret the professor's comments, thus both producing and interpreting text. To use Diana George's term, these groups were "Task-Oriented" groups, as they were "self-starting and self-perpetuating. . . . Their real strength lies in their willingness to talk and to listen to each other" (321). This willingness was immediately apparent. Anna, a native Bulgarian student who was particularly worried about second-language issues, told Schueler, "Please check my English. I worry that it's not so good." The other students were interested in reading each other's drafts as a means to generate ideas for their own revisions and to receive more general critiques, telling their partners, "Read it over and tell me what you think." At times the entire group was called upon to decipher the professor's handwriting or share an opinion. Although the conversations on this particular day were rushed, since the break lasted only a few minutes, these voluntary, impromptu peer review sessions occurred every time drafts of the major assignments were returned, and different students drifted in and out of these informal groups. While Dixie, Schueler, Anna, Katie May, and Beth were always involved, sometimes Twana was not; occasionally, other students, including Julie and Chris, joined the groups as well. Sometimes the students invited the professor or me into the group to answer a question or clear up some confusion.

In observing these peer groups, I saw patterns soon begin to emerge in the types of response the students gave each other. The students' feedback usually took one of three forms: the students would point out to their partner areas in which the partner's draft was more successful; the partner would point to his/her own paper as a model if the other student expressed concern about a particular element of his or her draft; and the partner would offer empathy, general encouragement, and reassurance to his or her peer.

Here is an example of the first type of exchange between Katie May and Beth. Katie May and Beth shared strong writing skills and dedication to the course; both women would eventually earn As. While both were skilled writers, their strengths lie in different areas, as this exchange suggests:

KATIE MAY: Your thesis is really good! That gives me an idea on how to make mine better.

BETH: Really? Thanks. I really like your paper, too. It's so funny, and you use dialogue a lot better than I did. This makes me think I should go back and add in some more quotes, tell the story better.

This exchange exemplifies the pattern I repeatedly observed in these impromptu peer review sessions, as the students became micro-sponsors of each other's literacy practices by pointing to a specific element of writing that their peer had done well and noting what they had learned from the other's example.

A snippet of conversation between Twana and Dixie illustrates the second pattern, in which one student offers her own paper as a model for how to deal with the other writer's concerns. Twana and Dixie were both single mothers and returning students; although Dixie had been out of school almost ten years longer than Twana, she enjoyed reading and writing and found more success in English class than Twana, who disliked reading and writing and struggled with both. In this exchange, Twana and Dixie discuss the problems Twana had in organizing her paper:

TWANA: She [Shanti] said my organization was bad. I knew it wasn't good when I wrote it, but I don't know how to fix it.

DIXIE: It does kind of skip around a lot. [pause] I had problems figuring out how to do mine at first, too. I wasn't really sure how to organize it, either. But what I did seemed to work if you want to look at it. She [Shanti] said it was good.

This phenomenon became a pattern among these informal groups: the students would offer their own drafts as models for the other students to use when revising, sponsoring concrete literacy practices. The students hadn't yet developed the vocabulary to explain *why* the writing did or did not work, but they knew when writing was or wasn't effective and could point to that effectiveness—traits that may explain the importance of modeling for these students.

The final pattern I observed among these students—the pattern of empathy, encouragement, and reassurance—can be seen in the following example, which occurred after Anna and Schueler read each other's papers:

ANNA: Were you able to understand it? I worry, you know. My English, it's not so good.

SCHUELER: Yeah, I was able to understand it! Your English is very good. It *is*. Don't feel like it isn't because she [the professor] made a lot of corrections. She does that to all the rest of us, and we all were born speaking English. I've had her for class before, and she just really wants the grammar to be correct. She's like that with everybody. It's not just you.

Here, Schueler praises Anna's writing and attempts to bolster her confidence, reassuring Anna about her language skills.

Schueler was certainly correct when he told Anna that her language use was very good; her skills in English were far greater than she gave herself credit for. Using his previous experience as a student in the professor's literature course, Schueler was able to contextualize the marginalia ("She just really wants the grammar to be correct. She's like that with everybody") in a way that would be meaningful and encouraging to Anna. He even went so far as to put his paper alongside Anna's so she could see that the amount of "red ink" on his paper rivaled hers—reinforcing his point that their professor "does that to all of us." While Schueler was the only student in the class who had previously taken a course with the professor, the way in which he contextualized the marginalia was not unique. Other students followed this pattern as well, using comments the professor made on their drafts to illustrate to their peers that they shared similar struggles. In these cases, the students seemingly "bought into" their professor's directives, acquiescing to the consumption metaphor of literacy by assimilating the literacy practices offered by the professor.

Katie May provides some of the most powerful examples of how the students negotiated multiple meanings and metaphors of literacy by cosponsoring a belief system that linked the development of literacy practices and the attainment of a college degree to the betterment of the local community. Katie May was an active participant, if not a leader, in the chain of micro-sponsorship I have described. When I asked her why she helped other students learn how to use their grammar handbooks, offered them feedback on their papers, and the like, she replied, "By helping one another we help ourselves and our communities, eventually." In her response, Katie May links the development of literacy practices with the betterment of the community. While Katie May might not be an example of Freire's conceptualization of literacy as power—*conscientizacao*, or critical consciousness—she makes a connection between assisting others in learning literacy practices and serving her community. This model of literacy resists the consumerist metaphor promulgated by the university and instead establishes literacy as a communal resource.

To return to Scribner's description of literacy as power, Katie May conceptualizes literacy as a way to improve the conditions in her community; for her, literacy attainment, as recognized by a college degree, "lifts up" other members of the community. Katie May frequently identified her aunt, a dentist for whom she worked, as a role model in her life; when I asked her to explain her aunt's influence, she responded:

> She's a role model to me, because she came from poverty and got her education, which she had to do. She didn't have much money going through college, so she made a lot of sacrifices. . . . She has a lot of money now, and she gives back to the community, in various ways. . . . She has a lot of compassion for others. It makes me want to be like that.

Katie May further explained that her aunt made donations of time and money to local charities, including her church, and worked with individuals in the area as well. She mentored local high school students, and she helped her family members financially when needed. She also functioned as a micro-sponsor of literacy for Katie May, offering Katie May a summer job in her practice, some financial assistance with school, and substantial guidance and advice about her college education. As Katie May put it, "She teaches me how to do school," and Katie May planned to follow her aunt's example and provide this type of support to others. She viewed helping her composition classmates in this light, but she also hoped to work in the community as her aunt did, "giving back" by becoming a pediatrician. Thus, the view of literacy expressed by Katie May in some segments of our interviews was one that conceptualized literacy as a means of social uplift, as well as a means of individual economic gain, clashing with the images in the bookstore that presented literacy as a means of individual, rather than communal, achievement.

It is in Katie May's comments that the link between literacy and the performance of identity becomes clearer. In her descriptions of why it is important to her to develop academic literacy practices—as "credentialized" by a college degree—and to help her classmates in developing those practices, Katie May consistently returned to the idea of "helping out" or neighborliness, one of the romanticized values Loyal Jones, a senior scholar and founder of Appalachian studies, ascribes to Appalachian identity in his book *Appalachian Values*.[4] Jones outlines ten values that he argues are especially important to Appalachians; although Jones notes these values are not uniquely or uniformly Appalachian, the title of the book implies otherwise. While I am uncomfortable with these essentialist views of Appalachianness, some values of which Jones writes—particularly neighborliness—proved to be significant in the Sciotoville classroom. It was through their performance of a romanticized Appalachian identity rooted in neighborliness that these students were able to grapple with the contact zones of literacy in which they found themselves. In other words, these students needed to maintain a romanticized Appalachianness in order to manage the identity conflicts they felt in the college literacy environment. For Katie May, in particular, the social nature of literacy was inextricably tied to her performance of a romanticized Appalachian identity; she integrated her performance of Appalachian and academic identities, using her Appalachian identity as a way to help herself—and others in the class—develop an academic identity.

Negotiating Identity and the Role of Talk

Taken together, the previous examples demonstrate how these students micro-sponsored each other as they negotiated the academic literacy practices they were encountering in their composition class, "inventing the university"—to use Bartholomae's phrase—for themselves in the process. These students' desire to make literacy social, communal, and a space for mutual help countered the institution's consumption metaphor of literacy as an individual achievement. But these students went beyond inventing the university; they *re*-invented Bartholomae's conceptualization of the university as exclusively focused on the importance of the student-teacher relationship in the development of academic literacy practices. Instead, the students' university was one that accounted for the importance of literacy sponsorship by peers in fostering development and success in the composition classroom.

For members of this class, literacy functioned as a social act, as it does for members of many marginalized communities, and neighborly talk about literacy played a critical role in this process. Numerous scholars have examined how literacy is inherently social and how talk functions as part of the literacy toolbox; in many marginalized communities, literacy learning and uses intimately connect community members to one another (Heath; Moss; Guerra; Cushman). For the Sciotoville students—who were primarily working-class, rural Appalachian women, some of whom were also returning adult students—their use of talk as a form of literacy sponsorship contributed to their negotiations of academic literacy practices. Katie May stressed in interviews how working with her peers on assignments enhanced her own learning: "It helps me to talk to other people. . . . I know I'm not the only one struggling," a fact that encourages her. Many of her peers made similar comments:

> AMY: Sometimes they can give you a better way to word something. You kind of get stuck on what you're doing, and somebody else looks at it and can say, "Oh, just move that around a little bit" or whatever.
> SARA: So to get more help for yourself?
> AMY (overlapping): Kind of like calling technical support.
> SARA: OK.
> BETH: I know how it feels when you don't understand something and someone can explain it to you on your level, rather than a nonstudent level. And so, if I understand something that somebody else doesn't understand, why not?

Later in the conversation, Chris added this comment about being helped by her peers:

> CHRIS: I was just thinking that at times I was checking to make sure I understood something, that I understood what was going on, that I understood what she [the professor] expected from me. To [pause] ask someone how they did it or what they did was something that was reassuring to me, it let me know [pause]
> SARA: That you were on the right track?
> CHRIS: Mmm-hmm.

While the Sciotoville students could not always articulate why talk was so important in this classroom, they seemed to understand intuitively the crucial role of talk in literacy events in general and in writing groups in particular. Their responses included the following:

- "I would hope to be treated this way if I needed help."
- "If you understand something and can explain it, that helps, because sometimes they [other students] just need it worded differently to understand it."

- "It's a two-way street. The students who come to class want to learn and so do I. There is nothing to be gained by not helping if you can."
- "We're all in this together. . . . I feel a responsibility to help others learn."
- "I know it's great to have something explained to me on my level. If I understand something, why not help someone who doesn't? Everyone's trying to better themselves."

For these students, literacy practices were an important way to perform a romanticized Appalachian identity and create a sense of working-class solidarity ("Everyone's trying to better themselves").

What emerges from the Sciotoville students is a belief system about literacy profoundly shaped by their performance of Appalachian identity—a performance that, in turn, shapes their performance of an academic identity. For these students, their performance of an Appalachian identity that is neighborly and "helps out" others played a significant role in their development of another metaphor of literacy: literacy as communion. In this metaphor, literacy is a communal resource, one to be shared among friends and neighbors—including "neighbors" in the classroom—so that all can advance from the unemployment office to the corner office.

While these students clearly assimilated some elements of their university's conceptualization of literacy as consumption, their behavior was mitigated by their communal understanding of literacy. Yes, the students continually emphasized the importance of literacy for securing "a good job" and "making lots of money," echoing the consumption metaphor. However, they also engaged in communal behaviors that focused on helping out their classmates by forming impromptu writing groups and teaching each other how to use their textbooks—important sites for the learning of academic literacy practices. It was through these acts of teaching each other academic literacy practices that they began to perform an academic identity as well. In short, these students moved from being solely learners and students of academic literacy to producers and micro-sponsors of academic literacy—an important shift in their performative identities.

Notes

1. Pseudonyms have been substituted for the names of all locations and individuals in order to protect participant anonymity.

2. "At-risk" counties meet the following criteria: their three-year unemployment rate is 125 percent or more of the U.S. average; their per-capita market income is 67 percent or less of the U.S. average; and their poverty rate is 125 percent or more of the U.S. average ("County Economic").

3. The professor of the course did not require peer review or utilize in-class writers' workshops.

4. Jane Greer, in chapter 5 of this volume, also discusses the Appalachian/rural value of "neighborliness."

Works Cited and Consulted

Bartholomae, David. "Inventing the University." *Cross-Talk in Composition Theory: A Reader.* Ed. Victor Villanueva. Urbana, IL: NCTE, 1997. 589–619. Print.

Brandt, Deborah. *Literacy in American Lives.* Cambridge: Cambridge University Press, 2001. Print.

Cushman, Ellen. *The Struggle and the Tools: Oral and Literate Strategies in an Inner City Community.* Albany: State U of New York P, 1998. Print.

Freire, Paulo. *Education for Critical Consciousness.* Continuum: New York, 1973. Print.

Gee, James. *Social Linguistics and Literacies: Ideologies in Discourses.* 2nd ed. London: Routledge Falmer, 1996. Print.

George, Diana. "Working with Peer Groups in the Composition Classroom." *College Composition and Communication* 35.3 (Oct. 1984): 320–26. Print.

Graff, Harvey. *The Literacy Myth: Cultural Integration and Social Structure in the Nineteenth Century.* Rev. ed. New Brunswick, NJ: Transaction, 1991. Print.

Greer, Jane. "Women's Words, Women's Work: Rural Literacy and Labor." *Reclaiming the Rural: Essays on Literacy, Rhetoric, and Pedagogy.* Ed. Kim Donehower, Charlotte Hogg, and Eileen E. Schell. Carbondale: Southern Illinois UP, 2011. Print.

Guerra, Juan. *Close to Home: Oral and Literate Practices in a Transnational Mexicano Community.* New York: Teachers College, 1998. Print.

Heath, Shirley Brice. *Ways with Words: Language, Life, and Work in Communities and Classrooms.* New York: Cambridge UP, 1983. Print.

Horton, Myles, and Paulo Freire. *We Make the Road by Walking: Conversations on Education and Social Change.* Philadelphia: Temple UP, 1990. Print.

Jones, Loyal. *Appalachian Values.* Ashland, KY: Jesse Stuart Foundation, 1994. Print.

Moss, Beverly J., ed. *Literacy across Communities.* Cresskill, NJ: Hampton, 1994. Print.

Moss, Beverly J., Nels P. Highberg, and Melissa Nicolas, eds. *Writing Groups Inside and Outside the Classroom.* New York: Lawrence Erlbaum, 2003. Print.

Pratt, Mary Louise. "Arts of the Contact Zone." *Profession* 91(1991): 33–40. Print.

Scribner, Sylvia. "Literacy in Three Metaphors." *Perspectives on Literacy.* Ed. Eugene R. Kintgen, Barry M. Kroll, and Mike Rose. Carbondale: Southern Illinois UP, 1988. 71–81. Print.

United States Appalachian Regional Commission. "Appalachian Region: Economic Overview." Web. 13 Apr. 2006.

——. "County Economic Status Definitions." Web. 13 Apr. 2006.

——. "Fact Sheet on Reductions in Poverty Rates and Distress in Appalachia for FY 2004." Web. 13 Apr. 2006.

United States Census Bureau. "Fact Sheet: Census 2000 Demographic Profile Highlights." Web. 13 Apr. 2006.

Villanueva, Victor. *Bootstraps: From an American Academic of Color.* Urbana, IL: NCTE, 1993. Print.

Webb-Sunderhaus, Sara. "A Family Affair: Competing Sponsors of Literacy in Appalachian Students' Lives." *Community Literacy Journal* 2.1 (2007): 5–24. Print.

13

Sustaining a Rural Pennsylvania Community: Negotiating Rural Literacies and Sustainability

Thomas Butler and Jacqueline Edmondson

Tom Butler is a superintendent in a rural Pennsylvania school located in a mountainous region of the state where most people work in metal and plastic industries. On a blustery winter morning in January 2008, he convened a meeting with elementary and middle-school reading teachers in his district to discuss how children in his rural community were being taught to read. The meeting table had special gifts for each educator: maple syrup, goat cheese fudge, and cookies from a local farm. The pastries came from a local woman and were still warm. Tom was sharing some of the gems the local community had to offer. His message was both implicit and explicit, and his agenda for the meeting was clear: he wanted the teachers to teach the children to read in ways that connected to their rural community, and he planned to spend the rest of the morning discussing how they could move in this direction. He wanted children to engage in rural literacies that would sustain the community.

In *Rural Literacies*, Kim Donehower, Charlotte Hogg, and Eileen Schell rely in part on Derek Owens's definition of *sustainability* as:

> an intergenerational concept that means adjusting our current behavior so that it causes the least amount of harm to future generations. Sustainability is also concerned with intergenerational equity: understanding the links between poverty and ecosystem decline . . . It means looking critically at our contemporary behaviors from the perspective of children living generations hence, and modifying those behaviors accordingly. (qtd. in Donehower, Hogg, and Schell 6)

Like Tom Butler, these researchers are interested in the interrelated economic, ecological, political, and social factors that will sustain rural communities, and they believe that literacy should be emphasized while fostering dialogue and action toward this goal (6–7). But they clearly distinguish between *sustainability* and *preservation*, which they astutely point out, "suggests locking cultural practices into the past" (20).

When Tom embarked on this project, he invited me, Jackie Edmondson, to participate. We had previously collaborated on rural education research (see Schafft and Jackson) and engaged in numerous discussions and shared readings over several years as Tom completed his dissertation work at Pennsylvania State University. Our shared effort to understand the connections between rural communities, sustainability, and rural literacies is the central work of this chapter. The research included Tom's lived experiences in this community and school, explanations teachers offered about their classroom practices, and our collaborative effort to consider these observations and explanations in relation to other research on rural education and rural literacies. To begin, a story from Tom's family provides some context for his understanding of rural literacies. That story is then extended to connect with challenges in the field of rural public education, including teacher education.

Tom Butler's Story and Vision

In 1942, my grandparents purchased the family farm. My great grandfather had sold the farm to the local tannery to make money during the Great Depression, so my grandfather had to buy it back in 1942. My grandfather worked at the local tannery during the day, coming home at nights to work on the farm. My grandmother worked during the day as a farm wife, doing the jobs necessary to maintain a healthy farm and care for her family. To purchase the farm, my grandparents had to borrow money from one of the New Deal government programs. The money was deposited into my grandparents' account, but there were stipulations that came with the money. One of the stipulations was a periodic visit from a "homemaker" who would come into my grandparents' house and advise my grandmother on how to improve the functioning of the home.

On a typical day in the summertime in the early 1940s, my grandmother started to gather the ingredients so she could make a pot of bean soup. The vast majority of the ingredients were homegrown, whether it was the onions and vegetables from the garden, the ham that was cured in the building beside the granary, or the "lard" that was rendered from the pig during butchering. While my grandmother stood over the stove caring for her pot of soup, she noticed two people come into the driveway. As they approached the door, she recognized them as the county extension specialists who came to inspect the farm as a condition for my grandparents' loan to buy the farm. My grandmother welcomed them into the house, and the female "homemaker" inspected the canned goods in the cellar to make sure that everything looked like it was done properly. She next commented that the soup my grandmother was making looked good and nutritious and that the baby would probably like it. With that, the two people left. My grandmother took no umbrage at the visit. She accepted it as part of her life on the farm.

My grandfather was not so welcoming to the gentleman who was going to "help" him become a "better" farmer. As was often the case when someone came onto the farm to tell my grandfather how to do his job, he impolitely told the man to leave. There are many family legends revolving around my grandfather kicking people off the farm if they tried to tell him what to do or they did not agree with his political opinions. My grandfather was working in the barn, and when he saw the man start walking toward him, he met him halfway and told him to leave.

Years later, my grandmother would state that she never minded the visits from the homemaker. When asked if the homemaker ever helped her learn anything new, my grandmother could not think of anything, but she did not mind seeing her come.

Rural areas have faced this quandary of expert knowledge versus local knowledge in some form or another for hundreds of years (Theobald). Outside experts read the locality through a different lens than local community leaders; often they look at rural communities as a source of resources for the economy, or as a series of social problems that need to be solved. This is not to suggest that there is no role for outside expertise in a rural community; however, the nature of the relationship between the outside expert and rural communities is crucial. As Donehower observed in her Haines Gap research, outside experts have more potential to contribute to change in rural communities if they approach their work thoughtfully and sensitively as a "cultural exchange" rather than as an outside expert who is "there to 'fix' local practices" ("Rhetorics and Realities" 72).

Tom's grandparents lived this reality. The New Deal program had as a requirement that "experts" would go into the home of a local farmer and his wife to give advice about how to run the household. Never mind that the accumulated years of experience between Tom's grandparents (both grew up on a farm) were the current manifestation of generations of accumulated agrarian knowledge passed down from one generation to the next, all with deep understandings, skills, and real time experience in rural life, the very things that the experts were supposed to "check" to make sure his grandparents were doing "right."

Unfortunately, rural America is still being bombarded with the "outside expert" message today, except now it is more codified. Rural knowledge and understandings, including those that involve food production and care for the land, are becoming obsolete because they are not given credence by "outside experts" or valued in a corporate marketplace (see Kingsolver, Kingsolver, and Hopp), and local knowledge is often ignored and dismissed. This is perhaps most evident in the struggle to engage locality in rural public schools. Indeed, the threat to rural education comes from outside experts who seek to standardize school knowledge through mandated curricula and tests, checking in on the schools as the extension agents did to Tom's grandparents. But the threat also comes from the inside as teachers accept dominant discourses of public education that have become pervasive and largely unquestioned.

The Conversation

As the conversation between Tom and the teachers in his school unfolded around the ways in which they teach reading relative to rural life, some powerful and common discourses were clearly articulated. We would like to consider these more closely in what follows and then connect these to Tom's wishes to realize a rural literacy that contributes to the sustainability of rural education and rural communities.

Discourses are commonly agreed-upon understandings, languages, and ways of being. Linguist James Gee explains that primary discourses, those of our family, are acquired, but our secondary discourses, those that represent the various groups and affiliations in our lives, are contextual and learned (156–57). Building on Michel Foucault's work, Iara Lessa explains discourses as "systems of thoughts composed of ideas, attitudes, courses of action, beliefs and practices that systematically construct the subjects and the worlds of which they speak" (285). As such, discourses have disciplinary effects, which means there is some shared knowledge that constitutes discourses, as well as disciplining effects, which help to direct people's behavior in particular ways (Foucault).

Secondary discourses are learned through public pedagogies that attempt to instruct people about the social order and commonly accepted meanings of the world. The messages and meanings transmitted through public pedagogies are imbued with ideologies that reflect the "symbols and cultural practices of the dominant culture that shape people's thinking such that they unconsciously accept the current way of doing things as 'natural' and 'normal'" (Bartolome xiii). These messages come through the media, through social organizations and institutions, through policies, and other powerful sources that are mediated or read through individuals' own lenses and negotiated among individuals in groups. The readings of these symbols and texts provide insight to the literacies found in rural communities (see Edmondson).

For example, during the recent 2008 primary campaign, presidential hopeful Barack Obama commented on rural communities in our state, a moment alluded to as well in the introduction to this volume:

> You go into some of these small towns in Pennsylvania, and like a lot of small towns in the Midwest, the jobs have been gone now for 25 years and nothing's replaced them. And they fell through the Clinton administration, and the Bush administration, and each successive administration has said that somehow these communities are gonna regenerate and they have not. And it's not surprising then they get bitter, they cling to guns or religion or antipathy to people who aren't like them or anti-immigrant sentiment or anti-trade sentiment as a way to explain their frustrations. (Obama qtd in Reid)

Obama's comments reflect commonly held misconceptions and generalizations about rural communities and peoples, messages often perpetuated through films like *Deliverance* and television shows like *My Big Redneck Wedding*. These messages confirm some people's understandings of rural life, while others resist these meanings and attempt to reshape the discourse. Either way, these public pedagogies work to influence how the public reads and interprets the issues and potentials in rural areas.

With the increasing influence of neoliberal ideologies, which value fast capitalism, the so-called free market, and individualism, information flows quickly and often unchecked, and the messages and meanings that potentially shape our discourses come faster and perhaps louder than in the past. As Henry Giroux has explained, there is

> a new kind of public pedagogy, one in which the production, dissemination, and circulation of ideas emerges from the educational force of the larger culture. Public pedagogy in this sense refers to a power ensemble of ideological and institutional forces whose aim is to produce competitive, self-interested individuals vying for their own material and ideological gain. (*Against* 113)

As these dominant discourses become incorporated into the fiber of human life, they are codified, as Tom noted, and increasingly difficult to question unless there is purposeful and deliberate attention to the contradictions of these discourses accompanied by systematic efforts to critically engage the world and unpack the ideologies and discourses that are commonplace.

For rural educators, there are powerful public pedagogies and commonly accepted discourses about teaching and schooling that can be difficult to counter without purposeful, indeed deliberate and subversive work (see chapter 10 in this volume). For example, there is a strong public discourse that values standardized curriculum reflecting suburban and urban lifestyles, accompanied by both implicit and explicit messages that rural children should aspire to this standard knowledge rather than local, place-based understandings and concerns (Gruenewald and Smith). Rural teachers are educated in teacher preparation programs that do little, if anything, to distinguish what it means to be rural or to teach in a rural community in comparison to an urban or suburban area (see Eppley; also see Brooke for interesting counterexamples). While some universities boast of their urban teacher preparation programs, few, if any, make note of similar efforts in rural areas.

Within this broader sociopolitical context, the responses to Tom's request of the teachers in his rural district reflect the public pedagogies they have experienced and many of the more dominant discourses about rural schooling that circulate in American society. In this way, these powerful discourses speak through these teachers and are not reflective of any individual's shortcomings or limitations. By making these explicit, our hope is that these discourses can be disrupted, counterdiscourses can be formulated, and new rural literacies with the direct goal of rural sustainability can be conceptualized.

The Discourse of Compliance

Some teachers at Tom's meeting accepted the state and federal governments' authoritarian stance in relation to public education. This acceptance was reflected in statements like, "we must be in compliance with the state," or "children will be at a disadvantage if we don't prepare them for the tests." Sometimes this compliance is reflected in discursive practices, including spending time in explicit test-preparation instruction. In some classrooms, teachers were beginning the day with forty-five minutes of test prep, a constant reminder to the teacher and the children about who and what would determine their worth. Much like Tom's grandmother, there was quiet resignation that the state is the authority, and while the state's recommendations may not provide much information or insight that is new, they must be tolerated. To go against this authority could mean a loss of jobs or money for the school. The risk was too great.

The state and the federal governments perpetuate this discourse by exerting their influence through threats, some real and others empty. The result is a culture of fear that, if unquestioned, brings either submission or open resistance and opposition. In many cases the former is commonplace, but over the past few years, the latter reflects a growing movement. Consider that thirty-seven states did not passively accept the tenets of No Child Left Behind, and many states have passed legislation opposing some provisions of the law. These states are not necessarily those armed with the most social, economic, and cultural capital; instead, as political scientist Bryan Shelley has demonstrated, these states tend to have lower poverty rates, larger Hispanic populations, fewer highly qualified teachers, less developed accountability systems, and larger numbers of Democratic legislators.

The discourse of compliance sometimes reflects passive acceptance of the status quo and an inability to, or lack of awareness that one can, question whose values are represented in current educational practices and what vision for the future they support. Other times, compliance reflects a sense of intimidation that the outside expert is really correct and that there are no other choices. This discourse is often accompanied by a monolithic interpretation of rural communities and schools that subordinates rural children and teachers to particular norms, rather than providing opportunities to celebrate the diversity of rural life. Such subjugation potentially robs communities of a language to dismantle the exploitation they have experienced, limiting the opportunity to expose contradictions in rural communities and education that could, in turn, open new possibilities.

As Murray Edelman has explained, "All governmental actions purposefully construct a spectacle that is misleading" (33). Yet to simply question the government is not enough. Henry Giroux, extending Theodor Adorno's work, reminds us that we must engage in ideological critique in order to engage the public good, and this applies to rural education as well:

> Critique also [has] to come to grips with the affective investments that tied individuals, including critics, to ideologies and practices of domination. Analyses of the deep structures of domination might help to provide a more powerful critique and healthy suspicion of various appeals to community, the public, and the social. Clearly, while it is imperative to reclaim the discourse of community, the commons, and public good as part of a broader discourse of democracy, such terms need to be embraced critically in light of the ways in which they have often served the instruments of dominant power. (*Against* 162–63)

As a public educator interested in sustaining rural community life, Tom recognized the need to move beyond compliance. To do so requires educators to be disruptive and challenge this status quo, but in ways that extend beyond the current discourses of schooling, two of which follow.

The Discourse of Scientific Management

Some of the teachers in Tom's school advocated for direct instruction models, particularly systematic instruction of phonics in the early grades. These teachers felt that curriculum coverage would ensure that students learn to read, an essential element in young children's learning. They valued the systematic teaching they could engage in when they relied on basal readers and prescriptive, scripted textbooks. Straying from the textbook would involve risk that was a bit different but somewhat overlapping with the risk related to compliance. To deviate from the textbook could jeopardize a teacher's sense of professionalism as it related to authority given to these texts.

Like child-centered pedagogy, scientific management has a long history in the field of education with roots in psychological studies of human learning that can be traced to Frederick Taylor's factory management, E. L. Thorndike's laws of learning, and other turn-of-the-twentieth-century psychological theories (see Shannon for more detailed explanations of these influences). Grounded in what is believed to be observable in relation to human learning, scientific management breaks complex endeavors like learning to read into discrete parts and then encodes these in instructional practices where the discrete parts are taught through repetition and testing, from the least complex to the most complex. The belief is that mastery of these individual parts will lead to the more complex whole; however, scientifically based studies of such processes have not led to such conclusions. Consider the interim report on the first two years of the Reading First program; students in Reading First schools were taught the five components of reading instruction as recommended by the National Reading Panel (phonics, phonemic awareness, fluency, vocabulary, and comprehension) through direct systematic instruction; but studies have yet to confirm that these students are significantly better at reading comprehension than children in schools without these programs (Reading First).

Teachers in Tom's district are not the only educators who subscribe to the rationalization of instruction that occurs with scientific management. Patrick Shannon reported that in his research, 90 percent of teachers accepted the rationalization of reading instruction:

> Many teachers and administrators reduced all the possible ways of teaching reading (the abstraction) to the directions within the scientifically managed reading programs. By following the directions and using the commercial materials, they were teaching reading because the directions, scripts, and procedures embodied the science of reading instruction and they led to students scoring highly on standardized reading tests. (39)

As Shannon further points out, this rationalization of instruction resulted in changes in institutional structures that made this practice seem natural for both personal and national benefit. Such practices are not unique to reading instruction, and the detrimental effects of scientific management can be seen in other areas of rural life, including farming, where over time practices have become specialized around goals of mass production. Michael Pollan points out that goals such as scientific management and efficiency do not need to involve a focus on speed or ease of implementation; instead, he uses the example of the Polyface Farm[1] to demonstrate how efficiency can be about sustainability (123–33).

The Discourse of Progressivism

Many teachers in Tom's school completed their teacher education programs in Pennsylvania during a time when thematic units and child-centered approaches were dominant. As the meeting continued, teachers in Tom's district began to recall with fondness their earlier work in classrooms when such things were evident: units where the entire classroom was transformed into a rain forest, an ocean, a wagon train, or a scene from "Encyclopedia Brown." These notions are attached to a more general philosophy of progressivism in education, which is grounded in a belief that attending to the child's nature is crucial if one is to effectively educate that child (Egan). Early progressive movements were firmly rooted in rural communities where there was widespread concern that because of the Industrial Revolution the United States was losing its rural roots (see Stock for examples). There is a tradition of rural schools embracing Progressivism's tenets from as early as 1910. These included a child-centered focus, efforts to address the "whole child," allowances for students to participate in decisions about the content of their education, expecting teachers to be curriculum-makers, and reliance on community (Leo-Nyquist).

Child-centered pedagogues often assume that their work is completed in the best interest of the child, often without questioning what "best interest" means or which child or construction of childhood they are considering. Building historically on work by G. Stanley Hall, John Dewey, Jean Piaget, and others, these educators advocate what is frequently called "developmentally appropriate practices" that are supposed to connect curriculum and instruction to children's interests and abilities, providing opportunities for self-expression.

Yet these pedagogies are not without concern. For one, they are often based on particular conceptualizations of "the child" that have historical, political, racial, and social roots that normalize understandings of children in middle-class constructs that may have little to do with children in rural communities (see Panelli, Punch, and Robson). These understandings of "the child" have led to particular theories of development that are universalized in ways that overlook problematic assumptions about children and learning (Egan), while simultaneously construing children who do not fall within these normalized parameters as delayed, disabled, or pathological. Children most susceptible to such labels are those who are peripheral to the dominant societal group, including minorities, second-language learners, and in this case we would argue, many rural children who are considered peripheral based solely on their identification as rural. For example, Annette Henry astutely noted how in child-centered classrooms teachers are most likely to build on the experiences of children who come to school with the most social and cultural capital, and in her case, this created inequitable opportunities for black children to learn in school (370). Such could also be the case in rural communities where there are differences in social class, culture, and race represented among the children in a public school. Attention to differentially distributed social and cultural capital would require teachers to engage place-conscious pedagogy in ways that do not privilege some local knowledge and commitments over others and do not silence some children's voices and interests.

Within the context of No Child Left Behind, engaging child-centered pedagogy is considered to be a subversive act; however, while such practices may have benefits for some children and some schools, we argue that it is not enough to sustain rural communities unless these practices are explicitly connected to the life of rural communities. This is not to suggest that rural education become parochial or isolated from the broader world; instead, there needs to be purposeful work to link the issues and conditions in rural communities to broader global matters that are inextricably intertwined (see chapter 9 in this volume). For example, studies of natural habitats and threats to natural habitats in rural communities, which include toxic landfills in many Pennsylvania rural communities, could be linked to threats to other natural environments, including the rain forest. What we wish to see is pedagogy that is undertaken with purposeful goals to better understand rural life so that it can be sustained (see Hogg). This necessitates developing an appreciation for how local citizens are understanding rural life, as well as making the connections between the local and the global as new and critical agrarian literacies are formulated.

Absent in the teachers' conversation was any mention of literacy in relation to sustainability of the rural community. The dominant discourses of schooling are strong in teachers' heads, but Tom raised some different possibilities in an effort to generate further discussion and deeper understandings. He proposed that the teachers should consider getting students involved in researching and writing about local history and current issues and events (see Brooke for similar suggestions about place-conscious education). The

teachers did not seem to immediately connect with these ideas, in part because it seemed to involve risk in a context where the stakes are high and
compliance is valued, and also because this was a new style of leadership for
many of the teachers. We realize this work will take some time, and we are
encouraged by many of the teachers who have held an ongoing interest in
this curriculum work, which is under way. Tom's discourse is subversive in
relation to the other, more dominant discourses, and as he continues the conversation with these teachers, he is attempting to find ways to link their own
stories, much like that of his grandparents, to a different kind of pedagogy in
his school. His hope is to find ways to open different spaces where teachers
can question the status quo and find the relevance and value of connecting
literacy instruction in schools to the sustainability of their community.

Designing Different Possibilities

> All experience has shown that mankind are more disposed
> to suffer, while evils are sufferable, than to right themselves
> by abolishing the forms to which they are accustomed.
> —Thomas Jefferson, "The Declaration of Independence"

Educators generally engage the hard work of teaching because they care
about children and hope to influence the future in some way. This was clear
in the conversations among teachers in Tom's district. We have often heard
teachers remark how they wish to do what is best for children; yet, there are
struggles over what this means and who should decide. The dominant discourses that were apparent in the teachers' talk throughout the meeting are
currently inadequate to realize strong connections to local rural literacies.
None of the discourses at the meeting will bring change; all protect the status
quo. However, Tom has not lost hope and as he continues to work with these
teachers, there are three further ideas that could extend his efforts into the
community and the profession.

1. Rural schools can think and act like charter schools.

We wish to be clear from the outset that we are *not* recommending that rural
schools *become* charter schools. We both share significant concerns about
the consequences charter schools bring in relation to the privatization of
public education and the potential undermining of the democratic project
of public schools (see Dingerson, Miner, Peterson, and Walters for discussion of these points). Instead, we suggest that rural schools *think and act* as
charter schools in at least two ways, and that these efforts can further the
understandings of rural literacies and sustainability in rural communities.

First, rural schools can design a charter that is negotiated in the community and sets the school apart from others in different rural communities as well as suburban and urban areas. This requires the rural community to articulate what it values in relation to public education, and to set those values out in a way that can demonstrate that the goals for the community are being achieved. Rural educators have engaged this work, including those at the Patearoa School, a one-room school in Central Otago on the South Island of New Zealand. At this school, curriculum included community projects and events with a focus on the rural community's values and expectations for education (see Wright). This is not easy work, and it will involve disrupting long-held notions about public schooling and education among teachers and the public (see Edmondson).

Second, rural schools with a local charter should operate as independently as possible to design curriculum and achieve their goals. Like charter schools, they should seek exception to particular state mandates and regulations, but they will also need to provide evidence that they are accomplishing what they set out to do. This conceptualization of schooling involves tremendous responsibility of educators on behalf of the community and its children and much harder work than complying with prescribed curricula and state mandates entails. This will also likely involve rethinking how resources are allocated, including building curricular planning time and community meetings into the fabric of the school and community.

2. Teacher education programs need to explicitly prepare teachers for work in rural communities.

The changes Tom hopes for—changes where teachers in rural communities work with members of the school board and the community to redefine the relationship between public schools and communities in ways that will sustain rural life—will not come easily. In part this will involve a new kind of teacher education. The discourses of public schooling are strong in all of our heads, and we will need to find ways to open spaces for educators to create and design schools differently than the schools they attended. Like the accumulated knowledge of farming, we have accumulated knowledges of schooling that are difficult to disrupt.

Without being overly prescriptive, we would suggest that teacher education directed toward the sustainability of rural communities involves explicit work understanding the interdependence of rural life, the connections to land and people that are valued in rural communities, the relationship between rural communities and the federal government and other outside entities, and advocacy work on behalf of rural schools and communities.

Such education would need to engage purposeful work in rural areas so that new teachers could come to understand the unique qualities and potential of rural life. Teacher education candidates would need to have deep knowledge of the topics that touch rural life, including ecology, economics, history, sociology, and political science and how these connect to the various content areas they wish to teach. This work is not for the faint of heart, and it runs counter to some images of rural teachers as quaint or having less status and intelligence than their suburban peers. However, this work is already under way in some rural communities where place-conscious education is taking hold (see Brooke). Sharing these experiences and efforts across time, communities, and place, including teachers' personal accounts of their work, will be important (Leo-Nyquist).

3. School leaders can (and should) open spaces for new discourses to be explored and new literacies to be developed.

The leadership Tom is providing is very different than many of his superintendent colleagues throughout Pennsylvania. Rather than spending his days counting (test scores, money, enrollments, etc.), Tom is offering opportunities for his teachers to engage in difficult intellectual work that can potentially disrupt the status quo and bring different possibilities to the children and community. He is providing space, time, and resources for teachers to come together to talk and plan, and he is open to their ideas and suggestions. Tom is also working in earnest as a public intellectual, addressing issues of change within the school and community, studying the problems in depth, searching for answers, and offering his ideas to the public both in oral and written forms.[2] This is not easy work, and the changes he wishes to see will certainly involve struggle for the long term, but there is hope, particularly as other rural superintendents reach out to Tom in solidarity around issues like opposition to Pennsylvania's proposal to require graduation examinations.

Rural communities, including Tom's, will need to change and adapt if they are going to survive, and Tom is well aware of this. In order to sustain life, these changes will need to be purposeful, planned, and proactive. Again, we find Giroux's comments instructive:

> Teachers are going to have to begin to mobilize; they can't do this alone—they can't talk about engaging educational problems and closing the door and inventing a neat pedagogy that nobody knows about. They're going to have to work inside and outside the schools; they're going to have to force policy to be changed. They're going to have to vote people on boards that have power that represent what they're doing. They're going to have to fight for the power that they have; they're going to have to realize that

education is not a method, it's the outcome of struggles. It's not a method: it's not some *a priori* discourse that you simply invent and then apply; it's in flux all the time. Different conditions demand different interventions, and they're going to have to understand that that question of difference is crucial. (Interview)

Tom is opening space for teachers to critically engage and disrupt their commonly held understandings and discourses, and as such, there is terrific potential for change. Strong leadership and community support, along with connections to other rural educators, can help to ensure that teachers are not overburdened with this work. We hope other school administrators and teachers will follow his lead. We think Tom's grandfather would approve as Tom and his teachers negotiate local understandings in relation to the broader discourses and literacies of our society.

Notes

1. Polyface Farm is in the Shenandoah Valley of Virginia. It is a family-owned, multigenerational, pasture-based organic farm that produces food for families in the immediate bioregion. It is a study in efficiency that is intended to preserve the land and region. Polyface purposely rotates poultry and livestock on its fields so that pastures and landscapes are healed and nutritional, and habitats for plants and animals are nurtured to enhance the land and products. Polyface is also an example of ongoing struggles against the authority of the USDA and the Virginia Department of Agriculture and Consumer Services. For readers not familiar with this farm, please visit the website: http://www.polyfacefarms.com/default.aspx.

2. Tom's work as a public intellectual includes the following: (1) avidly reading local and national newspapers; (2) writing for local and national audiences, including the general public and educators; (3) convening meetings for educators and the public to discuss issues and possibilities for change; (4) conducting research to deepen understandings of his rural community.

Works Cited

Bartolome, Lilia. *Ideologies in Education: Unmasking the Trap of Teacher Neutrality.* New York: Peter Lang, 2007. Print.

Brooke, Robert. *Rural Voices: Place-Conscious Education and the Teaching of Writing.* New York: Teachers College, 2003. Print.

Dingerson, Leigh., Barbara Miner, Bob Peterson, and Stephanie Walters. *Keeping the Promise?: The Debate over Charter Schools.* Milwaukee: Rethinking Schools, 2008. Print.

Donehower, Kim. "Rhetorics and Realities: The History and Effects of Stereotypes about Rural Literacies." *Rural Literacies.* By Kim Donehower, Charlotte Hogg, and Eileen E. Schell. Carbondale: Southern Illinois UP, 2007. 37–76. Print.

Donehower, Kim, Charlotte Hogg, and Eileen E. Schell. *Rural Literacies.* Carbondale: Southern Illinois UP, 2007. Print.

Edelman, Murray. *The Politics of Misinformation.* Cambridge: Cambridge UP, 2001. Print.

Edmondson, Jacqueline. *Prairie Town: Redefining Rural Life in an Age of Globalization.* Boulder, CO: Rowman and Littlefield, 2003. Print.

Egan, Kieran. *Getting It Wrong from the Beginning: Our Progressivist Inheritance from Herbert Spencer, John Dewey, and Jean Piaget.* New Haven, CT: Yale UP, 2004. Print.

Eppley, Karen. "Friction, Fiction, and Failure: Scientifically Based Research and the Rural." Master's thesis, Pennsylvania State U, 2007. Print.

Foucault, Michel. *The Archaeology of Knowledge*. Trans. A. M. Sheridan Smith. London: Tavistock, 1972. Print.

Gee, James. *Social Linguistics and Literacies: Ideology in Discourses*. New York: Taylor & Francis, 2007. Print.

Giroux, Henry. *Against the New Authoritarianism: Politics after Abu Ghraib*. Winnipeg, MB: Arbeiter Ring, 2005. Print.

———. Interview at McMaster University. Hamilton, ON. November 2006. Audio recording.

Gruenewald, David, and Gregory Smith, eds. *Place-Based Education in the Global Age: Local Diversity*. New York: Lawrence Erlbaum, 2008. Print.

Henry, Annette. "Five Black Women Teachers Critique Child-Centered Pedagogy: Possibilities and Limitations of Oppositional Standpoints." *Curriculum Inquiry* 26.4 (Winter 1996): 363–84. Print.

Hogg, Charlotte. "Beyond Agrarianism: Toward a Critical Pedagogy of Place." *Rural Literacies*. By Kim Donehower, Charlotte Hogg, and Eileen. E. Schell. Carbondale: Southern Illinois UP, 2007. 120–54. Print.

Kingsolver, Barbara, Camille Kingsolver, and Stephen Hopp. *Animal, Vegetable, Miracle: A Year of Food Life*. New York: Harper Collins, 2007. Print.

Leo-Nyquist, David. "Recovering a Tradition of Rural Progressivism in American Public Education." *Journal of Research in Rural Education* 17.1 (Spring 2001): 27–40. Print.

Lessa, Iara. "Discursive Struggles within Social Welfare: Restaging Teen Motherhood." *British Journal of Social Work* 36.2 (2006): 283–98. Print.

Panelli, Ruth, Samantha Punch, and Elsbeth Robson. *Global Perspectives on Rural Childhood and Youth*. New York: Routledge, 2007. Print.

Pollan, Michael. *The Omnivore's Dilemma: The Search for the Perfect Meal in a Fast-food World*. New York: Penguin, 2007. Print.

Reading First Impact Study. Interim report. Web. 7 July 2008. Reid, Tim. Barack Obama's 'Guns and Religion' Blunder Gives Hillary a Chance. Web. 30 June 2008.

Schafft, Kai, and Alecia Jackson. *Rural Education for the Twenty-First Century: Identity, Place, and Community in a Globalizing World*. University Park: Pennsylvania State UP, 2010. Print.

Shannon, Patrick. *Reading against Democracy: The Broken Promises of Reading Instruction*. Portsmouth, NH: Heinemann, 2007. Print.

Shelley, Bryan. "Rebels and Their Cause: State Resistance to No Child Left Behind." Paper presented at the 2006 meeting of the American Political Science Association. Philadelphia, PA. 2006. Print.

Stock, Catherine M. *Rural Radicals: From Bacon's Rebellion to the Oklahoma City Bombing* New York: Penguin, 1995. Print.

Theobald, Paul. *Teaching the Commons: Place, Pride, and the Renewal of Community*. Boulder, CO: Westview, 1997. Print.

Wright, Anne. "Preserving and Affirming Rural Values through the Curriculum." *Educational Forum* 68.1 (2003): 32–41. Print.

Afterword

Paul Theobald

This volume does nothing quite so well as problematize the rural piece— the rural chapter—of the ostensibly onward and upward epic that is the American story. For in that story, *rural* represents the place from which we have come en route to national greatness and international preeminence. Occupying this peculiar place in the story has had real consequences for rural people, as Kim Donehower, Charlotte Hogg, and Eileen Schell, editors of this book, note at its very outset. For those adamantly opposed to spending tax revenue that might redound to the benefit of rural people, they have a convenient cultural pronouncement to draw upon—rural people are the past, they live nowhere, they are of no consequence. Go door to door in any suburb in any state and you will find near-unanimous support for the consolidation of rural schools, whether or not those suburbanites have a clue about what conditions such a policy would create.

The essays in this volume offer intellectual leverage over this circumstance, over the condition of being rural in the United States today, for rural residents must live in a larger culture that is focused squarely on the future. Those with power use a vision of that future (rather than the study of the past) to make our policy choices. Predictably, we repeat a lot of mistakes as a result—but I want to frame this dynamic in a way that renders it somewhat more understandable. Hopefully, too, it will give readers additional insight into the significance of this book.

All American citizens see urban America as the locus of power. It is in the big cities, the state capitals, that the really big decisions are made. Because America is predominantly an urban/suburban nation, rural residents have far fewer representatives in the halls of power. We all know this. This is why we hear that plans to extend rural broadband access are actually plans to build "cyber bridges to nowhere." What Americans don't fully understand is that an urban locus of power has not always been the way of the world. Restricting one's gaze to the world of white Europeans, we can see that for many centuries power resided in rural locales. Landowning rural aristocrats (including the king), buttressed by clergy with tight familial connections, controlled Europe's policy-making bodies for centuries. The inevitable battle against feudalism was in fact a kind of urban versus rural contest for control over the policy arena. Sometimes, as in England, the contest unfolded slowly, over time, and with little bloodshed. Sometimes, as in France, it happened quickly and violently. Of course the experience of the North American colonies was huge in both cases. We were the first to experiment with nonfeudal government—which is another way of saying that we were the first to effect the switch from rural to urban in the locus of power.

In this contest for the upper hand in the policy arena, no tactics were off limits, including rhetorical devices of all kinds. To the urban industrialists of eighteenth-century England and New England, to the bankers and insurance dealers who underwrote their entrepreneurial efforts, to the shipping magnates who grew rich moving their products around the globe, the juxtaposition of gears turning the wheels of progress versus farmers plodding along behind slow-moving animals gave birth to the expression of living in the past, of being backward, of not keeping up with the times.

"Captains of industry" were elevated to high status while the status of rural dwellers dropped precipitously. The peasants of England became country bumpkins and yokels, while the rural American followers of Andrew Jackson (nicknamed "Old Hickory") became hicks and crackers. An early nineteenth-century journalist in England, William Cobbett, claims to have witnessed this status shift, and the rhetoric surrounding it, during his own lifetime. Said Cobbett, "By degrees beginning about 50 years ago the industrious part of the community, particularly those who create every useful thing by their labour, have been spoken of by everyone possessing the power to oppress them in any degree in just the same manner in which we speak of the animals which compose the stock upon a farm. This is not the manner in which the forefathers of us, the common people, were treated." Identifying the switch from use of the reference "the commons of England" to such phrases as "the lower orders" frequently used by England's elite, Cobbett blamed this development on "tax devourers, bankers, brewers, and monopolists of every sort." He noted further that one could hear these sorts of pejorative comments not only from England's wealthy urbanites, but also from "their clerks, from shopkeepers and waiters, and from the fribbles stuck up behind the counter" (qtd. in Hammond and Hammond 211).

There was more than bragging rights at work in this urban-versus-rural struggle. As England's population grew during Cobbett's long life, the demand for food was heightened and thus also its price. This was obviously good for the nation's rural interests, but it was bad for factory owners since they had to raise wages so that workers could afford to feed themselves. To get around this conundrum, the commercial and industrial interests began importing cheaper grain from abroad. Rural politicians, still in control of Parliament, countered this move by passing what became known as the Corn Laws, restricting the importation of foreign grain. Each such move on the part of the nation's lingering rural aristocracy came with more condemnation for obstructing progress, for impeding the nation on its route toward greatness.

As noted above, this dynamic played out in the United States too, in numerous ways, in locations all across the country. When farmers in New England protested the construction of dams used to power industrial operations because of subsequent flooding, urban industrialists carried the day. When farmers who borrowed inflated dollars worth 50 cents during the Civil War sought to pay back their loans with dollars of similar worth, the nation's banking industry demanded repayment of loans in dollars worth 100 cents. When farmers tried to buy an implement built in Europe, they found that American tariffs raised the prices of these products to protect American industries. When farmers banded together to create a cooperative warehouse for their grain, they found rail companies willing to undersell their operations until they were driven from business. I could go on and on and on in this vein. The point is that from the very outset of our history as a nation, there was a rural versus urban dynamic in place. And to the victors go the spoils. The epithets Cobbett identified in 1810, as Cynthia Ryan describes in chapter 3 of this volume, are still used to this day. To be *rural* in America is to be considered backward and inferior at some level. It has only been very recently that scholars have brought much focused intellectual attention to this issue. It has only been recently that scholars, like those who contributed to this volume, have attempted to "reclaim" the rural.

And this is no easy task. Identifying cultural lessons is deep, complicated, highly nuanced business. For example, rural dwellers are often thought to be predisposed to a condition called nostalgia, a malady culturally defined as the inability to generate the intellectual wherewithal required to see the past as something that must be left behind in the march toward the future, in the march toward progress. The inference is that nostalgia is an objective condition, something like the measles, instead of a cultural pronouncement, instead of being yet another powerful rhetorical device in the urban/suburban lexicon. The dominant urban/suburban perspective goes something like this: "It's those rural folk who succumb to nostalgia, to glorifying tough circumstances by selectively forgetting the hard work and drudgery that accompanies a rural life, or the racism and sexism that has never been far from it." Perhaps this indeed happens, but to make this dynamic the exclusive preserve of rural dwellers is just plain wrong. All humans, urban and rural, possess the ability to repress what they don't wish to recall. But when rural residents do it, it's because they're suffering from nostalgia, yet one more good reason to reject whatever request they might make in the policy arena: "Those nostalgic rural people have rose-colored glasses when it comes to their little schoolhouse, and that's why they oppose consolidation." Never mind that study after study has shown that school consolidation does not save money and that a massive study of school consolidation, published recently, demonstrates that small unconsolidated schools outperformed larger consolidated schools in terms of students' income later in life and further educational attainment, throughout the twentieth century (Berry and West).

One of the major themes of this book can be summed up by the simple phrase "place matters." There is growing scholarly recognition of this across a variety of academic disciplines. Identity formation, for instance, is directly related to place and, related to this, cultural norms are determined in part by conditions that exist in particular places. But neither norms for behavior nor an individual's identity are exclusively determined by conditions in a place. Both are portable, meaning that norms and identity conceptions can be brought to new places, in the process creating a clash of cultures and a long list of potentially problematic social, economic, environmental, and political fissures. Witness the circumstances in Wyoming's Wind River valley, or in the preindustrial-to-atomic-age transitions in northern New Mexico, both ably described in this volume by Marcia Kmetz and Damián Baca.

The slowly developing scholarly recognition of the significance of place in human lives has gradually come to suggest new curricular and instructional thinking. Of course, the term *new* only applies when this thinking is put alongside what currently passes for educational thought in various policy arenas in this country. Place-based education has been informed by a long list of contributors, from indigenous educational conceptions like *resolana*, to early curriculum theorists at the margins, such as Liberty Hyde Bailey, John Dewey, and others. And, as numerous contributors to this volume have noted, the critical pedagogy of Paulo Friere has also been a major force in the development of place-based pedagogy.

This growing emphasis on education oriented to a particular place has led to the serious study of local history—as the Arkansas Delta Oral History project ably demonstrates. This kind of pedagogical work has created a small renaissance of sorts in the area of rural history, juxtaposing it against the textbook version of the nation as a whole. Sanitized school textbooks overlook a long history of rural struggle against urban-oriented and fundamentally anti-community policy. This volume represents a kind of scholarly corrective to that history. Take, for instance, Carolyn Ostrander's account of the early Grange societies. If this movement receives any acknowledgement at all in standard U.S. history texts, it is only as a precursor to the Populist movement, which, in turn, is portrayed only as an interesting footnote to the Progressive era. The fact that the Grange was one of the earliest contributors to gender equality, to elevating the voice of women in American society, is a fact lost to most Americans—rural and urban. But had there been no Grange, there likely would have been no Mary Lease urging Kansans to "raise less corn and more hell." Without the aggressive Populist movement described by Cori Brewster in this volume, there would have been less traction for the advocates of women's suffrage. It should be noted that this democratic reform tended to occur first in the nation's most rural places. In fact, as Marty Strange has noted, the nation's rural dwellers were a major force in virtually every democratic movement that occurred in this country at least until the Great Depression (16). Since that point in time, the rural experience has been marginalized so effectively that there has been no rural voice. Thus the great need to reclaim the rural.

Of course the rural story, like the larger American epic, has been anything but "onward and upward." The rural experience has been marred by cultural clashes, particularly with indigenous peoples, as several contributors to this volume so clearly demonstrate. Resentments and stereotypes have lingered across generations. Valerie Mulholland's chapter reminds us that this is a circumstance that rural Americans have shared with rural Canadians. While this clash of cultures continues to cause serious problems, there is at least some evidence to suggest that through greater recognition of the complexities involved, disparate cultures can come together in the interest of creating better circumstances among all who share a particular place on earth.

In the end, "reclaiming the rural" is about recognizing the complexity of shared circumstances—a project that is almost by definition tied to the realm of education. Literacy looms large in this regard—in particular, recognizing the various kinds of literacy and the ends they serve. Sara Webb-Sunderhaus's research with undergraduates from rural Appalachia is particularly telling.

She demonstrates that her rural Appalachian students possess a communally focused literacy, and that elevating their recognition of this can help provide intellectual leverage over the larger cultural emphasis on a literacy of consumption. Or consider Cori Brewster's analysis of the types of agricultural literacy bought and paid for by agribusinesses. With this kind of sophisticated analysis of literacies, rural residents are better equipped to demand just treatment in the policy arena.

But getting there is difficult. As Susan Meyers shows in this volume, even the Mexican educational system has come to be dominated by the goals of national cohesion and capitalist development. The American system has considerably more momentum and more power to pursue these same goals. This is why place-based pedagogy remains at the margins of educational discourse in this country. This is why the excellent examples of this kind of work in rural Nebraska, described by Robert Brooke, are rare—the exception rather than the rule throughout the rural United States. This is why Thomas Butler struggled to have a substantive conversation about how students in his rural Pennsylvania school district ought to be taught to read, write, listen, and speak. But these "on the ground" efforts can contribute directly to changes in how rural people see themselves and their place in the world—a circumstance that can help rural America once again become a pivotal player in the kind of democratic reforms the twenty-first century will demand.

Works Cited

Berry, Christopher R., and Martin R. West. "Growing Pains: The Consolidation Movement and Student Outcomes." *Journal of Law, Economics, and Organization* 26.1 (2008): 1–29. Print.

Hammond, J. L., and Barbara Hammond. *The Village Labourer, 1760–1832*. London: Longmans, Green, and Co., 1912. Print.

Strange, Marty. *Family Farming: A New Economic Vision*. Lincoln: U of Nebraska P, 1988. Print.

Acknowledgments
Contributors
Index

Acknowledgments

We would first like to acknowledge Robert Brooke who started us on our collaborative work on rural literacies. Without his support, encouragement, and overarching vision, our work on rural literacies would have taken place in isolation and perhaps not come to full fruition.

Thanks also to all who contacted us after reading *Rural Literacies* and who generously shared your thoughts about our first book and your own research, teaching, and community work in rural areas. One of the benefits of this work has been seeing the term *rural literacies* pop up in the scholarly literature, conference programs, and dissertation titles in our field.

Working with our contributors has been a pleasure as well. Thank you for your hard work and for taking this long but rewarding journey with us. We have been enriched by learning what rural literacies, rhetorics, and pedagogies mean to you, your students, and the communities you come from and investigate.

We appreciate SIUP editor Kristine Priddy's support, advice, and encouragement along the way. Finally, we want to express our appreciation for each other. All three of us have been engaged in raising families, teaching, administering programs, and juggling the day-to-day responsibilities and obligations of our academic institutions. Our collaborative efforts have been satisfying and supportive.

Kim would like to thank her colleagues in the Department of English at the University of North Dakota for being models of collegiality and support, and especially her chair, Sheryl O'Donnell, for her passion for and commitment to rural literacies. Kim's thanks also go to her rural students, both graduate and undergraduate, and to the many rural people who have shared their stories with her and influenced her work, particularly Lisa Swanson Faleide. Kim is grateful to her parents, Wanda and Bill Donehower, and her aunt, Marilee

Moore, for their continued nurture and for their tolerance of an academic career that has taken Kim far from home. Last, Kim thanks Jack Weinstein for his patience and persistence in prodding her to write, and for creating a family, with Adina's and Mingus's help, out of which such work can happen.

Charlotte would like to thank her graduate students and colleagues at Texas Christian University for their discussions—sometimes on rural issues and sometimes not—that have pushed her thinking and expanded her perspectives. She thanks her parents, Carolyn and Bob Hogg (one who grew up urban, one who grew up rural), for demonstrating to her the importance of place. She is grateful to Chris Garland for the constancy of his support and to Dean, who reminds her daily how much more there is to life than work.

Eileen would like to thank graduate students Carolyn Ostrander, Kurt Stavenhagen, and Dianna Winslow in the Composition and Cultural Rhetoric doctoral program at Syracuse University. She has appreciated their conversations and discussions of rural literacies over the past few years, and is excited to see their work on rural issues, agriculture, and social movements begin to take shape and influence the field. Eileen would also like to thank her Washington state family and friends, most of them living in or near her hometown of Cashmere. She is thankful every day for the sense of place and community she found and still finds in her hometown. Finally, Eileen thanks her colleagues at Syracuse University and family (Tom Kerr and Autumn Kerr) in Syracuse, New York, for being a steadying force and a source of strength and companionship. *Nihil obstat.*

Contributors

Editors

Kim Donehower, an associate professor of English at the University of North Dakota, researches the links between rural literacy and sustainability, teaches courses in composition studies and English education, and directs the Red River Valley Writing Project. Her previous publications include *Rural Literacies* (with Charlotte Hogg and Eileen E. Schell, 2007) and essays in the *Journal of Appalachian Studies* and *Women and Literacy: Local and Global Inquiries for a New Century*.

Charlotte Hogg is an associate professor at Texas Christian University. Her work includes *From the Garden Club: Rural Women Writing Community* (2006), *Rural Literacies* (with Kim Donehower and Eileen E. Schell), and chapters in *Ethnography Unbound: From Theory Shock to Critical Praxis* (coauthored with Robert Brooke) and *Women and Literacy: Inquiries for a New Century*.

Eileen E. Schell is chair and director of the Writing Program at Syracuse University. Her publications include *Gypsy Academics and Mother-Teachers: Gender, Contingent Labor, and Writing Instruction; Rural Literacies* (with Kim Donehower and Charlotte Hogg); *Moving a Mountain: Transforming the Role of Contingent Faculty in Composition Studies and Higher Education*, coedited with Patricia Lambert; and *Rhetorica in Motion: Feminist Rhetorical Methods and Methodologies*, coedited with K. J. Rawson, in addition to numerous chapters, articles, and responses in *College English*, *CCC*, and elsewhere.

Authors

Damián Baca is an assistant professor of English and affiliate faculty in Mexican American studies at the University of Arizona. His publications include

Mestiz@ Scripts, Digital Migrations, and the Territories of Writing (2008) and *Rhetorics of the Americas: 3114 BCE to 2012 CE*, coedited with Victor Villanueva (2010).

Cori Brewster is an associate professor of writing and rhetoric at Eastern Oregon University and currently researches rural literacy sponsors and intersections between populism and white supremacy in progressive agricultural movements. She is a founding member of Oregon Rural Action, a grassroots community organization working for social justice, agricultural sustainability, and environmental stewardship in eastern Oregon.

Robert Brooke is a professor of English at the University of Nebraska–Lincoln, directs the Nebraska Writing Project, and is currently working on a collection extending place-conscious teaching to suburban communities. He has published four books and over fifty articles on the theory, teaching, and practice of writing, including *Rural Voices: Place-Conscious Education and the Teaching of Writing* (2003).

Thomas Butler received his doctorate in educational leadership from Pennsylvania State University, where he studied how globalization influences collaboration between rural schools and communities. He is currently a superintendent in a small rural school district in Pennsylvania.

Jacqueline Edmondson is an associate dean for teacher education and undergraduate programs at Pennsylvania State University. Her books include *America Reads: A Critical Policy Study* (2000), *Prairie Town: Redefining Rural Life in an Age of Globalization* (2003), *Understanding and Applying Critical Policy Study: Reading Educators Advocating for Change* (2004), *Reading Education Policy* (coedited with Patrick Shannon, 2005), and numerous biographies.

Laine Gates received her master's degree in cultural anthropology in 2010. She was the codirector for the Arkansas Delta History Project and is currently working at the University of Arkansas's Quality Writing Center and volunteering as a literacy tutor at a local community health clinic.

Christian Z. Goering is an assistant professor of secondary English and literacy education at the University of Arkansas, coordinates the English education program, and directs both the Northwest Arkansas Writing Project and Center for Children and Youth. He was recognized by the NCTE as a high school teacher of excellence and was named the Writing Conference's Judith C. Gilbert Outstanding Writing Teacher.

Jane Greer is an associate professor of English, women's studies, and gender studies at the University of Missouri–Kansas City, where she teaches courses on feminist rhetorics, the history of literacy, and composition. She is the editor of *Girls and Literacy in America: Historical Perspectives to the Present* (2003), and her research has appeared in *CCC*, *College English*, and numerous edited collections.

David A. Jolliffe is the Brown Chair in English Literacy at the University of Arkansas at Fayetteville, has taught courses in urban literacy and tutoring in city schools for the Steans Center for Community-Based Service Learning at DePaul University, and has written or edited several books on the theory and practice of rhetoric and the preparation of writing teachers.

Marcia Kmetz is a faculty member with Walden University whose work has appeared in *Rhetoric in the Rest of the West*, *Rhetoric Review*, and *Composition Studies*. Her current book project examines rural civic ethos in Hesiodic poetry, Ciceronian oratory, and modern rhetorical battles over mining and environmental issues in Butte and Libby, Montana, and water-rights disputes in Wyoming.

I. Moriah McCracken is an assistant professor of rhetoric and composition at the University of Texas–Pan American, teaches graduate and undergraduate courses in literacy and writing studies, and researches perceptions of rural students in university settings.

Susan V. Meyers holds an MFA from the University of Minnesota and a PhD from the University of Arizona, is the director of writing at Oregon State University, and is the recipient of a Monique Wittig Writer's Scholarship, an NEH grant, and a Fulbright Fellowship.

Valerie Mulholland is an associate professor of literacy and language in the Faculty of Education, University of Regina, in Saskatchewan. Her interests include literacy, autobiography, and postcolonial theory, and she teaches language, methods, and curriculum courses.

Carolyn Ostrander is a PhD candidate in composition and cultural rhetoric at Syracuse University studying rhetoric by and about women in the early Grange and the role of the Grange as a literacy and rhetorical sponsor.

Kelly Riley is a graduate of the University of Arkansas with master's degrees in both English and teaching. She currently works with an alternative high school student population in the Fayetteville Public Schools.

Contributors

Cynthia Ryan is an associate professor of English at the University of Alabama at Birmingham. Her research on intersections between medicine and media has appeared in *JAC: Journal of Advanced Composition*, *JBTC: Journal of Business and Technical Communication*, and *JAMA: Journal of the American Medical Association*, as well as *USA Today*, the *Chicago Tribune*, and *CR: Collaborations—>Results*. She is a coeditor of *City Comp: Identities, Spaces, Practices* (2003).

Hillary Swanton is a graduate of the University of Arkansas with degrees in English and anthropology and is currently pursuing teaching certification at Beaumont University in Nashville, Tennessee.

Paul Theobald is the Woods-Beals Chair for Urban and Rural Education at SUNY College at Buffalo. He is the author of four books on rural education, numerous journal articles in such publications as *Journal of Research in Rural Education*, *Journal of Thought*, and *American Journal of Education*, and many chapters in collections.

Sara Webb-Sunderhaus is an assistant professor of English at Indiana University–Purdue University, Fort Wayne, where she teaches undergraduate and graduate courses in writing, literacy, and folklore. Her work has appeared in *Community Literacy Journal, Composition Forum, Journal of Basic Writing, The Norton Book of Composition Studies*, and *Open Words: Access and English Studies*.

Index

farmers (*continued*)
interactions between, 60; membership-based organizations and, 37–38; networks in communities of, 63–64; organizing by, perceived as threat, 38–39; perspectives on changes in agriculture, 61; small, neoliberalist characterization of, 40; study participants and methodology, 56–57; values and concerns of, 68; as victims of capitalism in Farmers' Union teachings, 38
farmers' organizations, 19th-century, 37
Farmers' Union, 38
farming: changes in methods, early 20th century, 121; community-based notion of, 60–61; diversification strategies in, 64–65; effect of industrial techniques on rural residents, 103; efforts to dehumanize and depoliticize, 40; good judgment in, 58–59, 68; Indohispanic and Pueblo, 78; interpretations of progress, 53; limitations of neoliberalism in, 62; scientific management and, 231; successful, limiting ideologies of, 53–56; unpredictability of, 52–53
farming families, labor in, 108–10
Farm Plan advertisement, 59–60
farm publications: discursive shifts in, 55–56; editors' values and concerns, 68; soybean guru story, 61–62. See also *Progressive Farmer* (periodical)
federal government: and public education, 228–29; reclamation projects, 4–5; stimulus plan, 1; subsidies to tribes vs. to farmers, 28–29; western lands opened for individual ownership, 22–23
feedback patterns, in peer review sessions, 216–17
"first in time, first in right" doctrine, 24
First Nations: approach to inclusion of, in curriculum, 197–200; use of term, 191
Florida, Richard, 3
Ford, Bob, 177
formal language, 179
Fort Belknap Reservation, 23–24
Fort Bridger treaties, 18, 23
4-H organization: Farm Bureau links to, 39; *4-H Story*, 134–35; in "Growing

Great Kids," 62–63; integration of intellect with manual competence, 139; learning by doing, 123–24; literacy practices, 123–24, 132–33; *National 4-H Report Form*, 126, 127, 127–28, *133*; pledge, 121; Record Book, 135–36, *136*; *Record Book*, 124, 140; report forms, 125–31; report forms, evolution of, 138–40; standardizing the experience, 127–31; *Standard Report Form for 4-H Club Members*, 126, *128*; in Texas, 124–25; Van Buren family and literacy practices over time, 126–28, 130, *131*, *133*, 134–38
Foxfire program, 165–66
Framework for Understanding Poverty, A (Payne), 174, 178–81
Freire, Paolo, 79–80
"From Page to Stage" (workshop), 177
frozen language, 178–79
functional literacy, use of term, 69n. 3
Furman, Lucy, 93–94
Future Farmers of America (FFA), 39, 123–24
Future of Food, The (film documentary), 44
futurists, absence of rural in work of, 3

Garcia, Deborah Koons, 44
Gates, Laine, 183, 185
Gatewood, Willard, 175–76, 176
gender and rhetoric in rural and urban settings, 109–11
gender equality, in the Grange, 112–13, 117
gender inequity, in "Growing a Nation," 41
General Allotment Act, 18
Giroux, Henry, 227, 229, 235–36
"Going Green in Iowa" (*America's Heartland* episode), 44
Gonzales-Berry, Erlinda, 78
Graff, Harvey, 211
grain elevator discussions, 63–64
Grange, the: aims and organization, 108–9; Biblical justification for women's inclusion in, 113; degrees/levels of, 112; and innovations in American life, 108; language of rituals, 112; lecture topics, 115; meetings and rituals, 108–9; membership in, 117–18n. 5; opportunities for women, 111; oratory skill